First published 1987 by
Prentice Hall International (UK) Ltd,
66 Wood Lane End, Hemel Hempstead,
Hertfordshire, HP2 4RG
A division of
Simon & Schuster International Group

Printed by A. Wheaton & Co. Ltd., Exeter

British Library Cataloguing in Publication Data

Allen, Michael , 1943
Essential Management Accounting·
1 Managerial Accounting
I Title II Myddleton, D. R.
658.1'511 HF5635

ISBN 0-13-287871-2

1 2 3 4 5 91 90 89 88 87

CONTENTS

PREFACE

This book aims to meet the essential needs of students of management. It covers the key areas in management accounting in suitable depth, whilst recognising the time constraints of busy students.

The book is meant primarily for students on full-time and part-time MBA programmes, and on other courses in business management; but business managers generally will also find it helpful. The book explains what management accounting can and cannot do; and it should enable business managers to make better use in their own organisation of management accounting information, and indeed of management accountants.

Many of the chapters include problems for the reader to work through as he reads the text. This deliberate attempt to make the book more 'interactive' represents a big improvement over 'passive' reading, from the student's point of view.

The ten chapters have been written for use in the order in which they appear. Each chapter contains a summary at the end, together with review questions and answers. Some students may find that reading the summary and review questions first helps their understanding of the chapters. Others may prefer to use the chapter summaries and review questions to consolidate their knowledge after they have first read the text.

Chapters two to seven also contain a number of quantitative problems and exercises. Answers to the first two problems in these chapters are provided at the end of the chapters to enable the reader to self-test his understanding.

For teachers using this text there is a Teachers' Guide which suggests how to use the book as an integral part of an MBA Management Accounting course. The Teachers' Guide also contains answers for the problems where answers are not provided in the book itself. These problems may be suitable for setting as separate assignments.

The Glossary contains definitions of some two hundred words or phrases commonly used in Management Accounting. The reader is strongly recommended to consult the Glossary as he works through the book, whenever he comes across an expression he does not fully understand. Otherwise it is possible to prolong unnecessary confusion.

We would like to thank everyone who has offered helpful comments on the book in its draft form. This includes especially our academic colleagues at Cranfield, and students on the 1986/87 full-time MBA programme. We also owe thanks to Marjorie Dawe, who nursed the book from first draft to completion, and to Brigitte Courtney who prepared the book for the press. Of course, any errors are the responsibility of the authors.

M W Allen
D R Myddelton

Cranfield 1987

CHAPTER ONE

PLANNING AND CONTROL

1.1 FINANCIAL ACCOUNTING AND MANAGEMENT ACCOUNTING

It is assumed that the reader of this book will already be conversant with financial accounting but not with management accounting. In order to explain the essence of management accounting we shall first consider the nature of these two types of accounting and contrast them.

1.1.1 Financial accounting

Financial accounting classifies and records an entity's transactions, normally in money terms, in accordance with established concepts, principles, accounting standards and legal requirements. It then aims to present a 'true and fair' view of the overall results of those transactions. For a company the end result of financial accounting is a profit and loss account, a funds flow statement covering a period of time and a balance sheet at the end of the period. The company's auditors report on these financial statements. Figure 1.1 summarises the different financial statements contained in the published accounts of public limited companies.

Report of the Directors
Profit and Loss Account
Balance Sheet
Funds Flow Statement
Notes relating to the Accounts
Auditor's Report
Notice of the Annual General Meeting

Where a company has subsidiaries, group accounts are required.

Figure 1.1 Financial statements comprising a company's published accounts.

In recent years, membership of the EEC has influenced UK accounting practice. EEC directives have required changes to company law, including restrictions on the format and wording of company profit and loss accounts and balance sheets. These changes are now incorporated in the 1985 Companies Act.

Company accounts must also conform with accounting standards. In the UK there are currently in force twenty Statements of Standard Accounting Practice (SSAPs)*. These Standards, which are based upon common accounting practices, are the result of agreement between the six main accounting bodies (see Figure 1.2).

The Institute of Chartered Accountants in England and Wales (ICAEW)
The Institute of Chartered Accountants of Scotland (ICAS)
The Institute of Chartered Accountants in Ireland (ICAI)
The Chartered Association of Certified Accountants (CACA)
The Chartered Institute of Management Accountants (CIMA)
The Chartered Institute of Public Finance and Accountancy (CIPFA)

Figure 1.2 Main UK accounting bodies

The most basic standard is SSAP 2, which deals with four key accounting concepts.

(a) *Going concern concept*, which assumes that the business will continue to operate for the foreseeable future. Hence, actual historical costs (or possibly current costs) are used for 'valuing' assets rather than liquidation values.

(b) *Accruals concept*, which matches revenues as they are earned with expenses as incurred.

(c) *Consistency concept*, which requires the same treatment for similar items to allow proper comparison of accounts for different years.

(d) *Prudence concept* (or conservatism), which means that revenues are recognised only when reasonably certain, whilst expenses and estimated possible losses are provided for at once.

* Appendix A (p.316) lists all current SSAPs as at 30th June 1987.

1.1.2 Management accounting

Management accounting aims to help managers to run their organisations. Of course, accounting *alone* is not nearly enough: managers also need technical production data about technology and raw materials, market research on customers' wants and competitors' actions, information about the labour market, and much else.

Management accounting deals with two different things:

(a) the use of scarce resources, and
(b) how people behave.

It contributes to four main purposes, emphasising different time periods:

(a) Score-keeping	PAST
(b) Problem-solving	PRESENT
(c) Controlling	PRESENT
(d) Planning	FUTURE

Planning involves co-ordinating the activities of different parts of a business, gaining the agreement of various responsible managers to their part in the plan, and projecting possible outcomes of future events. Control involves monitoring the actual outcomes against the agreed budget, and where necessary taking corrective action.

The distinction between the various purposes may not be clear-cut. For example, many internal report forms are designed to help control as well as keep score, by both reporting 'actual' performance and comparing it with a 'standard' (budget). But different kinds of management accounting information may be better suited for particular purposes, as outlined in Figure 1.3.

The professional body representing Management Accountants is the Chartered Institute of Management Accountants, which possesses about 26,000 members. Many qualified management accountants also work as finance directors, financial controllers, or chief accountants. Similarly, members of the other accounting bodies may often act as management accountants.

Basis of Costs and Revenues	Past Facts	Future Estimates
1. Total	Financial accounting	Long-range plans
	Cost-plus contracts	Normal pricing decisions
	Reporting and analysing business unit performance	
2. Marginal		Special pricing decisions
		Alternative-choice decisions
		Capital investment decisions
3. Controllable	Reporting and analysing manager's performance	Budgeting

Figure 1.3 Uses for different kinds of accounting information

1.1.3 Contrasts

Financial accounting information is used to account externally to many potential users, as shown in figure 1.4:

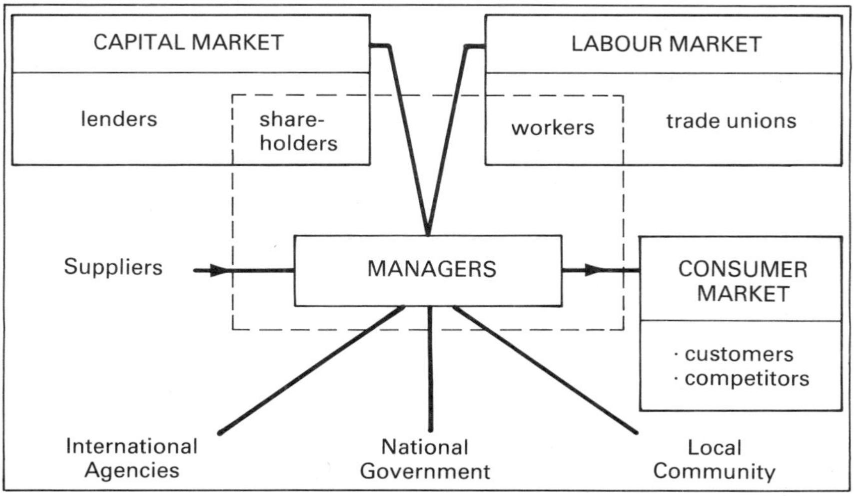

Figure 1.4 Users of financial accounts

Financial accounting, like management accounting, *summarises* data, mainly from operating information such as:

(a) purchases of materials
(b) production records
(c) labour payrolls
(d) fixed asset ('plant') registers
(e) sales and debtors
(f) cash

There are several differences between financial accounting and management accounting, as set out in Figure 1.5.

	Financial Accounting	**Management Accounting**
Governed by	Company law, SSAPs	Needs of managers
Users	External	Internal
Time	Past & present	Present & future
Period	Usually one year	As appropriate
Coverage	Whole company or group	Divisions and sub-groups
Emphasis	Accuracy	Speed
Criteria	Objective, verifiable, consistent	Relevant, useful, understandable
Unit of Account	Money	Money, or physical units
Nature of Data	Somewhat technical	For use by non-accountants

Figure 1.5 Differences between financial accounting and management accounting

Whereas the production of financial accounts is a legal requirement, management accounting is used only when its perceived benefits to internal managers outweigh its cost.

However, the absence of adequate management accounts (particularly costing systems and budgeting) has been identified as a major cause of company failure.

Management accounting is concerned mainly with the future, especially with planning and control of divisions, plants, sections and other business units. In contrast, published financial accounts deal with the past.

Accuracy is crucial in financial accounts, but matters less in management accounts. Managers cannot afford to wait three or four months for precise details of financial performance. Instead, they want prompt reports that are accurate enough not to be misleading. These may be expressed in units of output (product) and units of input (quantity of materials, man hours, etc.) as well as in money.

Ordinary managers must be able to understand management accounts. Financial accounts are supposed to convey information to a large external audience, but in practice they can be understood only by a fairly small number of experts.

1.2 KINDS OF ORGANISATION

1.2.1 Profit-seeking organisations

Most profit-seeking organisations aim to provide an adequate long-term financial return for their owners. If they do not the owners may either change the top management team or sell out to new owners who will. So directors and managers must be alert for opportunities to improve their firm's long-term financial return. Parts of the business that fail to meet the profit test must either be improved, or else curtailed, and their related fixed assets and working capital put to more profitable use. This is the pervasive *economic principle* of *opportunity cost*. (See section 5.3).

Every business is likely to have other aims which may not link directly with financial returns. These might include some of the following:

high market share
product (or service) leadership
very good company image
highly skilled, trained and motivated employees
use of the latest technology.

Although it is difficult to measure the financial return from achieving these 'non-financial' aims, to disregard them may well prevent the achievement of financial aims.

Let us consider a practical example of a profit-seeking organisation's aims.

In their 1985 Report and Accounts, Barclays Plc identified three aspects of their basic objective. The Chairman's Address identified Barclays intention to remain 'a *profitable* and *prudent* private sector, national and international bank, which is conscious of its *duty to the communities it serves*'.

In addition to their (chosen) aims most businesses are subject to constraints. Extensive legislation now relates to safety, environmental protection, minimum wages and redundancy terms.

Where top management is also the owner of the business, it may serve aims other than financial, e.g. the desire to run his own business. Profits might be foregone *in some cases* in order to achieve greater personal freedom. Where the owners of the business are not part of the management team, however, over-emphasis of managers' personal aims at the expense of financial returns is likely to lead to changes in management, ownership or both.

1.2.2 Non-profit-seeking organisations

Many organisations have primary aims which are non-financial in nature, as Figure 1.6 shows:

Organisation	Primary Aim
Charities	To improve the general welfare of those in special need.
Hospitals	Alleviation of illness and suffering.
Schools	Teaching useful knowledge and skills to students.
The Police Force	Prevention and detection of crime.
Ministry of Defence	Protection against foreign invasion.
Local Authorities	Satisfactory performance of obligatory and discretionary functions, within a limited budget.

Figure 1.6 Organisational aims

Non-profit seeking organisations do not have financial considerations at the top of their list. Still, effective use of management accounting techniques can enable them to achieve greater success in meeting their primary aims, for example, by achieving better value for money. Charities, for instance, should plan how to raise the desired amounts needed with the minimum input of time and cost. Then, how to achieve optimum satisfaction of the needy with the sum available. Hospitals (in the National Health Service) are provided with limited funds, but unlimited patients (often needing unlimited patience!). Optimum use of facilities and staff is desirable in maintaining the 'nation's health'. However, well-directed efforts on prevention of illness and accidents could reduce the needs for hospitalisation.

1.2.3 Responsibility centres

In order to let managers control units of 'manageable' size, many large organisations need extensive decentralisation. This may be of two different types:

(a) functional, e.g. production, marketing, distribution, etc.
(b) divisional, or product-oriented.

The economics of a business may dictate a functional form of organisation, where some important trade-offs can be decided only by top management. The divisional type of organisation can allow even fairly junior managers responsibility for profits. This improves motivation, and permits necessary trade-offs (e.g. in deciding on levels of stocks) nearer to local markets.

Responsibility centres have inputs and outputs. Three possible ways of viewing their objectives are:

(a) maximisation of outputs for a given volume and quality of inputs;
(b) minimisation of inputs for a given volume and quality of outputs;
(c) maximisation of the excess of outputs over inputs for a given level of investment.

In functional organisations it may be fairly easy to measure the inputs but not the outputs. In divisional companies it is common to set up 'profit centres' whose managers are expected to 'maximise profit', subject to constraints such as the balance between short-term and long-term profit.

An important difference between business units may relate to the destination of the outputs, whether they are sold on external markets or transferred internally to other units in the same organisation. In order to set up profit centres, suitable 'transfer prices' may need to be established for internal transfers (see Chapter 8).

1.3 PLANNING

Management accounting is vital for running any but the smallest business. Its various techniques provide a framework for solving problems, making decisions, planning and controlling the business. Figure 1.7 illustrates the important aspects of the planning and control process.

Important Aspects

Long-term planning	Company objectives Business definition - current and future Analysis of company Strengths and Weaknesses Assessment of 'external' Opportunities and Threats Competitive position Strategic market and product decisions Identifying resource needs - financial, physical and people
Short-term planning	Operating plans and programmes Budgets Reactions to market changes
Controlling	Reports Evaluation Problem-solving Decision making Effective action

Figure 1.7 The planning and control process

1.3.1 Long-term planning

Many bigger businesses make some attempt at long-term ('corporate') planning. It may start with basic questions such as 'What business should we be in?'. It will include an analysis of the firm's Strengths and Weaknesses and of the Opportunities and Threats (SWOT analysis) arising from the environment in which the business operates. The long-term plan will identify the products (or services) and the markets in which the business chooses to compete.

A long-term plan needs to take account of marketing, production (or provision of services), personnel, and administrative aspects of the business in addition to its financial considerations. Here we are concerned with how to express the company-wide long-term plan in financial terms. This should include planned profit and loss accounts, balance sheets and, possibly, funds flow statements, year by year for the whole period. How long is 'long-term'? Five years might be a typical 'long-term' period, but this time-span may be inappropriate for certain types of business. A life assurance company may need a 40-year plan, whereas in a fashion business the long-term might be only one to two years.

1.3.2 Short-term planning

Most organisations accept the need for budgeting as a disciplined approach to planning and control. Typically annual budgets are set for the coming twelve months, including details of production and sales volumes, sales revenue, cost of sales, marketing costs, administrative costs and finance costs. Detailed budgeted profit and loss accounts, together with cash flows and balance sheets are often sub-divided into monthly (or four-weekly) periods. This allows frequent comparison of actual results with budget.

At the lower level, the budgeting process is often a *negotiated* short-term plan for a manager of a responsibility centre, agreed with his organisational superior. For many managers, it may involve only costs, not revenues.

Achievement of budgets is important, but if conditions change it may be desirable to deviate from previously agreed budgets in order to achieve better results. The budget should not needlessly restrain managers from making worthwhile changes, although they may require approval if they want to spend more money.

1.4 CONTROL

Control, in the context of management accounting, is the process by which managers seek to ensure that firms obtain and use resources effectively and efficiently in the achievement of their goals. The goals of an organisation are actually those of top management: other employees have their own personal goals.

Effectiveness means how well a unit contributes to the organisation's objectives, whereas efficiency means 'optimising' the ratio of outputs to inputs. An organisation can be efficient in producing outputs which are not valuable, or it can inefficiently produce outputs that are valuable.

1.4.1 Process of control

The process of management control involves two related activities: planning and control. 'Planning' means deciding what to do, when and how. 'Control' is seeing that desired results are achieved.

A management control system will normally include at least four stages:

(a) *Programming*: choosing in broad terms which activities a company will undertake and what resources it will assign to each programme. Depending on a company's precise organisation, a product line or a whole plant may represent a 'programme'.

(b) *Budgeting*: preparing plans expressed in detailed quantitative terms covering a specific period (often one year). Budgeting translates plans from approximate numbers relating to programmes into precise money amounts relating to responsibilities of particular managers.

(c) *Accounting for operations*: this incorporates both broad programmes and specific responsibility centres. Accounting reports on the latter need not be only in terms of money.

(d) *Appraisal*: this is one major purpose of management control. Data on programmes form part of the input to future budgeting decisions; while data on responsibility centres are used to evaluate managers' performance (usually by comparing 'actual' performance with 'budget').

One important distinction in evaluation is between a business unit as an economic entity and the performance of its manager. A loss-making division may be assigned a 'good' manager, who may still be performing well even if the unit for which he is responsible is not. Equally important, it can be expensive for a business unit not to 'cash in' when conditions are favourable. This implies that a manager's performance may be reckoned poor even if his unit makes large profits.

Top management is concerned not merely with how good or bad the results actually were, but with how good or bad they 'ought' to have been; in other words, with suitable standards of performance. Many internal accounting reports (like external ones) may tend to over-emphasise short-term results; but nearly all managers in practice have to balance short-term against longer-term performance. Internal reports may also serve other functions such as keeping managers informed about what is happening, and helping to co-ordinate activities.

1.4.2 **Motivation**

A management control system should lead individuals to take actions which are not only in accordance with their own perceived self-interests, but are also in accordance with the goals of the organisation, as perceived by top management. This is sometimes called 'goal congruence'.

An individual whose personal goals conflict with those of the organisation might find more personal satisfaction ('fulfilment') by moving to another organisation whose goals are more in line with his own. Similarly, an organisation in setting recruitment policy might well concern itself with the personal goals of the people it proposes to employ.

There are two basic aspects to inducing individuals to act in accordance with organisational goals, crudely summarised as 'carrots' and 'sticks'. Absence of a carrot may sometimes be more or less equivalent to a stick, but not always. Figure 1.8 summarises generalisations about incentives.

---

* 'Carrots' motivate people more strongly than 'sticks'.

* Time-lags dilute incentives, hence rewards should follow action promptly.

* Motivation may flag where a goal is either 'too easy' or 'too hard'.

* Money may be less important than non-monetary rewards; but status may often be reflected by monetary reward levels.

* People tend more readily to accept and use reports of their performance which they regard as objective and unbiased.

* People's needs differ, hence management control systems and incentives need to be adapted to the personalities and attitudes of the people to whom they apply.

Figure 1.8 Incentives

1.4.3 Control Reports

A number of criteria should affect internal management control reports:

(a) *Personal responsibility.* It is people, not 'systems', that take action. Reports should, therefore, focus on the specific responsibility of individual managers, e.g. in distinguishing between 'controllable' and 'non-controllable' items. But even 'controllable' items may not be completely under any one person's control: all that is required is *significant influence.*

(b) *Suitable standards.* Actual performance may be compared with:
   i. pre-determined standards ('budgets');
   ii. historical standards (past actual performance); or
   iii. external standards (e.g. competitors' performance). Managers being evaluated need to accept the standards as reasonable.

(c) *Significance.* Modern technology can produce almost unlimited information about actual performance. Control reports should focus only on what is significant, often by means of management by exception.

(d) *Frequency.* The frequency of control reports should be determined by the significance of data and management's ability to take corrective action. For instance, sales and production levels are vital information whereas rent, rates and top management salaries need less frequent attention. Too frequent information may mean that managers are 'swamped' with data and have insufficent time to analyse, understand and take effective action.

(e) *Timeliness.* Management accounting may need to sacrifice accuracy in order to produce reports quickly.

(f) *Clarity.* Information should be communicated clearly. This implies not too much detail on any report; in particular, not reporting separately in every monthly report items which 'might come in useful' once every five years.

(g) *Integration.* The relationship between reports at different levels of the organisation should be clear. This enables managers to pursue items in more detail when necessary and avoids gaps in the system of responsibility accounting.

(h) *Forward-looking.* As well as comparing actual past performance with budget, it may often be useful for budget reports to provide 'latest estimates to the end of the year'. Another useful aspect of looking forward can be 'rolling budgets' which add a new twelfth month as each month passes, thereby retaining a budget for the next twelve months.

1.5 CHAPTER SUMMARY

Management accounting involves the provision, analysis and use of financial and other information in order to help managers run their businesses better. Managers should try to ensure that the benefits of management accounting outweigh its costs. In contrast, external financial accounting is legally required in order to satisfy shareholders, lenders, and other 'outside' users.

Management accounting deals with two different things:

(a) the use of scarce resources, and

(b) how people behave in business. It aims to help profit-seeking firms to earn good financial returns, and to help non-profit-seeking entities to use resources effectively.

Most firms accept the need for financial budgeting on an annual basis, as well as for longer-term planning. Annual budgets can help to co-ordinate the actions of managers with various responsibilities; and should be agreed in advance in order to secure commitment to achieving the desired results.

1.6 REVIEW QUESTIONS AND ANSWERS

1.6.1 Questions

1. What are the two main branches of accounting?
2. What are the main differences between the two main branches of accounting?
3. What is the primary aim for profit-seeking organisations?
4. If that aim is not achieved, what is likely to happen?
5. What other aims might profit-seeking organisations have?
6. What legal constraints are profit-seeking organisations subject to?
7. Identify three non-profit seeking organisations and their likely primary aims.
8. Why is management accounting relevant to non-profit seeking organisations?
9. Name two types of decentralisation.
10. What important aspects need to be considered in the long-term planning process?
11. What does 'long-term' mean?
12. What is the major management tool for short-term planning?
13. How are these short-term plans represented?
14. List four stages in a management control system.
15. Identify four common generalisations about incentives.
16. Identify five criteria that should affect internal management control reports.

Write out your answers. Then check with the answers over page.

1.6.2 Answers

1. Financial Accounting and Management Accounting.

2. Financial accounting is:
   (a) governed by Company Law and SSAPs;
   (b) for external users;
   (c) for the past (and present);
   (d) usually for one year;
   (e) concerned with the whole entity;
   (f) accurate;
   (g) objective, verifiable and consistent;
   (h) expressed in money terms;
   (i) somewhat technical (not easy to understand).

   Management Accounting is:
   (a) intended for managers' needs;
   (b) used internally only;
   (c) for the present and future;
   (d) for any appropriate period;
   (e) primarily for divisions and sub-groups;
   (f) required speedily;
   (g) relevant, useful and understandable;
   (h) in money or physical units;
   (i) for use by non-accountants.

3. To provide an adequate long-term financial return for their owners.

4. The owners may either change the top management team or sell out to new owners who will.

5. These include:
   (a) prudence;
   (b) duty to the community;
   (c) high market share;
   (d) product (or service) leadership;
   (e) very good company image;
   (f) highly skilled, trained and motivated employees;
   (g) use of the latest technology.

6. Legislation relating to safety, environmental protection, minimum wages and redundancy.

7. (a) Hospitals aim to alleviate illness and suffering.
   (b) Police aim to prevent and detect crime.
   (c) Ministry of Defence aim to protect the population against foreign invasion.

   (See also Figure 1.6 Organisational aims.)

8. Management accounting can help achieve better value for money.

9. (a) Functional;
   (b) divisional.

10. (a) Company objectives;
    (b) business definition;
    (c) analysis of company's strengths and weaknesses;
    (d) assessment of 'external' opportunities and threats;
    (e) competitors;
    (f) markets and products;
    (g) financial, physical and human resources needed.

11. Depends on the business. Maybe as little as one or two years (e.g. for a fashion business), or as much as forty years (e.g. for a life assurance company).

12. The annual budgets.

13. Details of budgeted profit and loss account, balance sheet, and cash flow.

14. Programming, budgeting, accounting for operations, and appraisal.

15. (a) Carrots motivate people more strongly than 'sticks'.
    (b) Time-lags dilute incentives.
    (c) Motivation may flag where a goal is either 'too easy' or 'too hard'.
    (d) Money may be less important than non-monetary rewards.

    (see also Figure 1.8 Incentives)

16. Any five from:
    (a) personal responsibility;
    (b) suitable standards;
    (c) significance;
    (d) frequency;
    (e) timeliness;
    (f) clarit;
    (g) integration;
    (h) forward-looking.

CHAPTER TWO

THE NATURE OF COSTS

2.1 INTRODUCTION

The cost of acquiring something is what must be given up to get it. This is often money, but may be goods, time or some other valuable resource. Cost, however, is not the same as value. Someone who buys a book for £6 is not valuing it at £6, but at more than £6. He might have been willing to pay as much as £10 for the book. (The difference of £4 is sometimes called the 'consumer surplus').

There are many reasons why a business wishes to measure its costs. The main purposes of costing are listed in Figure 2.1. Although identified under four major headings concerned with planning, controlling, decision making and reporting, these activities are very much interrelated, e.g. it is usually necessary to make decisions in order to plan.

---

1. FORECASTING, PLANNING AND BUDGETING
2. COST CONTROL
   - (a) Comparison of actual costs with:
     - (i) planned/budgeted/standard costs,
     - (ii) competitors.
   - (b) Implementation of cost reduction schemes.
3. DECISION MAKING
   - (a) Make or buy (applicable to both products and services).
   - (b) Setting of output levels and inventory levels.
   - (c) Aid to setting selling prices.
   - (d) Capital investment and disinvestment.
   - (e) Assessing changes to product or process.
4. ACCOUNTING REPORTS
   - (a) Monthly management accounts.
   - (b) Profitability of product/service/contract/ customer/project.
   - (c) Stock valuation (raw materials, purchased items, work-in-progress and finished goods).
   - (d) Published financial accounts.

Figure 2.1 Purposes of costing

When dealing with cost information one should beware of spurious accuracy. It is more important to get a rough idea of relevant costs than to make calculations to the nearest penny. Most costs can only be estimates. Indeed, some accountants are unwilling to provide any cost figures at all unless they know for what purpose managers are likely to use them!

Example 1: Economy Hire Cars Ltd owns a two-year-old car which, when not out on hire, shares a garage with three other cars. The annual garage rent is £2,400, insurance costs £200 a year, and the annual licence fee is £100. The car does 30 miles to the gallon, petrol costs 195p per gallon, and maintenance is reckoned to cost 2.5p per mile. Depreciation is £1,500 a year, and the car is expected to travel 20,000 miles next year. Figure 2.2 classifies expected operating costs for next year between fixed (see section 2.2.1) and variable (2.2.2) and between direct (2.3.1) and indirect (2.3.2).

	DIRECT (£)	*INDIRECT (£)*	*TOTAL (£)*
FIXED COSTS:			
Insurance	200		} 2,400
Licence fee	100		
Depreciation	1,500		
Garage rent		600	
VARIABLE COSTS:			
Petrol (6.5p/mile)	1,300		} 1,800
Maintenance (2.5p/mile)	500		
TOTAL COSTS	3,600	600	4,200

Figure 2.2 Car operating costs for next year

2.2 FIXED AND VARIABLE COSTS

2.2.1 Fixed costs

A fixed cost remains unchanged, for a given period, even when the volume of output changes. Thus, the cost of rent and rates for a retail shop will be the same whether business is booming or slack. However, this is true only within a given range of activity: for example, if business were to increase four-fold it might need to acquire larger premises and hence incur greater rental and rates costs. Such major changes in the scale of the business are infrequent so the fixed cost concept is of practical use for short-term planning such as annual budgeting.

Figure 2.3 shows that Economy Hire Cars Ltd's fixed costs (insurance, licence fee, depreciation and garage rent) remain at £2,400 regardless of the number of miles to be travelled during the next year.

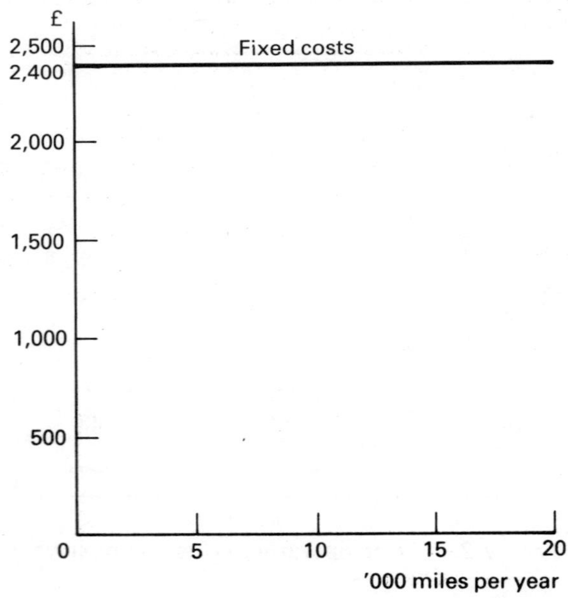

Figure 2.3 **Fixed costs for Economy Hire Cars Ltd**

Fixed costs do not vary with output volume changes, but due to inflation they are likely to change with time. For instance, the cost of Economy's insurance, licence fee and garage rent will probably increase annually. Depreciation based on historical cost may remain constant until the car has been written down to nil book value or until it is replaced. Fixed costs need to be reviewed periodically and any changes taken account of.

2.2.2 Variable costs

A variable cost is one which changes in proportion to the volume of output. Usually variable costs are regarded as a constant amount per unit of output. An example in a manufacturing business would be the cost of materials used in production of goods. The higher the level of production, the higher would be the cost of materials used; and the higher the volume of sales, the higher would be the materials cost of goods sold. The relationship between output and material costs would probably be linearly variable (i.e. directly proportional), unless the volume changed enough to affect material prices, e.g. bulk purchase discounts.

Economy's variable costs (petrol and maintenance) are 9.0p per mile or £1,800 for the 20,000 miles forecast (see Figure 2.4).

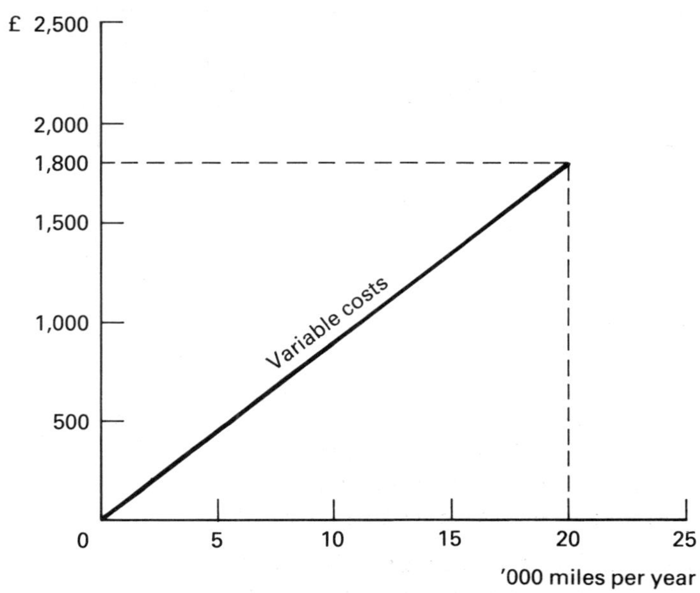

Figure 2.4 Variable costs for Economy Hire Cars Ltd

If Economy Hire Cars Ltd were to hire out the car at 25p per mile (petrol included), the company would be earning 16.0p per mile towards its other running costs. This difference of 16.0p per mile between the hiring out fee (or 'selling' price) of 25p per mile and the variable cost of 9.0p per mile is called the contribution. Contribution may be expressed on a per unit basis (e.g. 16.0p per mile) or in total, e.g. for 1,000 miles the contribution would be £160. In general terms, contribution (to fixed costs and profit) is equal to selling price less variable cost.

2.2.3 Semi-variable costs

Often the distinction between fixed and variable costs is not clear-cut. Some expenses may be semi-variable. Telephone, gas and electricity charges usually consist of a basic fixed charge plus a variable charge depending on usage (i.e. a 'two-part tariff').

Direct labour costs are often partly or wholly fixed even though they are still commonly treated as if they were wholly variable. When the workload falls due to a business slump or supplier strike, the workforce may be retained on full pay for a specified period. Some manufacturers even agree to make some payments to employees without the latter being required to attend work. And most employees, apart from the higher levels of management, expect overtime pay when the level of business activity requires more than the normal number of working hours. The wage rate per hour of overtime is often higher than the basic rate: perhaps 1½ times basic for evening work and Saturdays and double for Sundays. Figure 2.5 illustrates how a firm's manufacturing wages may be affected by changes in output.

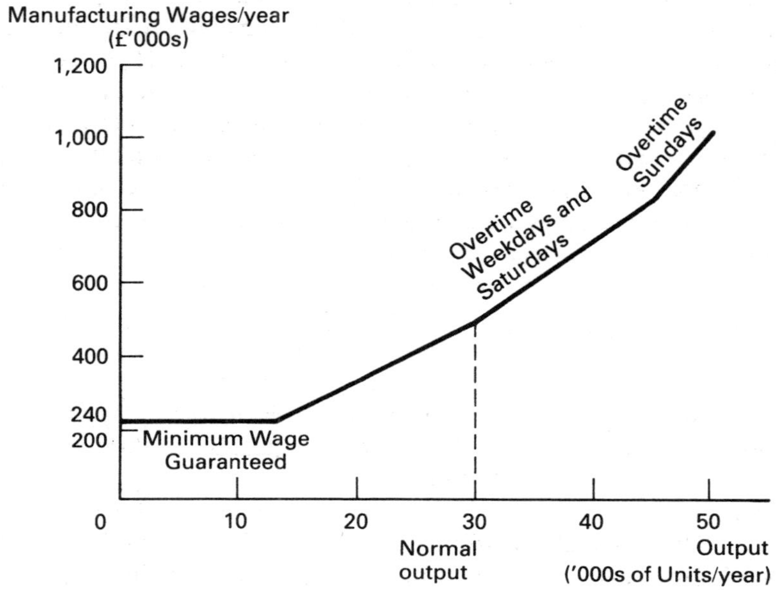

Figure 2.5 Manufacturing wages and output

2.2.4 Discretionary costs

Some costs belong in none of the three previous categories. Spending on advertising, training or research for example, results from management decisions, and is often called *discretionary*. These costs may change, not due to changes in volume, but as a result of management's 'discretionary' decisions. For instance, if sales volume fell, advertising expenditure might well be increased. Discretionary costs are not committed for the long term in the way that rent and rates are. For example, management may decide to reduce training expenditure by cancelling future programmes at very short notice. Expenditure on advertising, training or research is usually determined by management's subjective assessment of the (often long-term) benefits to the business compared with the (immediate) measurable cost.

Now consider the following case study.

Problem:

Pio's Pizza Parlour

Pio Sarno opened a pizza parlour in Hertfordshire, which he operated on his own. He leased the premises for two years at an annual cost of £3,000, paid in monthly instalments. Rates and the standing charges for electricity and gas amount to £65 per month. Pizzas are sold to customers at three times their (uncooked) cost from the supplier. Pio reckoned the usage charge for electricity and gas for last month was about £50. His pizza sales for the month were £2,400.

Analyse Pio's costs between fixed and variable. What were his contribution and profit for the month? Write your answer below.

Pio's Pizza Parlour - Costs Analysis

Fixed		Variable	
Item	Amount (per month)	Item	Amount (per month)
Total fixed =		Total variable =	

Contribution
(to fixed costs and profits) = sales revenue-variable costs
= -

= ______ per month

Profit = contribution - fixed costs
=

= ______ per month

Now check your answer, over page.

Solution:

Pio's Pizza Parlour - Costs Analysis

Fixed		Variable	
Item	Amount (per month)	Item	Amount (per month)
Lease	£250	Pizzas - uncooked	£800
Rates & Standing Charges	£65	Gas & Electricity usage	£50
Total fixed =	£315	Total variable	= £850

Contribution
(to fixed costs and profits) = sales revenue-variable costs
= £2,400 - £850
= **£1,550** per month

Profit = contribution - fixed costs
= £1,550 - £315
= **£1,235** per month

2.3 DIRECT AND INDIRECT COSTS

A further major classification of costs is their separation into either direct, or indirect costs.

2.3.1 Direct costs

When a cost can be easily and conveniently identified with a particular product, service or other specified activity, it is known as a *direct cost*. For example, the material cost in the manufacture of most products. With enough effort it might be possible to identify nearly all costs with specific operations. But a management accountant must always ask: is the resulting 'accuracy' worth the cost of getting the information?

Figure 2.2 shows that for Economy's car the direct costs are petrol, maintenance, insurance, licence fee and depreciation.

2.3.2 Indirect costs (overheads)

Indirect costs (or overheads as they are commonly known) are all those costs which *cannot* be easily and conveniently identified with a particular product or service. For instance, in a factory that produces a number of different products, the rent and rates of the premises are indirect product costs. In order to determine the total production cost of a particular product, the business could apportion the cost of rent and rates on some reasonable basis (see section 2.3.3).

In the Economy Hire Cars example (see Figure 2.2) the garage rent is an indirect cost. The annual garage rent of £2,400 has been apportioned (shared out) equally between the four cars occupying the garage.

Figure 2.6 shows the two ways in which costs can be classified.

	Fixed	Variable
Direct	Fixed/Direct	Variable/Direct
Indirect	Fixed/Indirect	Variable/Indirect

Figure 2.6 Classifying costs

Examples of each quadrant in Figure 2.6 are:

(a) Fixed/Direct - depreciation of equipment used on a single product.

(b) Variable/Direct - raw materials.

(c) Fixed/Indirect - factory rent for a multi-product factory.

(d) Variable/Indirect - energy costs for a multi-product organisation.

2.3.3 Apportionment of indirect costs

It is often useful to know the approximate total cost of a product or service. Comparing cost with selling price gives management an idea of product (or service) profit which can generate suggestions about how to run the business more profitably in future, e.g. by making changes to the product mix or customer mix. In order to make sound decisions, however, it is necessary to use costs which are *relevant* (see chapter 5).

Some common bases of apportionment are shown in Figure 2.7.

Cost	**Basis of Apportionment**
Rent and Rates	Floor space
Heating and Lighting	Floor space
Energy	Power rating of equipment and facilities
Depreciation of Plant and Equipment	Machine minutes used
Production Supervision	Direct labour minutes or cost
Indirect labour and expenses	Direct labour minutes or cost

Figure 2.7 Basis of apportionment of indirect costs

The apportionment of indirect costs usually involves two or more steps. For instance, rent and rates may firstly be apportioned on the basis of the floor space occupied by different departments, and then that proportion applied as a percentage of that department's direct labour costs. See Figure 2.8 for an illustration.

In most businesses indirect expenses may often most conveniently be allocated on some employee-related basis, such as number of personnel, direct labour hours worked, or total direct labour costs. Some businesses regard 'direct labour' as including only gross wages paid for directly identifiable productive output. Others will also include expenses such as employers' social security expenses (national insurance and pension contributions), holiday pay, and possibly other 'fringe benefits'. In total these can amount to a significant percentage of basic gross wages.

Apportionment of Rent and Rates

Step 1: Apportioning Rent and Rates cost to Departments

Department	Floor Space m^2	Apportionment (£'000)
A	200	10
B	600	30
C	500	25
D	700	35
	Total Rent and Rates =	100

Step 2: Applying departmental Rent and Rates cost to direct labour cost

Department	Direct Labour Cost (£'000)	Rent & Rates Cost (£'000)	Rent & Rates as a % of Direct Labour Cost
A	200	10	5
B	300	30	10
C	125	25	20
D	875	35	4

Figure 2.8 Apportionment of rent and rates to direct labour cost

The purpose of apportionment is to compile a reasonable estimation of the total cost for a product or service. Since judgement is involved in choosing the basis of apportionment, excessive complication, time and expense should be avoided. Because apportioned costs are *not* uniquely and unarguably correct, the total product costs should be regarded as indicative only. However, total product costs may help identify other alternatives that should be considered in more detail, e.g. out-sourcing instead of in-house manufacture; changes to materials, equipment or processes. Chapter 3 deals further with product (and non-product) costing.

Now consider the following case study.

Problems:

Pronto-Fix Garage

Pronto-Fix is a small garage dealing with motor car repairs and servicing. With the aid of three employees, the manager reckons that a total of 6,000 hours per year could be used effectively for repair and service work. The following budgeted information is available for the coming year.

	£
Total staff costs	42,000
Rent and rates	5,000
Depreciation of equipment	9,300
Electricity, gas and telephone	2,500
Advertising costs	2,700
Parts, materials, oils, etc.	45,000

Determine:

(a) the labour cost per effective hour;

(b) the overhead cost per effective hour to cover the cost of rent, rates, depreciation, electricity, gas, telephone and advertising;

(c) the gross labour cost per effective hour (for labour plus overhead);

(d) the price paid by the customer for six hours of labour time and £15 worth (at cost) of parts. Assume that Pronto-Fix add 20% to labour, overheads and parts to provide for financial charges and profit.

Write your answers on the next page.

Pronto-Fix Garage

(a) Annual labour cost =
Annual effective hours =
Labour cost per effective hour = $\frac{\text{Labour cost per year}}{\text{Effective hours per year}}$

= ______

= ______ per hour

(b) Total overheads (exclude parts, materials, oils, etc.) per year =
Annual effective hours =
Overhead cost per effective hour = $\frac{\text{Total overheads per year}}{\text{Effective hours per year}}$

= ______

= ______ per hour

(c) Gross labour cost per effective hour = labour cost per effective hour + overhead cost per effective hour

= £ per hour + £ per hour

= £______ per hour

(d) Total cost = (Labour hours x Gross Labour Rate per hour) + cost of parts

= (hrs x £ /hr) + £

= £ + £

= £______

Charge to customer = Total cost + 'Profit' margin

= £ + £

= £______

Now check your answer, over page.

Solution:

Pronto-Fix Garage

(a) Annual labour cost = £42,000
Annual effective hours = 6,000
Labour cost per effective hour = $\frac{\text{Labour cost per year}}{\text{Effective hours per year}}$

= $\frac{£42,000}{6,000 \text{ hours}}$

= £7.00 per hour

(b) Total overheads (exclude parts, materials, oils, etc.) per year = £19,500
Annual effective hours = 6,000
Overhead cost per effective hour = $\frac{\text{Total overheads per year}}{\text{Effective hours per year}}$

= $\frac{£19,500}{6,000 \text{ hours}}$

= £3.25 per hour

(c) Gross labour cost per effective hour = labour cost per effective hour + overhead cost per effective hour

= £7.00 per hour + £3.25 per hour

= £10.25 per hour

(d) Total cost = (Labour hours x Gross Labour Rate per hour) + cost of parts

= (6 hours x £10.25/hr) + £15.00

£61.50 + £15.00

= £76.50

Charge to customer = Total cost + 'Profit' margin

= £76.50 + £15.30

= £91.80

2.4 MARGINAL AND AVERAGE COSTS

2.4.1 Marginal costs

Marginal cost is the extra cost incurred as a result of producing one more unit of output. Within existing capacity constraints, marginal costs equal variable costs, *providing* that the extra output does not change the variable cost per unit. If, for instance, overtime is needed to produce additional output, then the marginal cost will exceed the previous variable labour cost per unit. Alternatively, marginal material cost would be lower if quantity discounts reduced the purchase price per unit.

When extra output requires additional fixed costs, the marginal cost may be extremely high.

For Economy Hire Cars Ltd the marginal cost is 9.0p per mile.

2.4.2 Average costs

The average cost is total costs divided by the total number of units of output. All costs are therefore considered whether they be fixed variable, semi-variable, discretionary, direct or indirect. So Economy Hire Cars Ltd's average cost per mile is expected to be 21.0p per mile (£4,200/20,000 miles).

Example 2: Geoffrey Boycott's career average is 56.0, higher than any other batsman who has scored more than 30,000 runs. But finally the time has come for Boycott's Last Innings. You do not have to be an expert cost accountant to see that if he is out for less than 56, his average will fall (slightly); while if he scores more than 56, or is not out, his average will rise. Only if he scores exactly 56, or is not out 0 (a rare event!), will his average remain at 56.0.

2.4.3 Marginal versus average costs

For many short-term business decisions, it is marginal rather than average, costs which are relevant.

Example 3: A nice example of the difference between average and marginal costs is given by the story of the office worker who went to have a haircut. When he returned the boss asked him where he had been.

Worker:	*To have a haircut.*
Boss:	*In office hours?*
Worker:	*Well, it* grew *in office hours!*
Boss:	*Not* all *of it, surely?*

Worker: *No, but then I didn't have it* all *cut off!*

In practice, different firms have widely different cost patterns. Unlike economists, accountants usually assume that marginal per-unit costs are constant, at least throughout the 'relevant range' of output. And business firms are trying to maximise profits, not to produce at minimum cost.

The distinction between marginal and average can be illustrated by reference to political arguments about British tax levels. Some people argue that British tax rates are high (by comparison with other countries), others that they are not. You might think this is simply a question of fact, about which it would be hard to continue arguing for decades on end. But the argument is still not over - because the participants often confuse average with marginal.

In terms of *average* tax levels, British taxes do not seem to be out of line with most other countries, certainly in the EEC: somewhat higher than Spain, somewhat lower than Denmark. But in terms of *marginal* rates of tax on incomes, for most of the post-war years British marginal rates of income tax have been considerably higher than most other countries. (Because those top marginal rates of tax actually yield very little revenue, they have not significantly affected the overall *average* weight of taxes).

Which is more relevant? It partly depends on the time horizon. If you are thinking of *emigrating* (a long-term decision) you will probably be concerned with *average* tax levels (among many other things, of course). But if you are wondering whether to work overtime this weekend, you will presumably be concerned with the rate of tax on your marginal earnings.

2.4.4 The importance of time

So far we have been discussing costs without much reference to time. But in the 'long run' a firm can change the scale of its operations. The short run is a period of time during which the inputs of some factors of production cannot be changed. The factor which is 'fixed' is often capital equipment, but it might be land or labour or materials. The calendar length of the short run may vary widely: it will be much shorter for a window cleaner than for a shipbuilder.

It follows that, in the long run, inputs of all factors of production can be varied.

A producer can alter plant capacity, a distributor can increase (or decrease) warehouse size, and so on. Thus, the 'long run' corresponds to the outlook facing a firm planning to enter, or remain in, business.

As we all know, another thing that takes time is learning. A firm's workers are likely to know better how to make a product after they have been doing so for some months than on their first day. This may enable a firm to reduce its marginal costs per unit. The learning relates more to the volume of output produced than to the lapse of time. This being so, the firm with the largest market share, and therefore the largest output per unit of time, should be learning at a faster rate than its competitors. If this does result in lower costs, a firm which is 'further down the learning curve' can either reduce its selling price, or make a higher contribution margin on each unit sold. Figure 2.9 illustrates the learning curve.

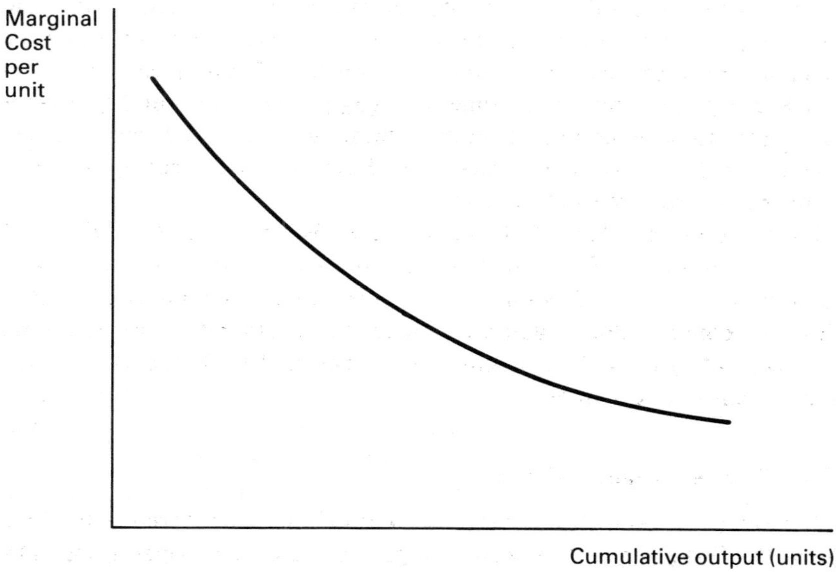

Figure 2.9 The learning curve

2.5 WHOSE COST?

Is the cost of running an organisation's centralised computer department fixed or variable? Is it direct or indirect? The answer depends upon whose cost is being determined.

When using its own computer equipment and salaried staff, an organisation's computer department cost is likely to be mostly fixed. But if the computer department charges other departments on the basis of their usage, they will regard these costs as variable. Hence the familiar dilemma: if departments are charged for computer costs, they may use 'too little' - given the existing facilities - but if not, they may use 'too much'.

Likewise, computer depreciation and staff salaries are direct costs for the computer department but appear to be indirect costs to other departments.

We need to identify the product, service, process, man, machine, section, department, plant, or company involved. The specific activity being costed is sometimes called the *cost objective*. Identifying 'whose cost' (= the cost objective) we seek, will enable us to determine whether a particular cost is fixed or variable, direct or indirect.

2.6 CHAPTER SUMMARY

Cost estimates are used to aid planning, control, decision making, and reporting. They can be classified in a number of ways: fixed and variable; direct and indirect; marginal and average

Fixed costs do not change when output changes (within the relevant range), whereas variable costs change in proportion to output. Some costs contain both a fixed and a variable element; while other costs are neither fixed nor variable, but depend on management discretion. Cost classification depends partly on the time-scale: no costs are 'fixed' forever.

Direct costs are those which can be traced to a specific activity (product, process, department, etc.), while indirect costs cannot (or not easily). In order to estimate total cost, the indirect costs must be apportioned between the various activities, on some reasonable basis.

Marginal cost is the extra cost resulting from one more unit of output, and may be relevant for certain business decisions. Average cost per unit of output is total cost divided by output volume.

2.7 REVIEW QUESTIONS AND ANSWERS

2.7.1 Questions

1. What are the main purposes of costing?
2. Define and give an example of each of the following:
   (a) Variable cost.
   (b) Fixed cost.
   (c) Semi-variable cost.
   (d) Discretionary cost.

3. What is a direct cost?
4. What is an indirect cost?
5. What is the distinction between an indirect cost and an overhead?
6. Why are indirect costs apportioned to products (or services)?
7. Explain the term 'basis of apportionment' and give two examples.
8. Give an example of each of the following types of cost:
   (a) Fixed and direct cost.
   (b) Fixed and indirect cost.
   (c) Variable and direct cost.
   (d) Variable and indirect cost.

9. What is marginal cost?
10. What is the distinction between marginal cost and variable cost?
11. How are average costs determined?
12. 'Since fixed costs are included in the calculation of average cost per unit, but not in the calculation of marginal cost per unit, the latter must always be less than unit average cost.' Do you agree?
13. What is contribution?
14. 'Because all costs are variable in the long-term, there is no such thing as a fixed cost.' Do you agree?
15. Are fixed costs the same every year?

16. How does the 'range of activity' affect fixed costs?
17. Is a discretionary cost a fixed cost?
18. Are the terms 'direct cost' and 'variable cost' synonymous?
19. Are indirect costs the same as fixed costs?
20. 'Accountants must be precise in their determination of costs.' Do you agree?

Write out your answers. Then check with the answers provided.

2.7.2 Answers

1. Planning, controlling, decision making, reporting.

2. (a) A variable cost is a cost which varies directly in proportion to output, e.g. material costs in a manufacturing concern.

   (b) A fixed cost is a cost which, within the 'relevant range' of output, is fixed for a given period, e.g. rates.

   (c) A semi-variable cost is a cost which is partly fixed and partly variable, e.g. electricity costs.

   (d) A discretionary cost is a cost which is neither fixed nor variable: it may change, but not necessarily in proportion to output, e.g. training, advertising, research.

3. Cost which is directly identifiable with a particular process, product or other specified activity.

4. Cost not directly identifiable with a process, product or other specified activity.

5. Indirect cost = overhead. There is no distinction.

6. Indirect costs are apportioned to products (or services) in order to know the approximate total cost.

7. The basis of apportionment is the common factor used in the process of sharing out indirect costs. Examples: floor space may be the basis of apportioning rent and rates; direct labour minutes may be the basis of apportioning indirect labour costs.

8. (a) Depreciation of equipment used on a single product.
   (b) Factory rent (for a multi-product factory).
   (c) Raw materials.
   (d) Energy costs (for a multi-product organisation).

9. The extra cost incurred as a result of producing one more (or one less) unit of output.

10. None, unless the additional unit of output necessitates additional fixed costs, and providing the variable cost per unit remains constant.

11. Total cost divided by the number of units produced.

12. No. At very high levels of output marginal cost may be greater than average cost, due to overtime premiums, etc.

13. Contribution (to fixed costs and profit) is sales revenue less variable costs. Contribution is expressed in total or on a per-unit basis (or per £ sales revenue).

14. No. Fixed costs are fixed (i.e. not normally changeable) in the short-term.

15. No. Due to management decisions, inflation and specific price changes, many fixed costs change each year.

16. Fixed costs are fixed only within the 'relevant range' of output. If the actual range of activity extends beyond the 'relevant range', the fixed costs may change.

17. No. A discretionary cost can be changed at management's discretion.

18. No. Whilst many direct costs are variable (e.g. materials) some direct costs are fixed (e.g. depreciation) and some variable costs are indirect (e.g. energy costs in a multi-product organisation).

19. No. Many indirect costs are fixed (e.g. rates) but some indirect costs are variable (e.g. energy costs) and some fixed costs are direct (e.g. depreciation of equipment used on one product).

20. No. In management accounting it is better to have approximate information quickly than precise information in three months' time. Also, total costs including overheads, involve subjective decisions about apportionment of overheads and are therefore not unarguably correct.

2.8 PROBLEMS

2.8.1 Questions

1. Park's is a small family-owned fish and chip shop selling fried fish and chips, fish cakes, sausages and pasties as well as wet fish, vinegar, sauces, canned soft drinks and other miscellaneous items.
During their most recent financial year, Park's made a profit of £18,000 as detailed below:

	£	£
Sales		
Fried fish	40,000	
Chips	20,000	
Other fried products	10,000	
Wet fish	10,000	
Other items	10,000	
		90,000
Expenses		
Fish for frying	28,000	
Potatoes	6,000	
Other fried products	6,000	
Frying oil and batter	2,400	
Frying equipment - depreciation	4,000	
Other equipment - depreciation	1,000	
Fish sold uncooked	10,000	
Other items	8,000	
Rent, rates, gas and electricity	6,600	
		72,000
Profit (before proprietor's drawings)		18,000

The following costs are regarded as fixed:

(i) depreciation (which is calculated on the straight line basis).

(ii) rent, rates and the standing charges for electricity and gas (£4,000 in total).

(a) What was the total of fixed and variable costs respectively?

(b) What was the contribution for the year? How much is this (on average) per £1 sales?

(c) What is the variable cost of a piece of fried fish sold for 80p? Assume that the frying oil and batter costs, as well as the variable electricity and gas costs, are apportioned in the same ratio as the expenses for fish for frying, potatoes and other fried products. What is the contribution on this piece of fish?

(d) Which costs are direct and which are indirect?

(e) What is the average cost of each £1 of sales?

2 Emilio De Camillo is a self-employed ice-cream salesman. The financial results of his first year in business are as follows:

			£
Sales of ice-cream and lollipops			36,000
Expenses		£	
Cost of goods sold ($^1/_3$ x Sales Price)		12,000	
Ice-cream van	: running costs	3,500	
	: depreciation	3,000	
			18,500
Profit (before proprietor's drawings)			17,500

Running costs include £1,100 for vehicle licence, insurance, garaging and routine maintenance. The remaining £2,400 relates to fuel, oil and vehicle repairs.

Depreciation has been calculated at 20% of vehicle cost.

Determine:

(a) the fixed costs for the year
(b) the variable costs for the year
(c) contribution, in total, and per £1 of sales
(d) the direct cost of £6,000 sales of lollipops
(e) total indirect costs for the year.

Would Emilio have made even more profit if he had bought two ice-cream vans (same price) and also recruited a driver-salesman at a cost of £8,000 per year if the latter made only £21,000 of sales? Assume the fixed costs are the same for both vehicles and variable costs are linearly variable.

3. A university has a permanent faculty of 50 lecturers, all on academic tenure (unsackable). Their total salaries amount to £800,000 a year. The university's fixed overheads are £450,000 a year. Other expenses total £200,000 at 'normal' capacity (reckoned to equal 80% of maximum capacity). At maximum capacity, total expenses would be £1,500,000.

(a) What are the marginal costs of offering courses which move the university from 80% to 85% of capacity?
(b) What is the marginal cost of a lecturer in Department A, who is otherwise teaching only 25 hours a year? (The standard teaching load is about 250 hours a year)
(c) What is the marginal cost of a lecturer in Department B, who is teaching 350 hours a year (reckoned to be the maximum feasible)? Outside teachers can be hired at £60 per hour. Would your answer be different if outside teachers cost £600 per hour? Why?

4. A public utility operates at 100% of capacity for only four hours out of 24, at 50% of capacity for a further eight hours, and at only 25% of capacity for the remaining twelve hours each day. Total operating costs are £132,000 per day. How

should costs be allocated? (Capacity actually used is shown in the following diagram).

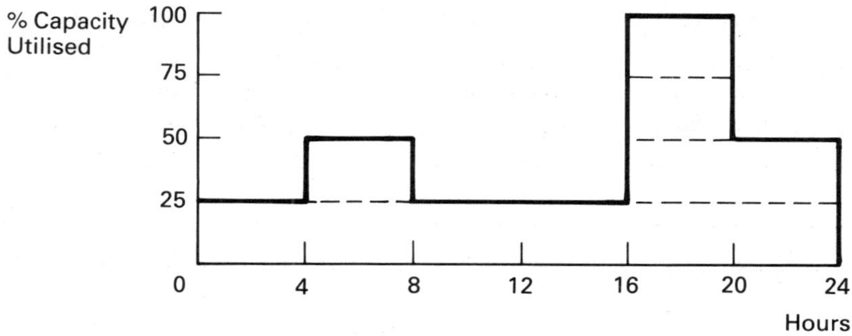

2.8.2 Solutions:

1. (a)

	£	
	4,000	(depreciation: frying equipment)
	1,000	(depreciation: other equipment)
	4,000	(rent, rates & standing charges)
Fixed costs =	9,000	

	£
Total expenses	72,000
Less fixed costs	9,000
= variable costs	63,000

(b) Contribution = Sales revenue - variable costs
= £90,000 - £63,000
= £27,000

Contribution per £1 sales revenue $= \frac{£27,000}{£90,000}$

= 30p

(c) Cost of fish uncooked $= \frac{£28,000 \text{ expenses}}{£40,000 \text{ sales}}$

x 80p selling price = 56p

Variable frying costs

	£
Frying oil and batter	2,400
Electricity and gas (£6,600 - £4,000)	2,600
	5,000

Variable fried product costs

	£
Fish	28,000
Potatoes	6,000
Other fried products	6,000
	40,000

$$\text{Frying costs} = \frac{\text{£5,000 frying costs}}{\text{£40,000 fried product costs}}$$

x 56p cost of uncooked fish = 7p

variable cost of fried fish = 56p + 7p = 63p

contribution = 80p - 63p
= 17p

(d)

Direct Costs	Indirect Costs
Fish for frying	Frying oil and batter
Potatoes	Frying equipment - depreciation
Other fried products	Other equipment - depreciation
Fish sold uncooked	Rent, rates, gas and electricity
Other items	

(e) Average cost per £1 sales

$$= \frac{\text{Total costs}}{\text{Sales revenue}} = \frac{\text{£72,000}}{\text{£90,000}}$$

= 80p per £1 sales

2. (a) Fixed costs for the year

	£
Ice-cream van depreciation	3,000
Vehicle licence, insurance, garaging & routine maintenance	1,100
Total fixed costs	4,100

(b) Variable costs for the year

	£
Cost of goods sold	12,000
Fuel, oil & vehicle repairs	2,400
Total variable costs	14,400

(c) Contribution = Sales revenue - variable costs
= £36,000 - £14,400
= £21,600

Contribution per £1 sales = $\frac{\text{Contribution}}{\text{Sales revenue}}$

= $\frac{£21,600}{£36,000}$

= 60p per £1 sales

(d) Direct cost of £6,000 sales of lollipops

= £6,000 x $^1/_3$ = £2,000

(e) Total indirect costs for the year = £3,500 + £3,000
= £6,500

Should Emilio buy two vans?		£	£
Additional sales revenue			21,000
Less additional expenses:			
cost of goods sold ($^1/_3$ x £21,000)		7,000	
driver-salesman		8,000	
ice-cream van:	running costs*	2,500	
	depreciation	3,000	
			20,500
Additional profit			500

* £1,100 fixed + ($\frac{21,000}{36,000}$ x £2,400) variable

Emilio would make an additional £500 profit. But is that enough to justify an outlay of £15,000 on an extra van? He is likely to get a better return on his money elsewhere.

CHAPTER THREE

PRODUCT COSTING

3.1 USES OF PRODUCT COSTS

Business managers often want to know the cost of products they make, or services they provide. In running a business, knowledge of costs can be helpful for a number of purposes. (See Figure 3.1).

(a) Planning financial resources required.

(b) Controlling costs - efficient use of resources.

(c) Carrying out value analysis exercises.

(d) Helping to set selling prices:
  (i) external;
  (ii) internal ('transfer prices').

(e) Valuing stock for financial accounts.

Figure 3.1 Uses of product costs

3.1.1 Planning financial resources

When planning for future periods, estimated costs are needed to complete budgeted profit and loss accounts and balance sheets. Cost information is also required for cash flow forecasts.

3.1.2 Controlling costs

Satisfactory business profits largely depend upon effective control of costs. Managers can compare actual costs against budgeted costs. If budgets are not being achieved management needs to take suitable action.

3.1.3 Value analysis

Efficient use of resources is not enough to achieve satisfactory long-term profits. Resources must also be used effectively.

Value analysis is a technique in which products are critically examined in order to promote ideas for cost reduction by changing either the materials and/or the manufacturing processes. The aim is to minimise product costs whilst retaining (or even improving) the product's functional performance and appearance. For example, plastic jug kettles are gradually replacing aluminium kettles: they are easier and cheaper to produce as well as having (arguably) an improved appearance.

3.1.4 Setting selling prices

Because private sector businesses need to sell their products at prices that exceed costs, cost information can be used to help establish minimum prices. Generally, the higher the price that can be obtained, the better. However, high prices might lead to low volumes.

Marketing people say that goods should be sold at a price that the 'market will bear'. Clearly if the market will only bear a price which is less than the marginal cost, then the item in question should not be produced. More about pricing in Chapter 4.

3.1.5 Stock valuation

Published accounts of UK companies must conform with the appropriate accounting standards. SSAP 9 requires balance sheets to show stocks at a cost which comprises:

(a) direct materials (cost of purchase);
(b) direct labour;
(c) production overheads;
(d) other attributable overheads.

3.2 FULL COSTING

Full costing aims to attribute all a business's costs (or perhaps just the manufacturing costs) to particular products. Direct costs can be directly identified with products; but indirect ('overhead') costs, by definition, *cannot* be directly identified with particular products. Hence there is a need first to apportion indirect costs to cost centres; and then to attribute the total costs of each cost centre to the various products which pass through it, on some more or less arbitrary basis.

The process of attributing *all* costs to individual products inevitably involves a degree of estimation. The results are by no means uniquely correct. The question, therefore, is whether they are close enough to be useful in running the business.

Section 3.3 discusses an alternative system of costing, which allocates only variable costs to products (known as 'marginal costing'). But many businesses prefer to use full costing.

3.2.1 Apportioning indirect costs to cost centres

A cost centre is a part of a business in respect of which costs can be identified and aggregated. It may be a whole factory, a part of a factory, or even single machines. Different cost centres may be appropriate for different levels of management decision. For example, possible cost centres are shown below for a company engaged in vehicle production:

Level of decision	Possible cost centres
* Group directors	Operating divisions: cars, buses, trucks
* Truck division directors	Truck factories A, B, C.
* Factory director	Truck assembly lines 1, 2, 3.
* Works manager	Welding machines, presses, lathes
* Press shop foreman	100-ton presses, 50-ton presses, etc.

Each cost centre should bear a 'fair share' of indirect costs. These should be apportioned on the most *realistic and convenient* basis that can be devised. The basis of apportionment might be:

(a) floor area (for rent and rates);
(b) employees (for indirect supervision, personnel costs);
(c) book value of assets (for depreciation of plant, insurance).

3.2.2 Absorption of indirect costs by products

Once all overhead costs have been apportioned to cost centres, they can be charged out to individual *products* by sharing out the cost centre's overheads among all units passing through that cost centre. The accounting term for this is absorption (because the products 'absorb' the overhead costs). It requires computing an overhead absorption (or 'recovery') rate, based on some notion of standard or 'normal' volume. That predetermined rate of overhead absorption is then applied to actual volume in order to determine 'actual' product costs. Common bases for overhead absorption are:

(a) direct labour (either hours or costs);
(b) units of output;
(c) machine hours.

Example 1: Suppose a business expects total overheads applicable to a cost centre will be £480,000 next year; and the cost centre is expected to operate at 80% of 'capacity' of 100,000 direct labour hours per year. Then overheads will be 'absorbed' at the rate of £6.00 per direct labour hour (i.e. £480,000/80,000 hours) for the purpose of product costing. Then for various purposes (such as quoting a price for a special job, or valuing stock at the end of a period) one may estimate the direct costs (material and direct labour) separately *and then simply add on the standard overhead absorption rate. This is often expressed as a percentage of the direct labour cost. So if labour costs were £4.00 per hour, overheads (@ £6.00 per direct labour hour) would represent 150% of direct labour costs.*

Example 2: Costs for a particular job include £7,000 for material, and £4,000 for direct labour. The standard overhead costs would be 150% of direct labour, i.e. £6,000; and total factory costs for the job would be £17,000 (i.e. £7,000 plus £4,000 plus £6,000).

Figure 3.2 shows the general approach:

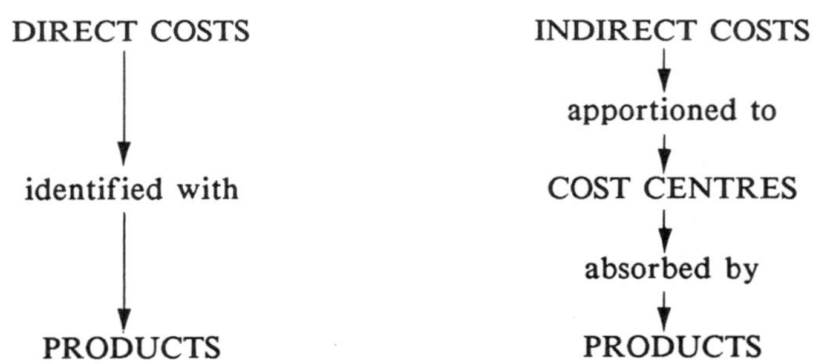

Figure 3.2 Absorption (full) costing

Now examine the following case study:

Easidig Garden Equipment Ltd (A)

Problem:

Easidig make shovels, spades and garden forks which they sell to local retailers. During the last three months they made and sold 8,000 forks, 7,000 spades and 5,000 shovels. The gross manufacturing labour cost (including holiday pay, sick pay, national insurance, etc.) is £4 per hour for each man. The manufacturing times and material costs are as follows:

	Fork	Spade	Shovel
Labour minutes per unit			
Fabrication	6	6	9
Assembly	3	3	3
Materials cost per unit			
Steel	£2.30	£1.80	£1.70
Wood	£0.50	£0.50	£0.60
Fasteners	£0.10	£0.10	£0.10

Total manufacturing overheads for the last three months were £39,000 and are recovered on direct labour minute.

Determine for each product:

(a) labour cost per unit;
(b) material cost per unit;
(c) manufacturing overhead cost per unit;
(d) total cost per unit.

Write your answers below.

(a) Labour cost per unit:

	Labour mins. per unit x	Labour rate	=
Fork	mins. x £	per hour/60	=
Spade	mins. x £	per hour/60	=
Shovel	mins. x £	per hour/60	=

(b) Material cost per unit:

	Steel		Wood		Fasteners		Total
Fork		+		+		=	
Spade		+		+		=	
Shovel		+		+		=	

(c) Manufacturing overhead cost per unit:

Labour mins./unit	x	no. of units produced	=	labour mins.
Fork	x		=	
Spade	x		=	
Shovel	x		=	
		Total labour minutes	=	

Manufacturing overhead cost per minute = Manufacturing overhead cost / Total labour minutes

=

= £ per minute

Therefore, manufacturing overhead cost per unit = manufacturing overhead cost per minute x labour minutes per unit.

	Mfg overhead £/minute	x	minutes	=	£/unit Mfg overhead
Fork		x		=	£
Spade		x		=	£
Shovel		x		=	£

(d) Total cost per unit:

	Labour	+	material	+	mfg overhead	=	total
Fork		+		+		=	£
Spade		+		+		=	£
Shovel		+		+		=	£

Now see over the page to check your answer.

SOLUTION

(a) Labour cost per unit:

	Labour mins. per unit		Labour rate
Fork	9 mins.	x	£4.00 per hour/60 = £0.60
Spade	9 mins.	x	£4.00 per hour/60 = £0.60
Shovel	12 mins.	x	£4.00 per hour/60 = £0.80

(b) Material cost per unit:

	Steel		Wood		Fasteners		Total
Fork	£2.30	+	£0.50	+	£0.10	=	£2.90
Spade	£1.80	+	£0.50	+	£0.10	=	£2.40
Shovel	£1.70	+	£0.60	+	£0.10	=	£2.40

(c) Manufacturing overhead costs per unit:

	Labour mins./unit	x	no. of units produced	=	labour mins.
Fork	9 mins.	x	8,000	=	72,000
Spade	9 mins.	x	7,000	=	63,000
Shovel	12 mins.	x	5,000	=	60,000
Total labour minutes				=	195,000

Manufacturing overhead cost per minute

$$= \frac{\text{Mfg overhead cost}}{\text{Total labour minutes}} = \frac{£39,000}{195,000 \text{ mins.}} = £0.20 \text{ per min}$$

Therefore, manufacturing overhead cost per unit = manufacturing overhead cost per minute x labour minutes per unit.

Manufacturing overhead

	£/mins.	x	mins.	=	£/unit mfg. Oh'd
Fork	£0.20	x	9	=	£1.80
Spade	£0.20	x	9	=	£1.80
Shovel	£0.20	x	12	=	£2.40

(d) Total cost per unit:

	Labour	+	material	+	mfg overhead	=	total
Fork	£0.60	+	£2.90	+	£1.80	=	£5.30
Spade	£0.60	+	£2.40	+	£1.80	=	£4.80
Shovel	£0.80	+	£2.40	+	£2.40	=	£5.60

3.3 MARGINAL COSTING

3.3.1 Contribution and profit

We saw in section 2.2 that variable costs are those which change proportionately with output, while fixed costs remain unchanged. In relating costs to revenues, it may be useful to attribute variable costs to products without trying to apportion fixed costs to products. This avoids arbitrary guesses about how the total fixed costs are to be apportioned as they are often not easily identified with particular products. In most cases any apportionment is likely to be arbitrary and subject to a large margin of error.

The excess of sales revenue over variable costs is known as contribution. This means 'contribution towards covering fixed costs and profits'. Of course, contribution is not the same as profit. In order to determine profit, the fixed costs, in total, have to be deducted from the total contribution of all the firm's products.

Figure 3.3 illustrates with an example, the numbers for which are set out in Figure 3.4. In estimating each product's contribution, there are three simple steps:

(a) For each cost centre, allocate variable costs to the appropriate product;

(b) For each product, total the variable costs from the various cost centres;

(c) For each product, deduct total variable costs from sales revenue, to give the product's contribution. Finally,

(d) Add together all the products' contributions, and deduct total fixed costs, in order to determine total profit.

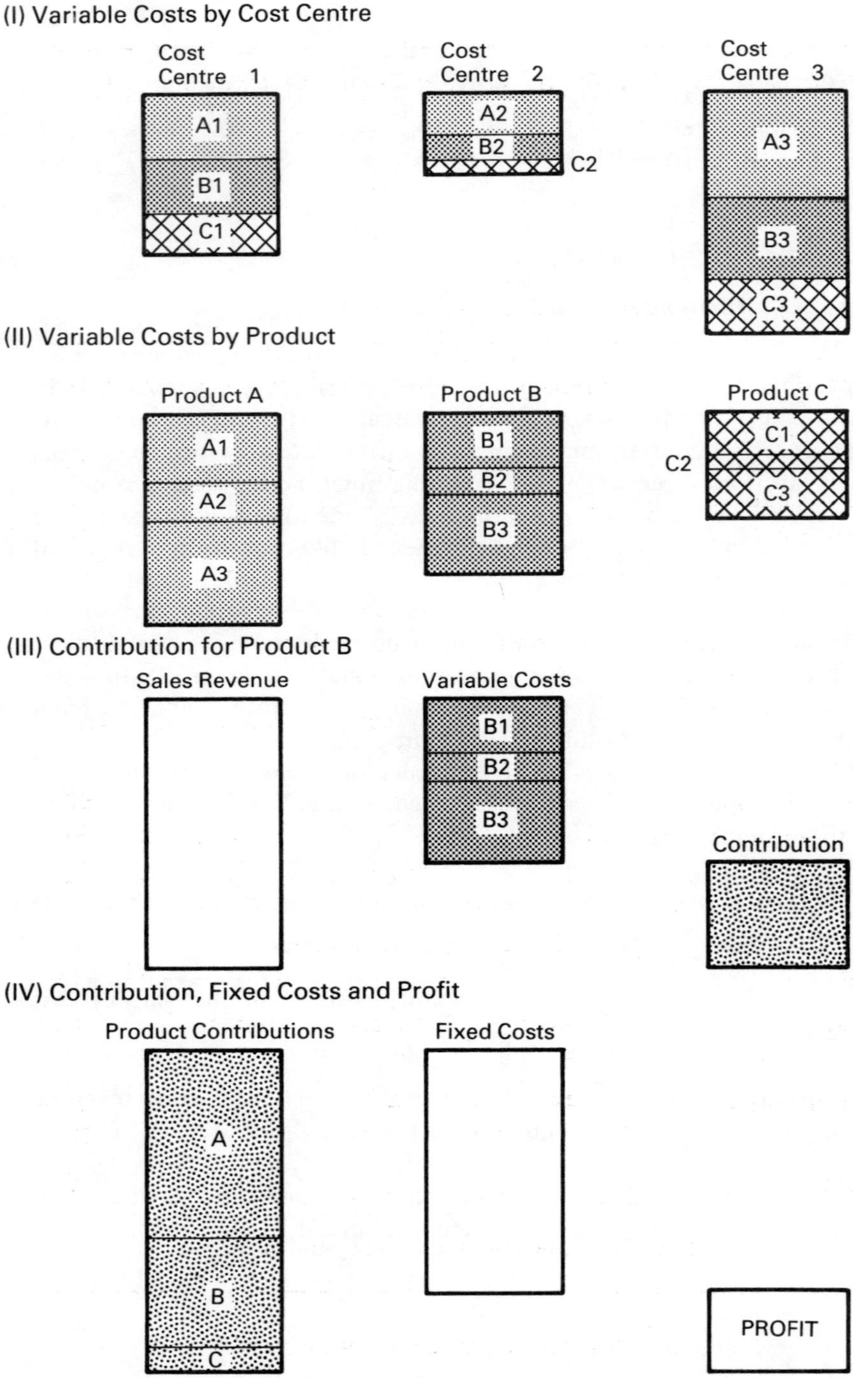

Figure 3.3 Variable costs, contributions and profit

£'000	Cost Centre 1	Cost Centre 2	Cost Centre 3
Product A	5	3	8
Product B	4	2	6
Product C	3	1	4
Total	12	6	18

(I) Variable costs by cost centre

£'000	Product A	Product B	Product C		Total
Cost Centre 1	5	4	3	=	12
Cost Centre 2	3	2	1	=	6
Cost Centre 3	8	6	4	=	18
Total	16	12	8	=	36

(II) Variable costs by product

£'000	Product A	Product B	Product C		Total
Sales Revenue	30	20	10	=	60
Variable Costs	16	12	8	=	36
= Contribution	14	8	2	=	24

(III) Contribution by product

£'000	Product A	Product B	Product C		Total
Contribution	14	8	2	=	24
Fixed Costs	NOT APPORTIONED			=	18
Profit				=	6

(IV) Contribution, fixed costs and profit

Figure 3.4 Variable costs, contributions and profit

3.3.2 The uses of marginal costing

Marginal costing is objective, in that it does not try to apportion fixed costs to particular products. It is fairly simple. It can apply to current and future situations, as well as for past evaluation. It focusses attention on products which appear to be making only small contributions (or even negative ones).

One of the main uses of marginal costing is in comparing actual current performance with the budgeted (planned) performance. We shall be discussing this kind of variance analysis in Chapter 7. It is helpful to be able to analyse a firm's planned total profit, in order to know which aspects of the business need further investigation and possibly corrective action. Since there will need to be regular reports, to be considered by managers who are not expert accountants, the simpler the analysis is to prepare and to understand, the better.

Because it is simple, the marginal costing approach can incorporate changes in information as soon as they are known. More complex methods may make this impracticable, so that they tend to be out of date.

In interpreting the results, one will usually be comparing an actual outcome with a *standard*. Very often this will be the budget, usually prepared and agreed before the start of the accounting period. It is not necessarily disastrous for a product to show a *small* contribution (though a negative contribution would be unusual in most firms). A new product may take time for sales to develop. Or an old product may be about to be phased out because its costs have been growing more rapidly than selling prices can be increased.

There are certain disadvantages with marginal costing. Perhaps the most important is that some people may tend to confuse contribution with profit. Thus, even a small positive contribution may be regarded as satisfactory. Since, however, fixed costs must be covered before a firm makes any *profit*, in total the positive contributions from all the firm's products need to be at least large enough to cover the fixed costs.

Marginal costing tends to be looking at fairly short-term aspects of a business, where the scale of operations is already fixed. Where decisions about changing the scale of the business are concerned, a good deal more information will be needed. Marginal costing is also more applicable where no major changes in stock levels are taking place.

In interpreting operating results in the light of marginal costing, it may be difficult to know how much contribution is 'required' from any product. But this should be resolved at the budgeting stage, difficult though it may be. The state of the markets for the various products is also critical. For example, if one product's costs increase (say because raw materials costs have increased more than expected), it may be impossible to raise selling prices, at least in the short term. It is true that some firms try to set their selling prices on the basis of variable costs plus a 'mark-up'. But (a) this 'mark-up' percentage may not be the same for all products, and (b) it may not be possible to maintain the level of mark-up for a product if selling conditions change.

Continuing the study of Easidig Garden Equipment Ltd., results for the last quarter are as follows:

Easidig Garden Equipment Ltd (B)

	Fork	Spade	Shovel
Sales (units)	8,000	7,000	5,000
Price per unit	£8.00	£7.00	£6.00
Variable costs			
Labour cost	£0.60	£0.60	£0.80
Materials cost	£2.90	£2.40	£2.40
Fixed costs			
Manufacturing overheads	£39,000		
Sales & Admin. costs	£25,000		

Determine:

(a) Contribution per unit of each product.
(b) Contribution in total for each product.
(c) Total contribution.
(d) Profit for the quarter.

Write your answers below.

(a) Contribution to profit and overheads
= selling price - variable costs

	Price/unit		Variable costs/unit		Contribution/unit
Fork		-		=	
Spade		-		=	
Shovel		-		=	

(b) Contribution in total for each product = Contribution per unit x number of units sold

	Contribution/unit	x	Units Sold	=	Contribution
Fork		x		=	
Spade		x		=	
Shovel		x		=	___________

(c) Total Contribution = ___________

(d) Profit = Total Contribution - total fixed costs
= -
= ___________

Now check your answers over the page.

SOLUTION

(a) Contribution to profit and overheads
= selling price - variable costs

	Price/unit		Variable costs/unit		Contribution/unit
Fork	£8.00	-	£3.50	=	£4.50
Spade	£7.00	-	£3.00	=	£4.00
Shovel	£6.00	-	£3.20	=	£2.80

(b) Contribution in total for each product = Contribution per unit x number of units sold

	Contribution/unit		Units Sold		Contribution
Fork	£4.50	x	8,000	=	£36,000
Spade	£4.00	x	7,000	=	£28,000
Shovel	£2.80	x	5,000	=	£14,000
(c)Total Contribution				=	£78,000

(d) Profit = total contribution - total fixed costs
= £78,000 - £64,000
= £14,000

3.4 FULL COSTING VERSUS MARGINAL COSTING

Both full costing and marginal costing are used in practice. Where indirect costs form a high proportion of total costs, management are more likely to make an effort to apportion them between products. But the extent to which some overheads can be identified with particular products is often a matter of degree. For example, factory rent may be apportioned on the basis of floor space, even though that is not the only possible basis. Or indirect supervision may be split between products on the basis of direct labour hours worked on each product, although it may not follow that supervision is split in exactly the same proportions.

Full costing does arrive at a 'profit' for each product, but only after more or less arbitrary apportionment of indirect costs. The accounting calculation, and resulting management reports, can be difficult to understand; especially since changes in stock levels can seriously distort the results.

Marginal costing is simpler to apply, and easier to understand, but it does risk pressure to 'shave' margins as long as a product is showing any positive contribution at all. If this is not carefully watched, the result can be that the overall total contribution of all a firm's products added together is not large enough to cover the total fixed costs. The result will then be a loss, of course. Figure 3.5 summarises the advantages and disadvantages of both full costing and marginal costing.

Full Costing	**Marginal Costing**
Advantages	*Advantages*
Indicates total costs of a product or service.	Easy to understand.
Identifies product profitability.	Simplifies budgeting and variance analysis.
Useful to compare with selling price.	Can quickly incorporate changes in cost.
	Avoids arbitrary apportionment of fixed costs.
	Identifies low contribution products.
Disadvantages	*Disadvantages*
Difficult to understand.	Over-emphasis on short-term results.
Complicated and time-consuming to use.	Possible confusion of contribution with profit.
Tendency to become out-of-date.	May encourage selling at below full cost.
Full costs are subjective, not uniquely correct.	
Potentially misleading when stock levels change.	

Figure 3.5 Full costing versus marginal costing: advantages and disadvantages

To show how the two approaches might differ, the fixed costs in Figure 3.4 are allocated below between products, on three different bases. Without knowing a good deal more about the business, we cannot tell which, if any, is 'correct'. (Indeed, it may be that even people who have worked in the business for years cannot tell either).

£'000	Product A	Product B	Product C		Total
(a) Fixed costs in proportion to sales revenue					
Contribution	14	8	2	=	24
Fixed costs	9	6	3	=	18
'Profit' ('loss')	5	2	(1)		6
(b) Fixed costs in proportion to variable costs					
Contribution	14	8	2	=	24
Fixed costs	8	6	4	=	18
'Profit' ('loss')	6	2	(2)		6
(c) Fixed costs apportioned equally					
Contribution	14	8	2	=	24
Fixed costs	6	6	6	=	18
'Profit' ('loss')	8	2	(4)		6

Figure 3.6 Three possible ways to apportion fixed costs

The three ways to apportion fixed costs as in Figure 3.6 might be justified as follows:

(a) apportioning fixed costs in proportion to sales revenue is reasonable if the fixed costs are salesmen's salaries;

(b) apportioning fixed costs in proportion to variable costs is reasonable if the fixed costs relate to supervision of manufacturing labour (assuming manufacturing labour is a large portion of variable costs);

(c) apportioning fixed costs equally over each product line might be reasonable where top management spends its time roughly equally over each of its products.

The choices available for apportioning fixed costs are many but two basic approaches are available:

(a) use one common basis for apportioning all fixed costs to products;

(b) use the most appropriate basis for apportioning each category of fixed cost.

3.5 COSTS FOR COMPARISON

If one wants to prepare estimates for costs of future operations, one can either use figures of past performance, or else construct estimated costs based on other information available within the firm. The first method uses historical costs, while the second uses standard costs.

3.5.1 Historical costs

In producing a cost statement of a firm's operations, it may be fairly simple to look at costs that have already been incurred. Often the data is readily accessible. The obvious danger in using past costs is that they may not reflect present circumstances if conditions have changed.

In using a statement of past costs as a basis for estimating the future, one is implicitly assuming the statement to be an acceptable basis. But what if the past period was atypical? It may have been an especially good year, or an especially bad one. What if particular costs are known to have changed since then?

3.5.2 Standard costs

An alternative to historical costs is to use standard costs as a basis for judging future operations. Standard costs are predetermined costs that should be attainable and are often expressed on a per unit basis. Establishing a standard (full) cost involves:

(a) determination of the quantity and price of materials to be used,

(b) determination of direct labour minutes and related rate of pay, and

(c) addition of an overhead charge.

If the job is new, estimates based on similar work might be used. When in production, actual information may be used, possibly supplemented by time study and method study. Past performance can also be modified to allow for desirable or expected changes, so that standard costs genuinely become a useful 'standard' against which to measure actual performance in future. Standard costs can also be used for other purposes, such as valuing stock or setting selling prices.

Example 3: A firm plans to sell 900,000 pressings in June of next year, which it must produce in April. The standard direct labour cost of producing them is to be calculated for the pressing cost centre. The following information is available: the firm works a 5-day 40-hour week, plus overtime. The presses can theoretically make 100 pressings per minute, but in practice the total output is reduced to 75 per minute because of breakdowns, etc. The projected wage-rate for press operators next April is £3.00 per hour, increased to £4.00 per hour if overtime is worked. The company will have one press and operator available for this work next April, which will contain 22 working days.

In order to calculate the standard direct labour cost, we must calculate the machine hours required to produce the parts. We know the presses can produce 75 pieces per minute, or 4,500 per hour. Hence the number of machine hours needed to produce 900,000 pressings is 900,000/4,500 = 200 hours. The number of press hours available in April is 22 x 8 hours, or 176 hours; so there will be a need for 24 hours of overtime.

The cost of the operator's wages will therefore be 176 hours @ £3.00 (= £528) plus 24 hours @ £4.00 (= £96), making a total of £624. Hence the standard cost of direct labour will be £624 on this job.

Using standard costs like this allows a firm to plan its use of financial resources. Budgets can be drawn up, which are useful as production can be predicted with fair accuracy. Obviously, standard costing depends on accuracy in both estimating and measuring actual costs. It also requires a fairly complex organisation for setting and monitoring standards, which not all organisations may require. It would be beyond the scope of many smaller companies; but larger business find some such approach necessary to help them plan their activities into the future.

Standard costs are more often used in high volume manufacturing where the product life is several years or longer.

3.6 COSTING SERVICES AND PROJECTS

This chapter has explained the important principles of costing, assuming a manufacturing organisation as the basis for the costing framework. Much of this chapter also applies to determining costs outside the manufacturing sector. We shall look at two other major areas to see how we can incorporate what we have learned to date.

3.6.1 Services

The cost of services may include little or no material costs. Moreover, most costs might well be fixed in the short-term.

Example 4: Consider a hotel with a restaurant and bar. The hotel offers three services:

(a) bedrooms (overnight accommodation);
(b) restaurant, open to residents and non-residents;
(c) bar, open to residents and non-residents.

Direct materials for these three services would include the following:

(a) bedrooms - bed linen, soap, toilet paper, tissues;
(b) restaurant - food, cooking oil;
(c) bar - drinks, cigarettes, crisps, nuts.

These costs are likely to be variable and can be allocated directly to one of these three services.

Staff costs are likely to be largely fixed, although extra personnel might be needed at busier times.

Most of the hotel's personnel costs can be identified directly with the business area concerned.

Other direct costs can also probably be identified. Those which involve substantial sums are likely to be used for a number of years will be capitalised and depreciated over their expected useful life. The remaining other direct costs will be expensed in the year in which the expense was incurred.

Some costs (rent, rates, financial charges, etc.) cannot be identified directly with any particular service. A cost summary is provided in Figure 3.7.

	Direct Costs			Indirect Costs (mostly fixed)
Service	Materials (variable)	Labour (mostly fixed)	Other costs (mostly fixed)	
a. Bedrooms	Bed linen Soap Toilet paper Tissues	Chambermaid	Furniture Televisions Telephones	Building rent (or depreciation) Rates Electricity Gas Water
b. Restaurant	Food Cooking oil	Chef Waiters Washers-up	Furniture Crockery Cutlery Cooking equipment and utensils	Laundry Maintenance Reception General Management Advertising Financial charges
c. Bar	Drinks Cigarette Cigars Crisps Nuts	Bar staff Washers-up	Glasses Bar equipment	

Figure 3.7 Hotel service costs - direct and indirect

In many service businesses profit is highly sensitive to volume. Thus, the hotel's profitability will be highly dependent on occupancy. With most costs fixed, the contribution (to cover fixed costs and profits) will be a large percentage of any additional sales revenue. See Figure 3.8.

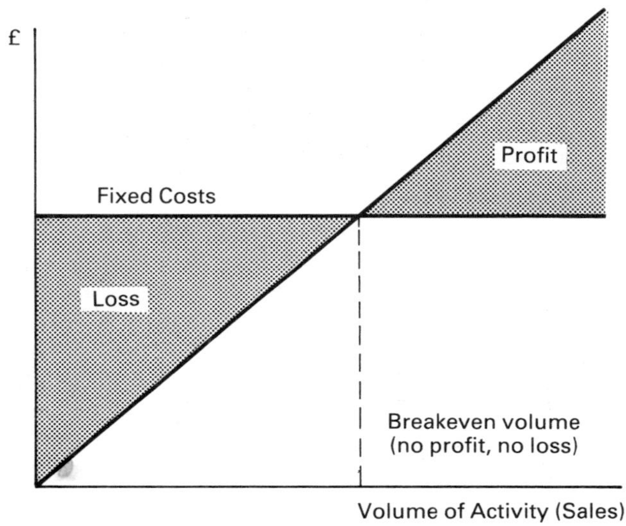

Figure 3.8 Effect of volume on hotel profitability

The key aspects of service operations will therefore be:

(a) the initial business strategy decision about the establishment and size of the business;
(b) generating a high level of facilities utilisation at a price needed to give, at least, satisfactory profits;
(c) controlling costs, whilst providing customer satisfaction.

3.6.2 Contracts and projects

Finally in this chapter, we need to consider the determination of costs for contracts and projects. Generally the term 'contract' is used in relation to standard products, and 'project' for non-repetitive work. Sections 3.1 to 3.5 are therefore applicable to contracts.

When determining project costs, job costing is used. This requires cost estimates for material, labour and manufacturing overheads, in order to establish an estimated manufacturing cost. The greater the use of common component parts the more accurate the estimated cost should be. For technically new business, the actual cost may differ widely from that estimated. A cost contingency for unknown (but expected) problems is therefore usually included in cost estimates.

For longer-term projects (5-15 years' duration) there are additional problems to those normally encountered in a manufacturing business:

(a) the effects of inflation over several years;
(b) greater uncertainty due to unfamiliarity with non-repetitive work;
(c) possible construction or installation activities in foreign countries;
(d) the longer-term exposure to currency fluctuations.

Fixed price projects involve considerable financial risk. Unexpected delays or unexpectedly high inflation will increase contractors' costs. If the project price is fixed, profit will be reduced. Contractors therefore seek a price which will be adjusted for inflation (often known as contract price adjustment or a cost escalation clause).

Projects containing technically new equipment, are frequently prone to unforeseen complications. These result in higher costs caused by having to carry out work later, and maybe a cost penalty for late completion. Also 'liquidated damages' may be incurred if the completed project fails to perform satisfactorily.

Additional uncertainties relating to weather conditions and working abroad mean greater risk in construction or installation.

3.7 CHAPTER SUMMARY

Knowledge of product costs helps in planning financial resources, cost control, value analysis, setting selling prices, and in valuing stock.

Full product costs include both direct and indirect costs. Indirect costs are first allocated to cost centres, from whence they are absorbed by products. Comparing full costs with product selling prices indicates profit.

Marginal costing takes account only of variable costs: it is simpler than full costing, in that it requires no arbitrary allocation of fixed costs. Product selling price less variable cost gives the contribution to fixed costs and profit.

Whether using full costs or marginal costs, it is helpful to compare actual costs against budgeted costs. The latter may be based upon historical costs or standard costs.

Either full costing or marginal costing techniques can be used to determine service costs, even though many services involve few material costs and may have a high proportion of fixed costs.

Estimating and controlling long-term project costs can be difficult, due to the time involved, the unique nature of the work, and often the problems of working abroad.

3.8 REVIEW QUESTIONS AND ANSWERS

3.8.1 Questions

1. Why do businessmen want to know product costs?
2. Why are cost centres needed for full costing?
3. On what basis should indirect costs be apportioned to cost centres?
4. Suggest three different bases for apportioning indirect costs.
5. What is 'absorption'?
6. Name three possible bases for overhead absorption by products.
7. What is the difference between direct and indirect costs?
8. What is the difference between contribution and profit?
9. What is marginal costing?
10. What are the key steps in determining a product's contribution?
11. How can one move from a product's contribution to a firm's overall profit?
12. Name two advantages of marginal costing.
13. Why may a small positive contribution be satisfactory?
14. Name two disadvantages of marginal costing.
15. Why may a small positive contribution be unsatisfactory?
16. What is the difference between full costing and marginal costing?
17. Name two reasons why historical costs may be unsatisfactory as standards.
18. What are standard costs?
19. Name three different purposes for which standard costs can be used.
20. What are the necessary conditions for standard costing?
21. Name two advantages of full costing.
22. In what major respects does costing for services differ from costing for manufacturing?
23. What additional factors have to be considered when estimating long-term project costs?

Write out your answers. Then check with the answers over page.

3.8.2 Answers

1. Product costs are used for planning required financial resources, controlling costs, value analysis, setting selling prices and valuing stock.

2. Because indirect costs cannot be identified directly with products; they need to be apportioned to cost centres and then absorbed by products on some reasonable basis.

3. The most realistic and convenient basis that can be devised.

4. (a) Floor area (e.g. for rates).
   (b) Number of employees (e.g. for indirect labour).
   (c) Book value of assets (e.g. for insurance costs).

5. Absorption is the charging out ('recovery') of indirect costs apportioned to cost centres, to individual products that pass through that cost centre.

6. (a) Direct labour (either hours or costs).
   (b) Units of output.
   (c) Machine hours.

7. A direct cost is directly identifiable with a particular process, product, or other specified activity, whereas an indirect cost is not.

8. Profit is contribution (to fixed costs and profit, i.e. sales revenue less variable costs) less fixed costs.

9. Marginal costing is the costing method which allocates only variable costs, not fixed costs, to products.

10. (a) For each cost centre, allocate variable costs to the right product.
    (b) For each product, total the variable costs from the various cost centres.
    (c) For each product, deduct total variable costs from sales revenue, to give the product's contribution (to fixed costs and profit).

11. Add together all the products' contributions, and deduct total fixed costs, in order to determine total profit.

12. (a) Easy to understand.
    (b) Simplifies budgeting and variance analysis.
    See also figure 3.5.

13. Because the next best alternative may be no contribution at all.

14. (a) Possible confusion of contribution with profit.
    (b) Encourages selling at below full cost.

15. A small positive contribution may still mean selling at below full cost. In the long-term the business cannot afford to sell all its products below full cost. In the short-term there may be no better alternatives.

16. Full costing takes into account all costs (whether fixed or variable) in determining a product cost, whereas marginal costing considers only variable costs.

17. (a) Past costs may have been unacceptable.
    (b) Costs may since have changed, due to changes in processes and/or materials.

18. Predetermined costs, maybe per unit, that 'should' be attained.

19. (a) Cost control, by comparing actual with standard.
    (b) Setting selling prices.
    (c) Valuing stock.

20. It must be possible to estimate accurately what future costs should be, probably on the basis of past costs. Also a fairly complex organisation is required for setting and monitoring standards.

21. (a) Indicates total costs of a product or service.
    (b) Identifies product profitability.

22. Service costs, unlike manufacturing costs, are often mostly fixed and may contain little or no material costs.

23. (a) The effects of inflation over several years.
    (b) Greater uncertainty due to unfamiliarity with non-repetitive work.
    (c) Possible construction or installation activities in foreign countries.
    (d) The longer-term exposure to currency fluctuations.

3.9 PROBLEMS

3.9.1 Questions

1. H Graham plc produces a steel and glass telephone shelf. There are three main processes: machining, painting and assembly. The direct costs are expressed as costs per unit of output:

	Machining	Painting	Assembly
Direct labour	20p	10p	30p
Direct materials	40p	10p	20p

The firm is currently making 10,000 shelves a year; sales revenue is £35,000; and related overheads amount to £14,000 a year.

(a) Apportion the overheads on the basis of direct labour, and draw up a table showing the cost apportioned between the three processes.
(b) What is the profit per shelf?
(c) What would be the effect of an increase in H Graham's production and sales of telephone shelves?

2. (See Q1.) H Graham plc has adopted a system of attributing costs to cost centres which yields the following total annual costs:

	Machining £	Painting £	Assembly £
Direct labour	10,000	12,000	6,000
Direct materials	20,000	10,000	4,500
Variable overheads	12,500	12,000	8,000
Fixed overheads (at 60% of factory cost*)	25,500	20,400	11,100

* Factory cost = direct costs + variable overheads

The telephone shelf passes through all three cost centres, and is attributed a proportion of each's costs (since several products pass through each cost centre). The shelf's costs are determined on the following bases for each cost centre:

Direct labour: 20%, 25% and 15% of direct labour respectively.
Direct materials: 20% of the direct materials in each case.
Variable overheads: according to each cost centre's proportion of total direct labour for telephone shelves.
Fixed overheads: 60% of factory cost.

The shelf sells for £3.50, and production and sales are currently running at 10,000 units a year.

(a) Draw up a full costing statement for the telephone shelf, showing the costs per unit.
(b) What is the profit per unit?
(c) What profit would you expect if selling price remained the same, but the sales volume and the variable costs increased by 10%?

3. A light engineering firm has received an inquiry for 10,000 components, which would need to be turned, milled and ground. Each 100 components will require 10 metres of 12mm diameter steel bar, at a cost of 90p per metre. Turning output is 30 pieces per minute, milling 60 pieces per minute, and grinding 15 pieces per minute. Only one machine of each type is available, each staffed by a skilled machinist paid £3.00 per hour.

At the machine outputs above, works fixed overheads would correspond to 45p per 100 components. The variable overheads can be apportioned as 100% of direct labour costs. Company policy is to charge a selling price which is 10% above total standard costs.

(a) Calculate the standard cost for the order.
(b) Calculate the proposed selling price per 100 units.
(c) What are the main advantages and disadvantages of this system of determining
   (i) product cost, and
   (ii) selling price?

4. The Managing Director of Thompson Tailors is thinking of abandoning production of one of the company's four lines of trousers, on the basis of a costing statement (reproduced below) which shows Style C as losing £5,000 a year.

	Style			
£'000 per year	A	B	C	D
Direct labour	20	14	10	16
Direct materials	20	16	12	12
Variable overheads	20	20	8	12
	60	50	30	40
Fixed overheads	30	25	15	20
Total cost	90	75	45	60
Sales revenue	94	110	40	76
Profit (loss)	4	35	(5)	16

(a) Does the information shown justify abandoning style C?

(b) Suggest an alternative presentation of the data. What recommendations for action does this new presentation suggest?

(c) If style C is abandoned, suppose the fixed overheads are re-allocated between the remaining styles in the same proportions as now. What new decision is implied? What is the ultimate result of following this approach?

5. Martin Simpson Ltd sells portable radios. Different price and marketing strategies are used in the three national sales territories (North, Midlands, and South). The table below shows the results, together with transport costs, for each territory:

	North	Midlands	South
Number of sales p.a.	40,000	50,000	30,000
Price per radio (£)	90	80	100
Marketing expenditure (£'000)	800	1200	1000
Transport cost (£'000)	200	100	200

The variable cost of production per radio (i.e. direct labour, direct materials, and variable overheads) is £50. Fixed overheads are running at £1,200,000 per year.

(a) What is the present contribution of each sales territory?
(b) What is the firm's present profit?
(c) What would be the effect of raising the price by £10.00 in each area, assuming that this would not reduce the sales volume?

6. Wilton Green Ltd, makers of ornamental household and garden goods, had recently diversified into car accessories. There were four main reasons:

(a) The car accessory market was an area of rapid expansion.
(b) The firm had a good working knowledge of the local car industry.
(c) The existing plant could be readily adapted to the new products.
(d) The labour force was both skilled and adaptable.

After some product rationalisation, the firm was struggling to achieve the right balance between products, and also to overcome the problem of unused capacity. The main problem, however, was how fast, and how much extra production they could squeeze out of the factory without drastically altering the firm's cost structure?

At present the firm's fixed overheads were £720,000 p.a. The present level of budgeted sales was £275,000 per month, but market expansion could raise this figure to £395,000 per month. As a result of such a rise in sales, direct material costs would rise from £30,000 to £44,000 per month, while the monthly wage bill would rise from £44,000 to £85,000.

The increase in plant utilisation would cause variable overheads to rise as follows:

	At present sales £'000/month	Estimated at forecast sales £'000/month
Maintenance	22	43
Stores	20	30
Factory Admin.	18	26

All the cost changes above are those which would fully utilise the firm's installed capacity.

As the firm's accountant, you are asked to:

(a) prepare a marginal costing statement from the data given.
(b) prepare a statement to the Board proposing a course of action, with reasons.
(c) What misgivings might you have about the analysis in (b) above?

7. 'Business is getting worse', said the Managing Director of Flexi-Lamp Ltd, a firm which made adjustable reading lamps. The reason for the remark was the latest profit and loss statement for the period January to September of the current year (shown below).

The Sales Manager had just received a special order for 5,000 lamps at a contract price of £26.00 each. He put this proposal to the Managing Director, who said: 'This really is the limit! A special order at less than the cost price of £29.20 per lamp, as well as an extra £4,000 fixed overhead cost for a special design!'

Flexi-Lamp Ltd - Profit and Loss Statement: January to September

	£	£
Sales revenue (15,000 units @ £50 each)		750,000
Less costs:		
Materials (15,000 units @ £3.40)	51,000	
Labour (15,000 units @ £15.00)	225,000	
Manufacturing overheads:		
Variable (15,000 units @ £1.80)	27,000	
Fixed (9/12ths of £360,000)	270,000	
Admin, selling & distribution overhead @ £21,000 per month	189,000	
		762,000
Net profit (loss)		(12,000)

A unit cost statement is set out below:

	£ per unit
Direct materials	3.40
Direct labour	15.00
Manufacturing overheads:	
variable	1.80
fixed (based on 40,000 units a year)	9.00
= total production cost	29.20

Required:

(a) Should the firm make the special order? Give your reasons.
(b) Should the firm accept orders of this type in the future?

8. Refer to Easidig Garden Equipment Ltd on page 57. What would be the cost of each product if manufacturing overheads were recovered on the basis of each product's labour plus material cost?

9. The Roundabout Hotel has forty bedrooms, a sixty seat restaurant and a bar which will accommodate up to eighty people. A recent cost analysis has identified the following cost structure:

Fixed costs per year:

Accommodation	£100,000
Restaurant	£30,000
Bar	£15,000
General (i.e. indirect)	£40,000

Variable cost per £1 revenue:

Accommodation	3p
Restaurant	25p
Bar	40p
General	2p

(a) What is the average fixed cost per day of:

(i) a hotel bedroom;
(ii) a restaurant table for four;
(iii) a space in the bar?

(b) What is the hotel cost for:

(i) one night in a £30 per night bedroom?
(ii) a dinner party of four spending £60?
(iii) a stag party of ten spending £50 in the bar?

3.9.2 Solutions

1. **H Graham plc**

	Machining	Painting	Assembly	=	Total
	£	£	£		£
Direct labour	2,000	1,000	3,000	=	6,000
Direct materials	4,000	1,000	2,000	=	7,000
Overheads	($^2/_6$)4,667	($^1/_6$)2,333	($^3/_6$)7,000	=	14,000
(a) Total costs	10,667	4,333	12,000	=	27,000
Sales revenue				=	35,000
Total profit				=	8,000

(b) Profit = £8,000/10,000 = 80p per shelf (£3.50 - £2.70 per shelf)

(c) Assuming overheads are fixed, each extra 100 shelves would produce £220 extra profit (£350 sales revenue less £130 variable costs).

2. **H Graham plc**

Telephone Shelf: Total Costs

		£	£
(a) Direct labour -			
machining: 20% x £10,000	=	2,000	
painting: 25% x £12,000	=	3,000	
assembly: 15% x £6,000	=	900	
			5,900
Direct materials: 20% x £34,500	=		6,900
Variable overheads:			
machining: 20% x £12,500	=	2,500	
painting: 25% x £12,000	=	3,000	
assembly: 15% x £8,000	=	1,200	
			6,700
= factory cost			19,500
Fixed overheads: 60% x factory cost			11,700
			31,200

Telephone shelf: total costs = £31,200

cost per unit	=	£31,200/10,000	£3.12 per unit
selling price	=		£3.50 per unit
(b) profit per unit	=		£0.38

If sales volume increased by 10%,	
sales revenue would increase by 1,000 x £3.50 =	£3,500
variable costs would increase by 1,000 x £1.95 =	£1,950
(c) profit would increase by	£1,550

Thus profit would rise from £3,800 (£35,000 - £31,200) to £5,350 - i.e. by 40.8%.

CHAPTER FOUR

COSTS AND REVENUES

4.1 RELATING COSTS TO REVENUES

Cost prediction and control are sometimes dealt with in isolation from revenue. At some level in the business, however, managers need to look at the interaction between costs and revenues.

In the long run revenues must exceed costs if the business is to remain viable. Since market forces determine prices, in effect they also set a limit to maximum long-term costs for a given volume of output. Very few firms can be sure of their ability to pass on whatever costs they incur to customers in higher prices, in the long run.

Both costs and revenues vary with output; and the efficient firm making what the market wants will be keen to know which level of output is likely to maximise profits. This chapter deals with short-term tactics, where the scale of the business is limited by its existing facilities. Chapter 10 will deal with strategic issues.

4.2 COST/PROFIT/VOLUME ANALYSIS

A *breakeven chart* is a graphical presentation of a firm's (or a product's) costs and sales revenue, showing the volume of output needed for sales revenue to equal total costs. At that volume of output, the firm (or product) is said to 'breakeven' - when it is making neither profit nor loss. We shall first consider costs for a firm, then sales revenues, and then profit or loss. Throughout we shall look at results for a whole firm. It is often very difficult to apportion some indirect costs between products; hence it can be hard to place much reliance on the results of breakeven analysis product by product.

4.2.1 Costs and volumes

In drawing breakeven charts, it is usual to make some sweeping simplifying assumptions. (We shall consider relaxing them later). So to start with, we shall assume that *all* a firm's costs can be regarded either as variable or fixed. As we discussed in Chapter 2, these terms refer to how costs vary with output. Variable costs are those which do vary linearly with output; while fixed costs are unchanged even if output changes.

Given those simplifying assumptions, it is not difficult to draw a picture showing how the firm's total costs will vary with output. For instance, suppose that a firm's variable costs amount to £0.80 per unit of output, and that fixed costs amount to £30,000 a year. Then we can draw a chart showing how costs in total will vary with output, as shown in Figure 4.1. Note that normal practice is to show volume of output on the horizontal axis, and money amounts on the vertical axis.

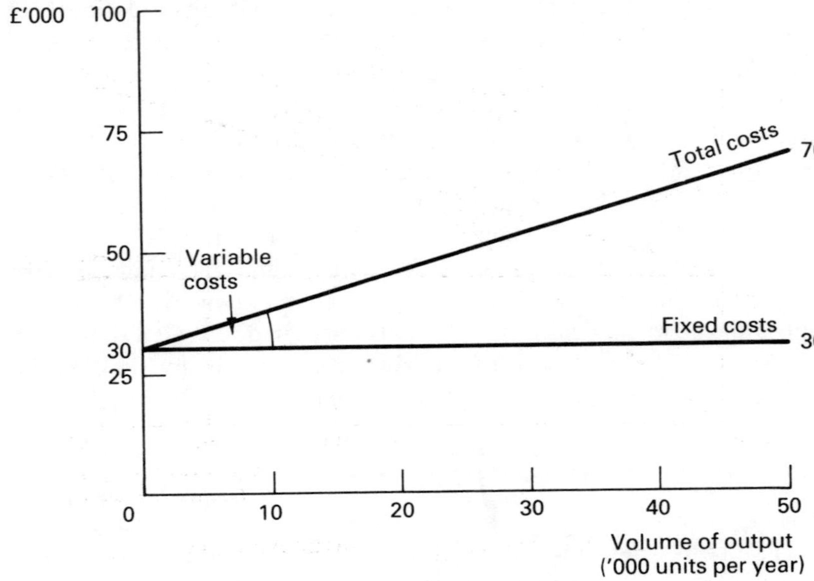

Figure 4.1 Costs and outputs

4.2.2 Profit and Volume

To complete the breakeven chart, we must include sales revenue in the picture as well as costs. Let us assume there is only a single product, with a selling price of £2.00 per unit. We also assume no change in stock levels. These simple assumptions (some of which we shall modify later) allow us to complete the breakeven chart in Figure 4.2.

Figure 4.2 shows that the 'breakeven point' comes at 25,000 units of output. At that level, sales revenue of £50,000 exactly equals total costs of £30,000 fixed costs plus £20,000 variable costs. Above that level, sales revenue exceeds total costs, and the firm makes a profit. At any level of output below 25,000 units a year, costs exceed sales revenue, and the firm makes a loss.

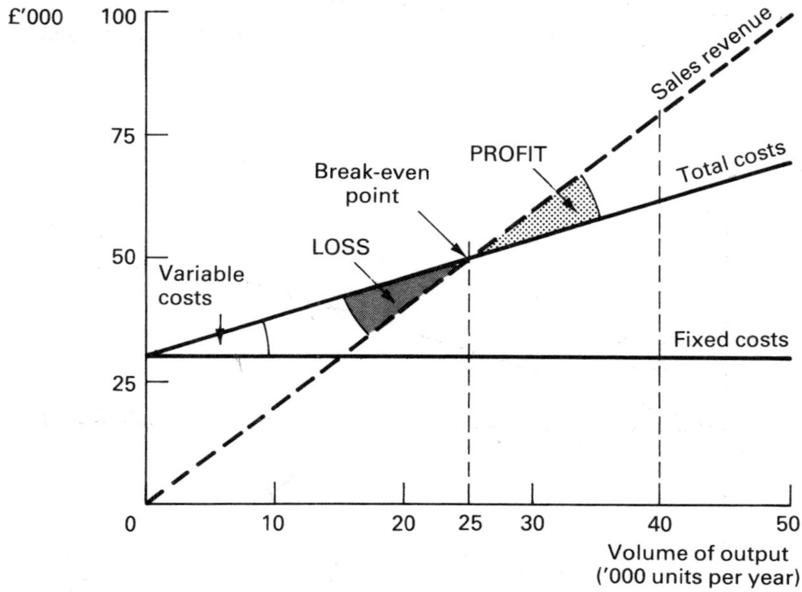

Figure 4.2 The completed breakeven chart

If the firm is planning to produce and sell, say, 40,000 units next year, the line drawn on the chart shows that the profit should be £18,000. We can check this in two ways. We know that total sales revenue will be £80,000 (= £2.00 x 40,000) and that total costs will be £62,000 (= fixed costs £30,000 + variable costs £32,000). Or we can say that the *margin of safety* is 15,000 units - this is the excess of planned output above the breakeven level of output. On our assumptions, the extra profit for every unit sold above the breakeven point is £1.20 (= £2.00 - £0.80). And £1.20 x 15,000 units is £18,000.

Breakeven charts may alternatively be constructed by drawing the variable costs first and then adding on the fixed costs. (See Figure 4.3).

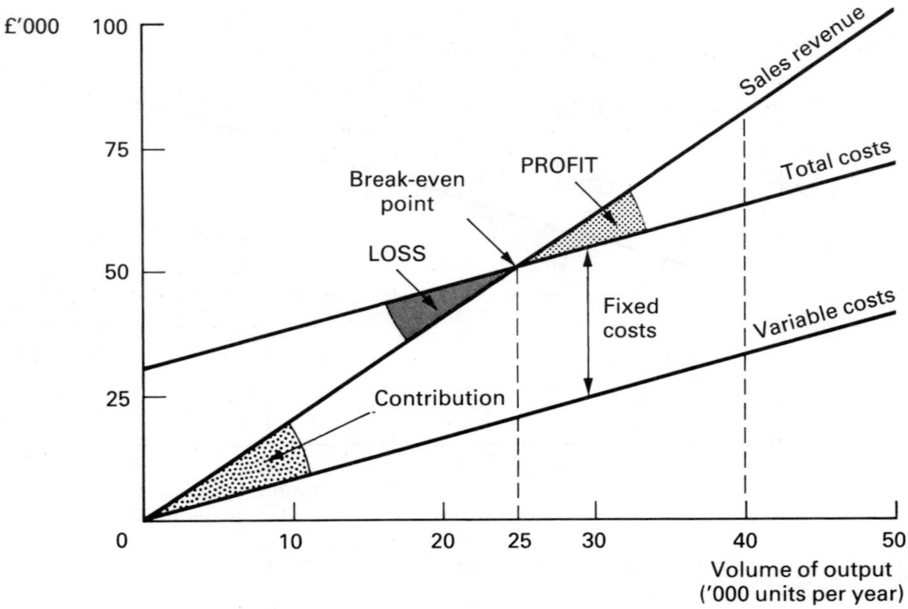

Figure 4.3 Breakeven chart - highlighting contribution

The construction used in Figure 4.3 has the advantage of highlighting the contribution to fixed costs and profit. The total cost line is, of course, the same as in Figure 4.2.

4.2.3 Algebraic Analysis

The information we need to draw a breakeven chart also allows us to calculate the breakeven point, by using simple algebra. We know that at the breakeven point, profit is *zero*, so that total costs exactly equal sales revenue. We can split total costs between fixed and variable costs. This allows us to use the contribution per unit (in our example, £2.00 - £0.80 = £1.20) to calculate the breakeven point: we simply divide total fixed costs by the contribution per unit.

At the breakeven point:

Sales revenue	=	total costs		
Sales revenue	=	variable costs	+	fixed costs
Sales revenue	-	variable costs	=	fixed costs

Suppose we call breakeven output 'x' units:

Then: $£2.00x - £0.80x = £30,000$

$£1.20x = £30,000$

$x = \frac{£30,000}{£1.20} = 25,000$ units

In general terms, if : x is the breakeven level of output,
: s is the selling price per unit,
: v is the variable cost per unit,
: F is the total fixed costs,

then sales revenue S = sx
and variable costs V = vx

At the breakeven level of output,

$$S = V + F$$
$$S - V = F$$
$$sx - vx = F$$
$$x(s-v) = F$$
$$x = \frac{F}{s-v}$$

Thus, to calculate the breakeven level of output, we simply divide the total fixed costs by the contribution per unit.

If the company needed to achieve a profit before tax of £12,000 we could also establish the level of output to do this by adding the profit before tax (P) to the fixed costs. The profit breakeven level of output is then given by: $x = \frac{F + P}{s-v}$ which is $\frac{£42,000}{£1.20}$ = 35,000 units.

It is worth being able to handle the algebra, which really is not at all complicated, because working out the breakeven point itself (and certain other implications of the data) is usually much quicker than having to draw a breakeven chart and read off a rough estimate of the answer.

4.2.4 Changing the assumptions

One of the main uses of the breakeven chart is as an aid to profit planning. The chart, subject to its limitations, allows managers to see the effects of variations of cost/revenue/volume factors on profit projections. A change in assumptions about volume alone can, of course, be read straight off the chart. For example, refer back to Figure 4.3. Suppose that actual volume of output (and of sales) were to be 45,000 units next year, instead of the planned level of 40,000 units? What would the profit amount to if other assumptions remained the same? This can be read off the chart as just under £25,000. (The precise amount can be calculated at: 20,000 x £1.20 = £24,000).

Or suppose that the selling price per unit were reduced from £2.00 to £1.80 in an attempt to boost sales volume. What would happen to the break-even point? Figure 4.4 shows that it would rise from 25,000 units to 30,000 units (= £30,000 fixed costs divided by the new contribution per unit of £1.80 - £0.80 = £1.00).

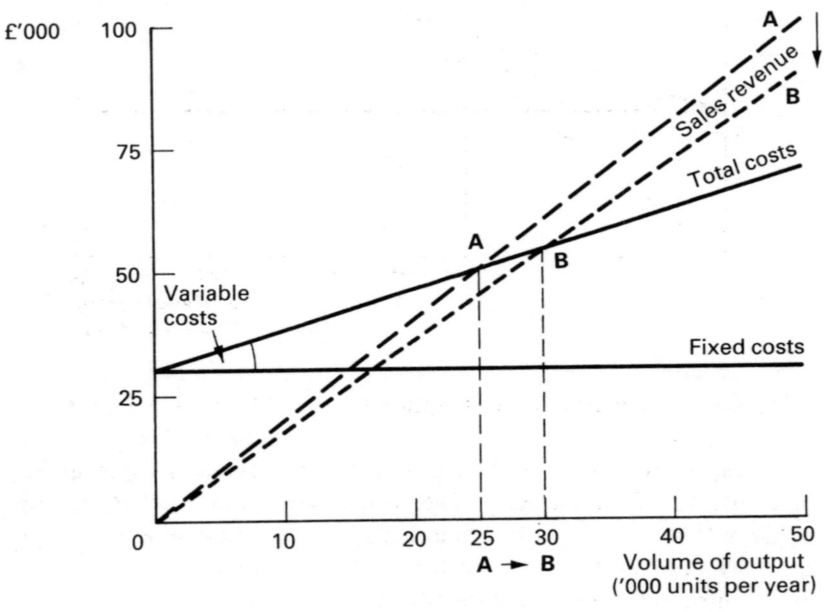

Figure 4.4 Breakeven chart with new selling price per unit

The original selling price per unit is drawn with the thick dashed line (A). The new selling price line is shown by the thinner dashed line just below it (B). The breakeven point shifts from point A to point B, i.e. from 25,000 to 30,000 units.

Now suppose we retain the original selling price of £2.00 per unit, but that the variable costs per unit can be reduced from £0.80 per unit to £0.50. (This is perhaps an unrealistically large reduction; but it makes it easier to see clearly on the chart). As a result, the contribution per unit increases from £1.20 to £1.50; and the breakeven point *falls* from 25,000 to 20,000 units.

In Figure 4.5 the original total cost line is shown as solid, and the revised total cost line (C) is shown as a dashed line just below it. The breakeven point moves from point A to point C.

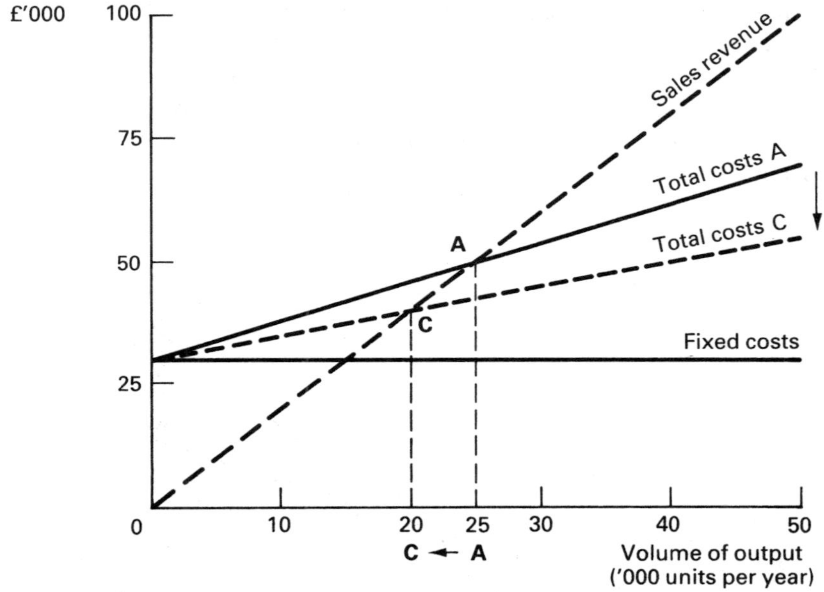

Figure 4.5 Breakeven chart with new variable costs per unit

Of course, it would be possible to combine the two changes in another chart; and other variations could easily be employed. Thus, on the very simple assumptions we have made, it is possible to portray the results of any given output level in terms of profit or loss.

Now examine the following case study:

Cleen Window Service

Problem

Cleen Window Service is a two-man partnership which cleans house windows. Their annual fixed costs are £2,100 and they normally charge £1.30 per house. Variable costs amount to about 5p per house.

How many houses will they need to window clean in order to cover their fixed costs? How many will need to be cleaned per year to provide them with an income of £140 per week each (before tax)? Draw the breakeven chart. Write your answer below.

To cover fixed costs:

Fixed costs = contribution (= contribution per house x number of houses).

$$\text{Therefore, number of houses} = \frac{\text{Fixed costs}}{\text{Contribution per house}} = \_\_\_\_\_\_$$

$$= \_\_\_\_\_\_$$

To provide for an income of £140 per week each:

$$\text{Number of houses} = \frac{\text{Fixed costs per year + total income per year}}{\text{Contribution per house}}$$

$$= \frac{\_\_\_\_ + \_\_\_\_}{}$$

$$= \_\_\_\_\_\_$$

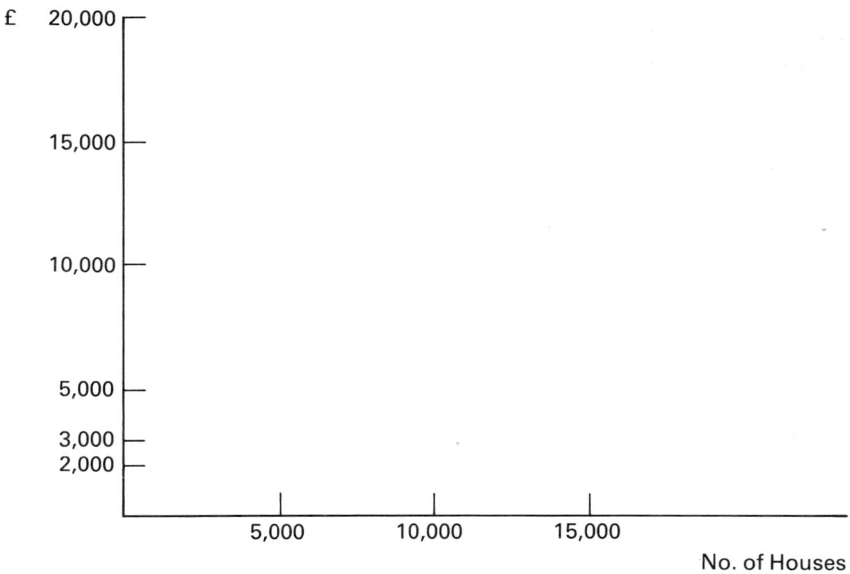

Breakeven chart for Cleen Window Service

Check your answer overleaf.

SOLUTION

To cover fixed costs:

Fixed costs = contribution (= contribution per house x number of houses)

$$\text{Therefore, number of houses} = \frac{\text{Fixed costs}}{\text{Contribution per house}}$$

$$= \frac{£2{,}100}{£1.25}$$

$$= \underline{\underline{1{,}680}}$$

To provide for an income of £140 per week each:

$$\text{Number of houses} = \frac{\text{Fixed costs per year + total income per year}}{\text{Contribution per house}}$$

$$= \frac{£2{,}100 + £14{,}560}{£1.25}$$

$$= \underline{\underline{13{,}328}}$$

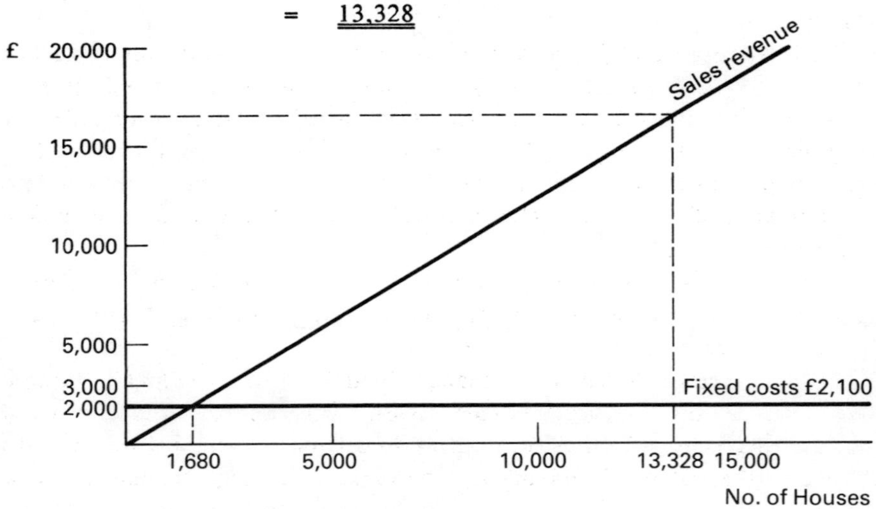

Breakeven chart for Cleen Window Service

4.3 THE NEED FOR CAUTION

We have seen how to draw a breakeven chart; and how to read off the breakeven point, and the amount of profit or loss at any given level of output. But perhaps we should remind ourselves of the assumptions we have been making. Taken together they probably amount to a severe simplification of reality; hence any conclusions need to be interpreted with considerable caution.

We have assumed:

(a) A single selling price per unit.
(b) An unchanging sales *mix* of products, if there is more than one product.
(c) A single unchanging variable cost per unit (unchanging *per unit*, hence varying *linearly* with output).
(d) Fixed costs which remain the same at all levels of output.
(e) No changes in the level of stock (with all output assumed to be sold).

In practice, the mix of products may well change over time, and the selling price may need to be reduced in order to increase volume significantly.

The variable cost per unit may also not remain exactly the same per unit throughout the entire range of output being considered: it may tend to fall because of quantity discounts and other economies at higher levels of output; or it may tend to increase because of overtime at higher levels of output. (Obviously, it would be a convenient coincidence if these effects happened to cancel out across the whole range of output!)

Fixed costs will often increase in a 'step-function' as output increases, as we shall see in section 4.4; they are 'fixed' only for a limited range of output.

Finally, stock levels may change, which rather spoils our simple assumption that output equals sales. Because of the financial accounting rules which require firms to attribute some period ('fixed') costs to the value of end-of-period stocks held, any change in stock levels affects cost of goods sold, and hence profit. The required use of SSAP 9 means that the fixed costs incurred during a period may not equal the fixed costs charged in the company's profit and loss account.

In breakeven analysis, we are concerned with the behaviour of costs (and revenues) as output changes. The basic distinction is between 'variable' and 'fixed' costs. Variable costs would normally consist of

(a) direct labour,
(b) materials, and
(c) some 'overheads'.

Fixed costs would normally consist of the remaining overheads. We have already noted that the terms 'direct' and 'indirect' refer to how closely costs can be *identified* with particular products, not to whether or not they *vary* with output. For example, certain fixed costs, such as depreciation, may be identifiable with a particular product and would therefore be a *direct* cost in this instance. On the other hand, some overheads, such as production supervision costs, may not be identifiable with particular products (and are therefore indirect costs), but may still be regarded as varying more or less linearly with output.

Thus, it may not always be clear whether overheads are to be regarded as fixed or variable. All one can do is make (and state) what seems to be the most appropriate assumption. If 'fixed costs' are stated separately, then any other item referred to as overheads is likely to be variable.

4.4 MORE COMPLEX ASSUMPTIONS

Figure 4.6 sets out a breakeven chart which includes more complex assumptions about three of the points just mentioned.

(a) Sales revenue per unit falls slightly as volume increases, so that the sales revenue curve slopes down to the right.
(b) Variable costs per unit fall to begin with, as quantity discounts begin to apply, but then increase as overtime costs outweigh this effect.
(c) Fixed costs increase in a step function as output increases.

It is clear that these changes, taken together, result in a much more complicated breakeven chart. As a matter of practice, it is quite common for breakeven charts to be drawn using very simple assumptions; but they will then be considered more or less valid *only for a rather limited range of output*.

In Figure 4.6, while it is not necessary to go into the detailed numbers, one conclusion seems fairly obvious. The chart is worth using only between output levels of 15,000 and 40,000 units a year; in other words, over the range for which fixed expenses are £30,000. Below an output of 15,000 units no profit appears to be possible (the best outcome is breakeven, exactly zero profit, at 15,000 units); and above 40,000 units, because fixed costs jump by £12,500 to £42,500, total costs exceed sales revenue - and the position gets worse as output increases. Sales revenue per unit starts declining, and variable costs per unit start increasing.

Indeed, in Figure 4.6 there are no fewer than three breakeven points: at 15,000 units, at just under 28,000 units, and a transition from profit into loss at 40,000 units. This is perhaps more realistic than the charts we were looking at earlier; but evidently much harder to use and interpret.

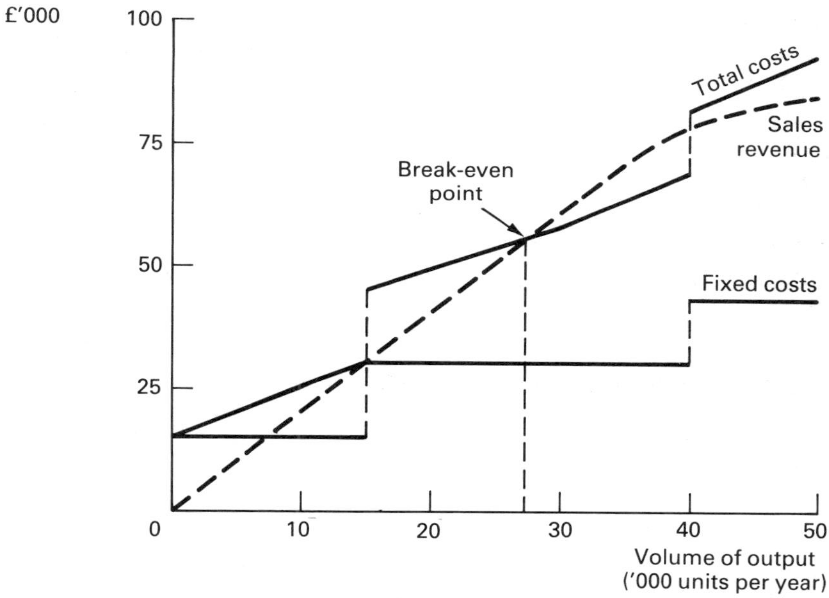

Figure 4.6 A more complex breakeven chart

4.5 PRICING

In setting prices, a business will be aiming for a satisfactory profit. Prices will be affected by:

(a) the benefit which customers receive;
(b) what it costs to make the product;
(c) what competitors are charging.

4.5.1 Costs and Prices

Many businesses price their goods and services on the basis of full cost plus a percentage mark-up. Even though apportionment of overheads cannot be precisely accurate (see section 3.2) full costing does have the advantage of covering all a business's costs in the long run. Indeed, if competitors' prices are unknown, the cost-plus approach may be the only reasonably objective basis for price quotations.

Example 1: Robinson's Heating and Plumbing have been asked to quote for supplying and installing a gas central heating system for a large house. The company builds up its quoted price of £3,072 as follows:

	£
Cost of gas boiler, radiators, pipes, etc.	*1,600*
Installation cost: 80 hours @ £6 per hour	*480*
Overheads @ 100% of labour cost	*480*
Estimated total cost	*2,560*
Plus: 20% mark-up	*512*
Quoted price	*3,072*

When business is extremely competitive, some firms may be willing to quote on the basis of variable costs only for a short time until business improves. Their reasoning is that in hard times any contribution towards fixed costs is better than none. (But of course the danger is that times may remain 'hard', so that total contributions may fail to cover fixed costs over a long period of time).

4.5.2 Price Elasticity

Firms may set prices after guessing how much of their product they can sell at different prices. *Figure 4.7* sets out the estimated price/volume relationship ('price-elasticity of demand') for Uni-Product Ltd's only product. *Figures 4.8* and *4.9* show graphically the estimated price-elasticity of demand, and the total sales revenue varying with quantity sold. For most products and services, an increase in price results in a fall in the quantity sold. But the total sales revenue may increase (see Figure 4.9).

Selling price £ per unit	Sales volume '000 per year	Sales revenue £'000 per year
4	10.0	40.0
5	9.0	45.0
6	8.0	48.0
7	6.5	45.5
8	5.0	40.0
9	4.0	36.0
10	3.2	32.0

Figure 4.7 Uni-Product Ltd. Unit selling price v. sales volume per year and total sales revenue per year

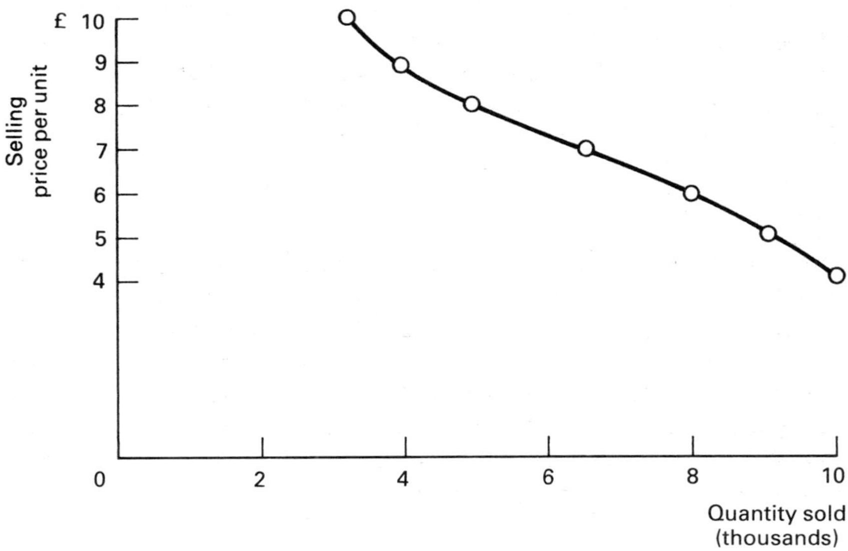

Figure 4.8 Selling price versus quantity sold

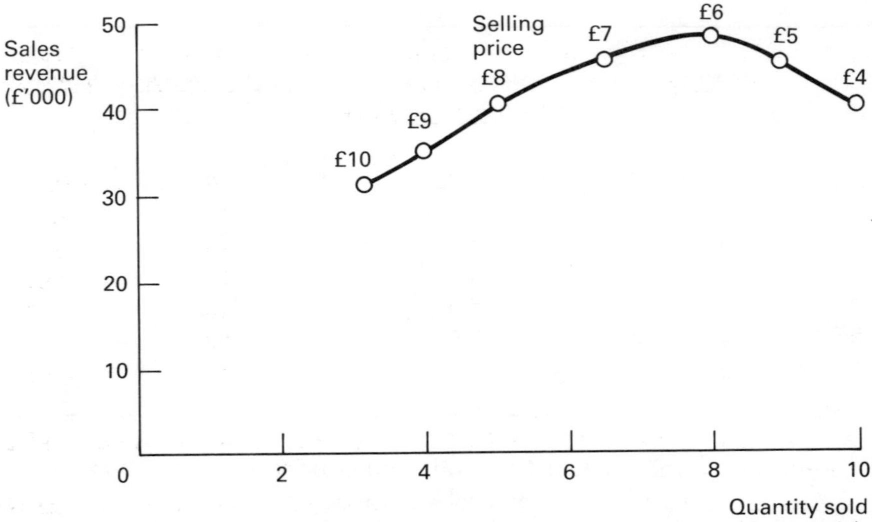

Figure 4.9 Sales revenue versus quantity sold

4.5.3 Improving Profit

Figure 4.9 shows which price will maximise total sales revenue (about £6). But maximising sales revenue is less important than maximising *profit*. Assuming no change in fixed costs, we can achieve maximum profit by maximising *contribution*.

Example 2: Uni-Product Ltd has fixed costs of £20,000 per year, and variable costs of £3 per unit. Given the price-elasticity estimates in figure 4.7, what is the selling price per unit which will maximise profit?

To answer this question, we can list the total contribution at each price (and deduct £20,000 to show total profit at each price).

Selling price £/unit	*Contribution per unit*	*x*	*Sales volume '000 units/yr*	*=*	*Contribution £'000/yr*	*Profit £'000/yr*
4	*1*		*10.0*	*=*	*10.0*	*-10.0*
5	*2*		*9.0*	*=*	*18.0*	*-2.0*
6	*3*		*8.0*	*=*	*24.0*	*4.0*
7	*4*		*6.5*	*=*	*26.0*	*6.0*
8	*5*		*5.0*	*=*	*25.0*	*5.0*
9	*6*		*4.0*	*=*	*24.0*	*4.0*
10	*7*		*3.2*	*=*	*22.4*	*2.4*

Figure 4.10 charts the annual contribution and profit at each level of sales volume.

We can calculate the breakeven sales volume for Uni-Product at the expected profit-maximising selling price of £7.00 to be 5,000 units. Thus, if sales are actually 6,500 units, profit is the contribution of £4.00 per unit x 1,500 (= £6,000).

Now suppose that fixed costs total only £12,000 per year; but that variable costs are £4.50 per unit. The position is then as shown below:

Selling price £/unit	*Contribution per unit*	*x*	*Sales volume '000 units/yr*	*=*	*Contribution £'000/yr*	*Profit £'000/yr*
4	*(0.50)*		*10.0*	*=*	*-5.0*	*-17.0*
5	*0.50*		*9.0*	*=*	*4.5*	*-7.5*
6	*1.50*		*8.0*	*=*	*12.0*	*0.0*
7	*2.50*		*6.5*	*=*	*16.3*	*4.3*
8	*3.50*		*5.0*	*=*	*17.5*	*5.5*
9	*4.50*		*4.0*	*=*	*18.0*	*6.0*
10	*5.50*		*3.2*	*=*	*17.6*	*5.6*

Now the expected profit-maximising price is £9.00 per unit (at which the expected profit is £6,000, the same profit - by chance - as before). And now what is the breakeven sales volume at the profit-maximising selling price? £12,000/£4.50 = 2,667 units. Thus, profit is 1,333 units x £4.50 = £6,000. This time, figure 4.11 charts the annual contribution and profit at each level of sales volume.

A firm needs to consider the implications of changes in selling price, viz:

(a) How will existing competitors react?
(b) Will new competitors enter the market?
(c) How will customers react? Will all customers react in the same way?
(d) How long will selling price levels remain the same?

Businesses whose costs are mostly fixed, such as cinemas, schools, computer software companies, may aim at maximising sales revenue as a proxy for maximising profit. With relatively low variable costs, sales revenue and contribution will be almost the same. Hence, revenue maximisation, which is easy to understand as a general operating principle, will result in almost optimum profits. But where a significant proportion of costs varies with output this is unlikely to be true. In that case, maximising sales revenue is unlikely to be an optimum policy in order to maximise profits.

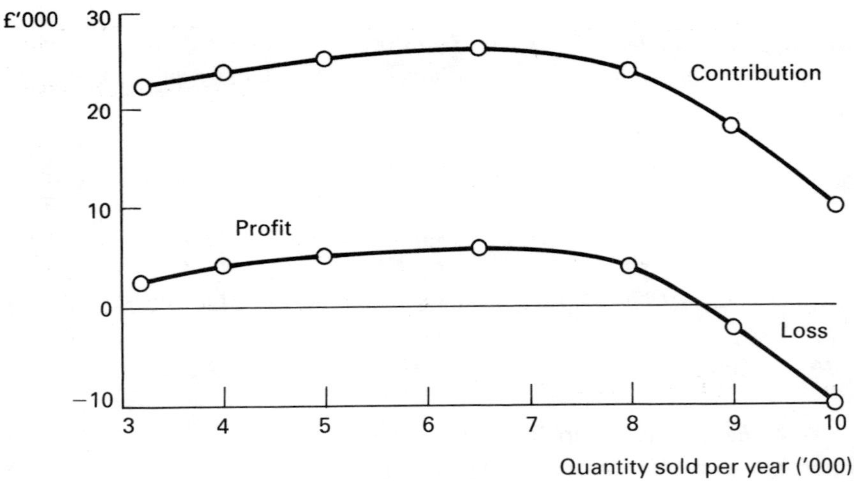

Figure 4.10 Contribution and profit versus sales volume

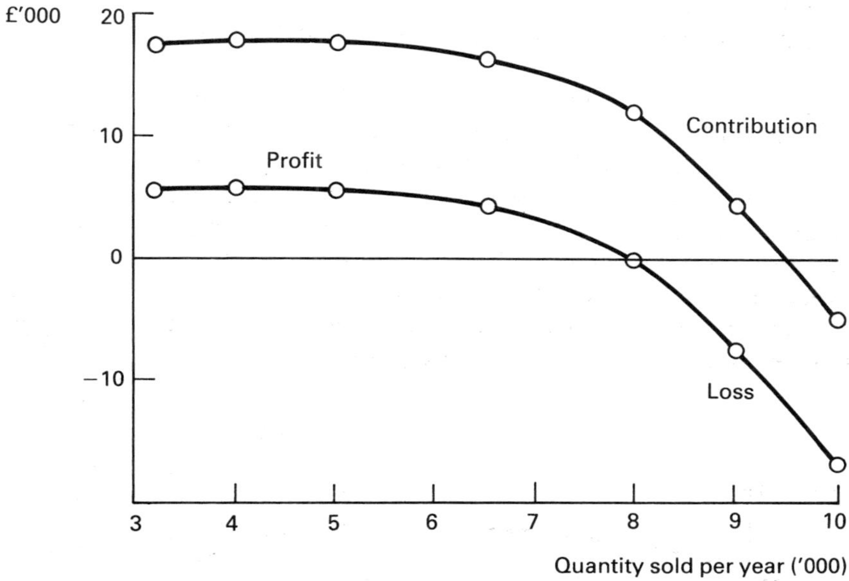

Figure 4.11 Contribution and profit versus sales volume

Consider the following case:

Discount Bookshop

Problem

Discount Bookshop buys and sells second-hand books. They are considering changing their pricing policy which currently is to sell books at 70% of the new-book-price. It is believed that reducing prices to 40% of the new-book-price will treble sales. However, before a final decision is made the following data has been gathered to assist with the decision.

Number of books sold per year	16,000
Average 'new book price'	£10.00
Average cost to Discount Bookshop	£2.20
Average selling price (at present)	£7.00
Fixed costs per year	£30,000
Other variable costs (average per book sold)	£0.05

Estimated effect of reducing selling prices:

Average selling price	Books sold per year
£7.00	16,000
£6.00	23,000
£5.00	33,000
£4.00	48,000
£3.00	80,000

What pricing policy do you recommend?
Write your answer below.

Average Selling price	Contribution per book	Books sold per year	Contribution per year
£7.00			
£6.00			
£5.00			
£4.00			
£3.00			

Maximum contribution (and profit) occurs at an average selling price of

at which profit = __________ per year

Now check your answer over page.

SOLUTION

Discount Bookshop

Average Selling price	Contribution per book	Books sold/year	Contribution per year
£7.00	£7.00-£2.25 =£4.75	16,000	£4.75x16,000= £76,000
£6.00	£3.75	23,000	£86,250
£5.00	£2.75	33,000	£90,750
£4.00	£1.75	48,000	£84,000
£3.00	£0.75	80,000	£60,000

Maximum contribution (and profit) occurs at an average selling price of £5.00

at which profit = £60,750 per year (see Figure 4.12)

Therefore, books should be sold at 50% of new price.

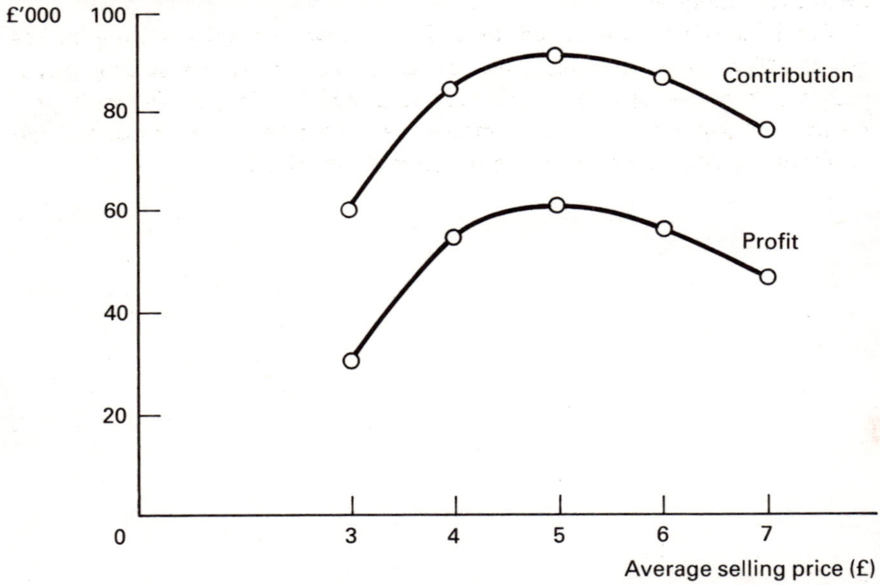

Figure 4.12 Discount Bookshop - estimated contribution and profit

4.6 CHAPTER SUMMARY

It is often useful for management to know how costs vary with output. A breakeven chart shows how changes in output affect total costs and sales revenue; and it shows the 'breakeven' level, at which total costs exactly equal total sales revenue. One can also calculate the breakeven point by algebra: it is the output volume resulting from dividing total fixed costs by the contribution per unit.

Breakeven analysis assumes

(a) that sales price is constant;
(b) that sales mix is constant;
(c) that variable costs vary directly with output;
(d) that fixed costs are known for the forecast range of output;
(e) and that output volume equals sales volume (i.e. there are no changes in stock levels).

These rather restrictive assumptions make caution essential in using breakeven analysis.

Profit-seeking firms need to estimate how changing selling prices might affect sales volume, sales revenue, and profit. As selling prices increase, sales volume normally declines; but profit may increase as a result. Maximising profits means maximising contribution, not maximising sales revenue, for a given level of fixed costs.

4.7 REVIEW QUESTIONS AND ANSWERS

4.7.1 Questions

1. What is a breakeven chart?
2. What information is needed to construct a breakeven chart?
3. What is the 'breakeven' point?
4. What goes on the horizontal axis of a breakeven chart?
5. Name five simplifying assumptions usually made in breakeven analysis.
6. What is the 'margin of safety'?
7. In drawing a breakeven chart, how would you determine a suitable scale:
   (a) for the vertical axis?
   (b) for the horizontal axis?
8. What is the algebraic formula for calculating the breakeven point?
9. At breakeven, what do total variable costs equal?
10. What is the breakeven point for a firm whose costs are:
    (a) all fixed?
    (b) all variable?
11. What will happen to the breakeven point:
    (a) if variable costs per unit rise;
    (b) if fixed costs fall;
    (c) if sales volume increases;
    (d) if contribution per unit falls;
    (e) if selling price per unit rises?
    Explain *why* in each case.
12. Explain how each of the simplifying assumptions in breakeven analysis may be unrealistic.
13. Under what circumstances can 'fixed' costs change?
14. Why would changes in stock levels (i.e. output different from sales) affect profit?
15. Why might variable costs per unit:
    (a) rise; or
    (b) fall as output increases?
16. How can there be more than one breakeven point?

Write out your answers and then check with the answers over the page.

4.7.2 Answers

1. A chart which graphically presents a firm's costs and sales revenue at different levels of sales volume and from which the volume of output needed to 'breakeven' can be (approximately) determined. The level of profit or loss at different levels of sales volume can also be approximated.

2. Fixed costs (total), variable costs (per unit) and sales revenue (per unit) for the firm's 'relevant range'.

3. The level of output at which there is neither profit nor loss.

4. Volume of output, either in money or units.

5. (a) Single selling price per unit.
   (b) An unchanging mix of products, if there is more than one product.
   (c) A single unchanging variable cost per unit.
   (d) Fixed costs remain the same at all levels of output.
   (e) No changes in stock level.

6. The excess of planned output above the breakeven level of output.

7. (a) Determine the greater of sales revenue and total costs for the maximum output level to be considered, and divide this number by the length of the vertical axis available.

   (b) Identify the maximum output level to be considered and divide this number by the length of the horizontal axis available. The horizontal axis and the vertical axis should be of similar length.

8. Breakeven level of output (x) = $\frac{F}{s-v}$

   Where: F is total fixed costs
   s is the selling price per unit
   v is the variable cost per unit

9. Total sales revenue less total fixed costs.

10. (a) When sales revenue equals fixed costs.
    (b) Zero.

11. (a) Breakeven point will rise (assuming variable costs per unit are less than sales revenue per unit), because more units will need to be produced for the total contribution to equal total fixed costs.

    (b) Breakeven point will fall because less total contribution is needed to equal the lower total fixed costs. Moreover, the percentage fall in breakeven will equal the percentage fall in fixed costs.

    (c) No change, since actual volume does not affect breakeven volume.

    (d) Breakeven point will rise because more units will need to be sold for total contribution to equal total fixed costs.

    (e) Breakeven point will fall because contribution per unit increases.

12. (a) Selling price per unit may need to be reduced in order to achieve the desired level of sales. In multi-product firms the sales mix is unlikely to be exactly the same as that predicted in constructing the breakeven chart.

    (b) Variable cost per unit may change, e.g. due to bulk buying (i.e. reduced variable cost) or overtime premiums (i.e. increased variable cost).

    (c) Actual maximum capacity may be different from 'theoretical' maximum capacity, thereby necessitating an increase in fixed costs within the ('theoretical') relevant range.

    (d) It is unlikely that stock levels will be exactly the same at the end of the period considered as they were at the beginning.

13. Fixed costs change when operating outside the relevant range. Also, due to inflation and specific price changes, they are likely to increase year by year.

14. Because the financial accounting rules (SSAP 9) require firms to attribute some fixed costs to the value of the closing stock level, any change in stock levels affects cost of goods sold, and hence profit. The fixed costs incurred during a period will therefore *not* equal the fixed costs charged in the period's profit and loss account.

15. (a) Overtime premiums or diminishing returns.
    (b) Bulk purchases at a discount.

16. Because fixed costs are not fixed for all levels of output, but increase in a 'step-function' as output increases.

4.8 PROBLEMS SECTION

4.8.1 Questions

1. Fixed costs are £300,000 a year. Sales price per unit is £18.00. Variable costs are £240,000. Present output is 40,000 units a year.
   (a) What is the breakeven level of output?
   (b) What will the breakeven level of output be (all other information remaining in each case as in (a) above) if:
      (i) fixed costs increase to £400,000 a year?
      (ii) variable costs increase by £2.00 per unit?
      (iii) sales price per unit falls to £16.00?

2. A company's fixed costs are £400,000 a year. Contribution is £10.00 per unit. Sales price is £25.00 per unit. Can you tell what the breakeven point is?
   (a) If yes, what is the breakeven point?
   (b) If no, what additional information do you need?

3. A firm has fixed overheads of £100,000 per annum. Direct costs and variable indirect costs taken together average £2 per unit, and the firm's plant can make up to 50,000 units per year. The finished product sells for £6.00.
   (a) Draw a breakeven chart showing the firm's present position.
   (b) What is the breakeven output?
   (c) What is the margin of safety at 45,000 units production?
   (d) How much profit would be made at 90% of capacity?

4. Fixed costs are £30,000 a year. Variable costs are £0.50 per unit. Selling price is £1.80 per unit.
   (a) Draw the breakeven chart.
   (b) What is the breakeven point?
   (c) Compare the breakeven chart with Figures 4.2, 4.3 and 4.4.

5. Sales revenue is £840,000 a year. Variable costs are £10 per unit. Fixed costs are £350,000 a year. Present output is 30,000 units.
   (a) Draw a breakeven chart. What is the breakeven level?
   (b) Confirm your graphical derivation *both*
      (i) by algebra, and
      (ii) by arithmetic.
   (c) What happens to the breakeven level if (separately)
      (i) fixed costs fall to £300,000 a year;
      (ii) variable costs per unit fall to £8.00;
      (iii) sales price per unit increases by £5.00?

(d) What happens to the breakeven level if all three of the changes in (c) above happen together?

6. Ronald Stamp Ltd had just completed its third year of trading. The maximum capacity of the firm now stood at 80,000 units of production a year. At this level, direct material and labour costs totalled £255,000; fixed overheads amounted to £60,000 for production, £50,000 for general administration, and £40,000 for selling and distribution; and variable overheads, which had fluctuated at first, had now settled at a level of £145,000 a year at capacity.

   Finished products were sold at £10 per unit. Unfortunately, in the year just ended (to which the above figures apply), Ronald Stamp had only been able to produce and sell 50% of its total capacity. The market position was now beginning to improve, and in these more favourable conditions the firm hoped to increase its output and sales to 75% of capacity. From a breakeven chart determine:
   (a) the breakeven volume;
   (b) the margin of safety at 50% of total capacity;
   (c) the increase in profit if the firm moves 50% of total capacity to 75%;
   (d) the new margin of safety.

7. A company's fixed costs are £400,000. Sales revenue is £1,200,000 a year. Variable costs, at £8.00 per unit, currently total £480,000. How would the margin of safety change if labour-saving equipment were installed which reduced variable costs by £2.00 per unit, but which increased fixed costs by £100,000 a year?

8. Hicks and Marshall produce briefcases which sell for £20 each. Fixed costs amount to £24,000 a year. Variable costs per unit are: materials £5; direct labour £4; variable overheads £3.
   (a) What is the annual breakeven level of sales?
   (b) Normal sales volume has been about 3,600 units a year. If the sales price per unit were reduced to £18, it is estimated that the number of briefcases sold would increase by 25%.
      (i) What would the breakeven level of sales then be?
      (ii) What would it be if the sales volume rose by $33^1/_3$%?

9. After several very competitive years in the domestic electrical appliances field, J H Baxter Ltd was finding it more and more difficult to compete. The firm was operating at its present capacity of 60,000 units per year. Variable costs were as low as

they could possibly be, at £6.00 per unit; and in the short run it was impossible to trim the fixed overheads below £60,000 a year.

The Managing Director wanted to know how best to increase profitability, hoping that in the short run there would be no other changes involved. He was considering three alternatives:

(a) Try to squeeze another 20% of capacity out of the firm, by working overtime. This would add another 30p per unit to direct labour costs as a result of overtime premiums.
(b) Raise the existing selling price of £7.50 per unit by 10%.
(c) Drop the selling price by 10% to stimulate sales. In this third case, the firm would have to determine how much more output would be required to maintain its present profit level.

Required:

(a) Examine the three alternatives listed above and plot them on a breakeven chart, together with the firm's original position.
(b) Which alternative do you think would be best for the firm? Why?
(c) Explain any weaknesses which you believe exist in the analysis.

10. Scott Ltd makes and sells two products, A and B. Because of the nature of the production process, two As are made for each B; and all planning is done on the basis that the number of units sold will also be in the proportion 2 to 1. Costs are as follows: variable costs per unit - A £4, B £6; fixed costs £300,000 a year. Each A sells for £12, each B for £10.
    (a) Counting two A's + one B as one 'unit', on an aggregate basis, what is the breakeven number of 'units'?
    (b) If fixed costs are split £160,000 to A and £140,000 to B, what is the breakeven number of units for A and for B?
    (c) How would fixed costs have to be split between A and B in order for the breakeven number of units for A to be the same as for B?

11. Charles's annual breakeven output is 45,000 units. If sales volume is 20% above that level, profit is £36,000. Variable costs are one third of selling price. Draw the breakeven chart.

12. A company's variable costs are £6.00 per unit. Sales volume is currently 40,000 units. Fixed costs are £100,000 a year. Would you recommend an improvement in product quality which would increase variable costs to £8.00 per unit, if that would enable the

company to sell 15% more units at the present selling price of £15 per unit?

13. Crookall Equipment Ltd is currently operating at 75% of capacity, and making an annual profit of £3 million, which is 10% of its total costs. The firm's fixed overheads are £5m per year. The production director has suggested modernising the firm's production processes and buying new machinery. This would increase fixed overheads by £10m a year, but would reduce the variable costs in such a way that the profit at 75% of capacity would remain unchanged.
    (a) Construct a breakeven chart to show the present situation and the proposed alternative.
    (b) At what per cent of capacity is the new breakeven point?
    (c) What is the effect of the new proposal on the firm's range of profitable operation?
    (d) What other factors would you consider before deciding whether to modernise as proposed?

14. Sparko Ltd makes small electrical goods. One of its relatively new lines, 'Bristle' electric toothbrushes, has been selling better than expected (at £5.00 each). In fact, it has been so successful that the firm recently had to turn away a large French order because the factory was already fully extended. The department concerned has already reached its present capacity of 40,000 units a year, at an annual fixed cost of £45,000. The variable costs of production per unit are: direct labour £1.50; material and components £0.50; and other variable costs £0.50.

    The company has been investing heavily in developing a completely new type of electric toothbrush. In about three years this should provide as good a product at a reduced price; but would probably require a new production process. The company has also been spending money to improve its distribution and marketing, in order to take advantage of the evident potential for growth in the market.

    The Managing Director sees three possible courses of action open to him:
    (a) to continue as at present, producing under great strain;
    (b) to increase production by going over to a two-shift system. Recruiting extra labour would not be a problem, and instead of present 8-hour day there could be two 8-hour shifts. The trade unions would insist that the workers' take-home pay be improved; and direct labour costs per unit would probably

rise by 20%. It is hoped that the 100% increase in hours worked would increase output by at least 50%;

(c) to build a new plant on available nearby space, and so allow capacity to expand by at least 50%. Such a venture would increase annual fixed costs by £30,000, but total variable costs in the new plant would be only £1.80 per unit.

Required:

(a) Draw the three alternatives on a breakeven chart.
(b) What should be done? Why?
(c) What assumptions are you making?
(d) What other courses of action might you consider?

15. Fergus Clothing Ltd makes fashionable men's clothing. Its current product is a fur-trimmed coat which retails at £21. Variable costs of production amount to £10 per unit, and the overheads exhibit the following pattern:

Output in units	Overhead costs (£)
Up to 100	1,000
101 to 200	1,500
201 to 300	2,500
301 to 400	3,000

(a) What is the minimum number of coats the company must sell to ensure a profit of 10% on costs?
(b) From market research the company knows it cannot expect to sell more than 350 coats a year. How many should be made in order to maximise profits?

16. The following equations represent the relationships between costs and revenues for a particular mass-produced product. You may assume that production volume equals sales volume (i.e. that there are no changes in levels of stocks held).

$$\text{Total costs} = C = 4 + \frac{w}{3}$$

$$\text{Total revenue} = R = \frac{w}{2}$$

C and R are money amounts in thousands of pounds, and w is the volume of production in thousands of units.

Required:

(a) the selling price of a unit;
(b) the breakeven level of production;
(c) profits at a production level of 30,000 units;
(d) the 'contribution' of each unit sold (to cover fixed cost and profit);
(e) the extra production required to maintain profits if fixed costs rose by 50%;
(f) the change in the breakeven level of production (as in (b) above) if the selling price could be raised by one-sixth.

17. Cheetah Bikes Ltd make motorcycles for the North American market. The current budget gives:

Fixed costs - £5 million
Variable costs - £1,500 per unit
Selling price - US $3,000 per unit
Production output - 20,000 units
Sales - 20,000 units
Exchange rate - £1 = US $1.50

No forward currency deals are planned.

(a) What is the breakeven level of sales?
(b) How much profit is budgeted?
(c) What would be the profit if the exchange rate was:
  (i) £1 = US $1.80?
  (ii) £1 = US $1.20?
(d) What would be the new breakeven sales volumes in (c)(i) and (c)(ii) above?

18. The Roundabout Hotel has recently analysed its cost structure, as follows:

    Fixed costs - £185,000 per year
    Variable costs - 20p per £1 of revenue (based upon an average mix of activities)

    (a) What is the breakeven level of revenue?
    (b) How much profit will be made if:
        (i) revenue is £300,000 per year?
        (ii) revenue is £500,000 per year?
        (iii) revenue is £200,000 per year?
    (c) If fixed costs were increased by £100,000 how much would the breakeven revenue be increased by?
    (d) What must the level of revenue be to achieve a profit before tax of £175,000?

4.8.2 Solutions

1. (a)

Sales price	=	£18	per unit
Variable costs	= £240,000/40,000 units	£6	per unit
Contribution	=	£12	per unit

$$\text{breakeven level of output} = \frac{\text{fixed costs}}{\text{contribution per unit}}$$

$$= \frac{\text{£300,000 a year}}{\text{£12 per unit}}$$

$$= \underline{\text{25,000 units per year}}$$

(b) (i)

$$\text{Breakeven level of output} = \frac{\text{fixed costs}}{\text{contribution per unit}}$$

$$= \frac{\text{£400,000 a year}}{\text{£12 per unit}}$$

$$= \underline{\text{33,333 units per year}}$$

(ii)

Sales price	=	£18	per unit
Variable costs	=	£8	per unit
Contribution	=	£10	per unit

$$\text{breakeven level of output} = \frac{\text{fixed costs}}{\text{contribution per unit}}$$

$$= \frac{\text{£300,000 a year}}{\text{£10 per unit}}$$

$$= \underline{\text{30,000 units per year}}$$

(iii)

Sales price	=	£16	per unit
Variable costs	=	£6	per unit
Contribution	=	£10	per unit

$$\text{breakeven level of output} = \frac{\text{£300,000 a year}}{\text{£10 per unit}}$$

$$= \underline{\text{30,000 units per year}}$$

2. (a) Yes. Breakeven point $= \dfrac{\text{fixed costs}}{\text{contribution}}$

$= \dfrac{\text{£400,000 a year}}{\text{£11 per unit}}$

$=$ <u>40,000 units per year</u>

CHAPTER FIVE

RELEVANT COSTS FOR DECISIONS

5.1 BUSINESS DECISIONS

Many business decisions can be improved by looking at their financial impact. This Chapter is primarily concerned with decisions for which the financial consequences can be assessed with reasonable accuracy. Precise information relating to future periods is seldom available and may not be worth the extra cost of collection even if it were.

The major business issues for which relevant cost information can be used to give better decisions include:

Make-or-Buy decisions
Use-of-capacity decisions
Capital investment decisions

These three areas are dealt with in sections 5.4, 5.5 and 5.6 respectively.

5.2 WHAT MAKES COSTS RELEVANT?

When making business decisions managers should consider only the costs and revenues affected by the decision. Some available cost and revenue information may be irrelevant or even misleading. Figure 5.1 summarises the four basic features that determine which costs and revenues are likely to be relevant.

Relevant	Irrelevant
Future	Past
Incremental	Unchanged
Cash Flows	Accounting Profits Depreciation Charges Accounting Book Values
Whole Enterprise	Costs moved from one department to another.

Figure 5.1 Features of relevant and irrelevant costs and revenues

We now discuss each of these features in detail.

5.2.1 Future

Only *future* costs and revenues are relevant not past ones.

Example 1: The Up Front women's clothes shop which sells women's fashion wear, bought a consignment of 200 new fashion dresses for £8 each. The shop had sold fifty of the dresses for £15 each, but with an unexpected change in fashion the remaining 150 dresses just could not be sold at that price. The shop owner, Maurice, reckons that at £10 each he could sell another 50 dresses; at £8 each another 100; and at £6 each he could sell all 150 dresses. Or he could leave any unsold dresses in the store room until the fashion changed back! What should Maurice do?

If Maurice sold 50 dresses at £10 each he would receive only £500. At £8 each, 100 dresses would fetch £800. If Maurice dropped the price to £6 each, the 150 dresses would sell for £900, which is the maximum cash receipts for the three alternatives.

At £6 each, an accounting loss *of £2 is made on each dress (£6 sales price less £8 purchase price). But unless there are any prospects of fashion changing back again, or unless the dress material has some scrap value, the £6 price (to yield £900 sales revenue) looks like the best (least bad) of the three alternatives.*

In theory it would be better to sell 50 dresses at £10 each, then another 50 at £8 each and the final 50 at £6 each (= £1,200 in total). However, the practice of gradually reducing prices might prevent potential customers buying at all, as they await the next price reduction.

5.2.2 Incremental

Only *incremental* (additional) costs and revenues should be considered. Costs and revenues which remain unchanged are ignored.

Incremental costs are also referred to as differential or avoidable.

Example 2: KPC Limited acquired a specialised machine for £100,000 two years ago, and had since made modifications costing £18,000. A major customer has just notified the company that they will not be needing the products made on the machine beyond the next three months. No other products use the machine nor is any other use seen for it in its present state. A senior production engineer suggests four alternatives for the machine as follows:

(a) keep it in store in case it might be useful in future;
(b) sell it for scrap for £2,000;
(c) cannibalise it (i.e. remove useful parts) at a cost of £400, thereby avoiding £5,000 future expenditure in respect of overhauling other machines;

(d) spend £20,000 carrying out further modifications to the machine in order to avoid buying another (different) machine for £45,000.

Three maintenance men are employed (at a total cost of £54,000 per year) in the machine shop. No change in their number or salary is expected whichever alternative is chosen.

The resultant expenditures and savings are shown in figure 5.2.

Alternative	*Further expenditure*	*Savings or Receipts*	*Net Savings/ Receipts*
(a)	*Nil*	*None, unless the machine can be used at some future date.*	*Nil*
(b)	*Nil*	*£2,000*	*£2,000*
(c)	*£400*	*£5,000*	*£4,600*
(d)	*£20,000*	*£45,000*	*£25,000*

Figure 5.2 Alternative expenditures and savings

In each case we ignore the past costs ('sunk costs') of £118,000 and the unchanging maintenance costs of £54,000. Only the incremental (avoidable) further expenditure and the future savings or receipts matter in the decision now. Alternative (d) appears to be the best, giving a net saving of £25,000 (£45,000 savings - £20,000 further expenditure).

However, to help in making better future decisions, some lessons *might be learned from* past *ones. For example, is it wise to invest in specialised equipment to satisfy the orders of one customer, without an adequate long-term sales contract?*

5.2.3 Cash flows

Cash flows should be used rather than accounting profits, depreciation charges, or accounting book values. The main advantage of the cash flow approach over the P&L account is that the timing of cash flows can be considered before reaching a final decision. Allowing for timing differences in cash flows can be dealt with by discounting them. (See section 5.6).

Example 3: The Four Ps Advertising Agency acquired a ten year lease on a suite of offices in the City of London four years ago, for a cost of £500,000. For financial accounting purposes the net book value of the lease stood at £300,000 (= £500,000 - (£500,000 x 4/10)). The Agency was considering moving to the new city of Milton Keynes where it was felt that its business could be conducted equally well, and operating savings (excluding lease costs) of about £35,000 per year could be made compared with London. The move itself would cost £10,000. Suitable leasehold premises were available at £240,000 for an initial period of six years. However, the leasehold premises in London could be sub-let for the remaining six years for a sum of only £180,000. Does it make financial sense to move? Figure 5.3 summarises the cash flows involved.

Cash Flows (£)	*Timing*	*Event*
+ £180,000	*Now*	*Sale of London lease*
- £240,000	*Now*	*Cost of new lease in Milton Keynes*
- £10,000	*Now*	*Cost of moving to Milton Keynes*
- £70,000	*Now*	
+ £35,000 per year	*Each of the next 6 years*	*Operating cost savings*

Figure 5.3 Cash flows resulting from move to Milton Keynes

In return for a £70,000 net cash outflow now, cash inflows of £35,000 per year could result for the next six years (= £210,000), giving a total net cash benefit of £140,000. So unless there are other significant factors (e.g. loss of customers, company taxation effects, staffing problems, etc.) moving to Milton Keynes appears the better (financial) alternative.

The book value of the London leasehold premises is irrelevant, even though the decision to move to Milton Keynes will result in a first-year accounting book loss of £120,000 (£300,000 net book value - £180,000 realisable value). But managers may sometimes be tempted to sacrifice long-term benefits in order to avoid reporting short-term losses, which in reality have already been incurred.

The move to Milton Keynes would affect profits for the next six years as shown in figure 5.4.

	Year 1	*Years 2-6*	
Book Loss on Sale of London lease	*(£120,000)*	-	
Savings in London lease depreciation £300,000/6	*£50,000*	*£50,000*	
Cost of Milton Keynes lease depreciation £240,000/6	*(£40,000)*	*(£40,000)*	
Cost of moving to Milton Keynes	*(£10,000)*	-	
Savings in Operating Costs	*£35,000*	*£35,000*	
	(£85,000)	*£45,000*	*per year*

Figure 5.4 Effect on profits by moving to Milton Keynes

Over the years the effect on profits is:

(£85,000) + £225,000 (= 5 years at £45,000 per year)

= +£140,000

The six-years net result is the same as that for the cash flow approach. The difference between accounting profits/losses and cash flows boils down to timing differences. This is always true, providing at the end of the period under review, there is no difference between the alternatives in the assets held by the business. (In our example both leases expire in six years' time and are therefore directly comparable).

5.2.4 Whole enterprise

The whole enterprise should be considered, not just the department making the decision.

Example 4: Static Products Ltd are considering withdrawing one of their product lines. This will result in the release of 2,000 square feet of floor space in the centre of the plant for which they have just signed a ten-year lease agreement. The remaining four product lines, which currently use 8,000 square feet of floor space, are not expected to increase in sales volume, nor are any new products likely to be introduced in the foreseeable future. If floor space costs £40,000 (£20 per square foot) per year, what will be the incremental saving in floor space costs if the product line is dropped?

The answer is none. Lease costs for the business will not be reduced. Unless Static Products can find an alternative use for the floor space there is no incremental (or opportunity) floor space cost saving. The floor space costs 'saved' by the discontinuation of one product line are merely shared between the remaining four product lines.

If the company had (incorrectly) included the floor space cost in the product costs for its decision, they might well have dropped the product line instead of retaining it (at least for the time being). With this line of (incorrect) reasoning other product lines might then follow as the total floor space costs are shared amongst fewer product lines. Using the full costing approach might lead to the whole plant eventually being closed down, when in fact continuing (for the time being) would have been financially better.

5.3 OPPORTUNITY COST

In section 2.1 it was stated that 'the cost of acquiring something is what must be given up to get it. This is often money but may be . . some other valuable resource'.

Suppose a business owns equipment that it is currently not using. A manager wishes to use this equipment on a marginal project, arguing that no cost should be charged against his project because the asset is idle. Is this reasonable?

Before we can properly answer this question, we need to determine if there are any further alternatives for the equipment. Could the equipment be sold? Could it be used on a different project? When we have identified the alternative uses of the equipment, we can choose the best. The other alternative uses are then forgone in favour of the course actually taken. The 'next best' (or second best) alternative is known as the opportunity cost. It is the use to which the equipment would be put if the favoured choice was not available.

It is important to know the opportunity cost in advance of the decision, to ensure that the proposed course of action is (expected to be) the best.

5.4 MAKE-OR-BUY DECISIONS

Businesses must often decide whether to make a product themselves or to buy it from another firm. If there is confidence that suppliers and in-house sources can equally well provide:

(a) the required technical competence
(b) the desired level of quality
(c) prompt and reliable delivery

(d) necessary support services

then the financial aspects may be decisive.

Example 5: Simon Goode, the purchasing officer of Dynamic Products Ltd recently discovered that the manufacturing cost of TRM units were £6.50 each. He invited two suppliers to tender for the part and received quotes of £4.58 and £4.70 per unit. Apparently Dynamic Products could make significant savings by purchasing the TRM unit rather than making it.

Before submitting his proposal to the Make/Buy Committee, Mr Goode took another look at the detailed cost sheet, shown in figure 5.5.

TRM Unit	£
Labour Cost (12 minutes at £4.00 per hour)	*0.80*
Material Cost	*0.90*
Manufacturing Overhead (at 600% of Labour Cost)	*4.80*
Total Standard Manufacturing Cost per unit	*6.50*

Figure 5.5 TRM unit cost sheet

Given that Manufacturing Overhead is 80% fixed and 20% variable, what should Simon Goode recommend ?

We need to identify the relevant costs for this decision. How much will Dynamic Products actually save if the TRM unit is bought out? Only 20% of the overheads are variable.

This amounts to 96p per unit (£4.80 x 20%). So the actual savings amount to £2.66 per unit (80p labour, 90p material and 96p overhead). Since the cheapest outside quote is £4.58, the recommendation should therefore be to continue making the TRM unit.

If the manufacturing overhead had been only 20% fixed then the total savings would have been 80p + 90p + £3.84 = £5.54. The decision would then have been reversed, i.e. recommend buying. Before reaching a final decision, other relevant issues (e.g. alternative uses for the resources released by buying the TRM units, potential supplier price increases, quality and delivery performance, etc.) need to be considered.

Financial information is important but often so are other (non-financial) factors.

It is clear that using full cost information may lead to bad decisions. Because many firms maintain standard (full) cost information, there is a constant danger of misusing it for decisions. The damage done may be worse than that resulting from less sophisticated approaches, e.g. 'gut feel'.

Now consider the following case.

Shrival Engineering Ltd

Problem

Shrival Engineering have suffered from falling demand in recent years and now find that they have spare capacity in their foundry and machining operations. Two years ago, a decision was made to buy, rather than produce in-house, a cast and machined iron component. The following financial information indicates that the purchase price is still cheaper than the in-house manufacturing cost.

	In-house cost per unit	**Purchase Price per unit**
	£	£
Material	3.45	N/A
Mfg. Labour	3.00	"
Mfg. Overhead	7.50	"
Total:	13.95	12.95

Manufacturing overhead is calculated at 250% of manufacturing labour cost. The 250% overhead rate is made up as follows:

Depreciation charges	90%
Supervision	8%
Non-productive labour	80%
Utilities	40%
Rates	12%
Other	20%
Mfg. overhead rate	250%

Depreciation and rates are reckoned to be fixed overheads. The remaining overheads are partly fixed and partly variable, as follows:

Supervision	75% fixed, 25% variable
Non-productive labour	50% fixed, 50% variable
Utilities	20% fixed, 80% variable
Other	90% fixed, 10% variable

Should Shrival Engineering continue to buy the component (cast and machined) from their outside supplier?

Write your answer below.

The decision should be based on the additional costs of producing the component in-house. The only additional costs involved appear to be the variable costs.

	Variable cost per unit £
Material	....
Mfg.Labour	....
Mfg.Overhead	
Depreciation	....
Supervision	....
Non-productive labour	....
Utilities	....
Rates	....
Other	....
Total Manufacturing Cost	

Purchase price = £12.95 per unit, therefore the company should

....

Now check your answer below.

Solution

The decision should be based on the additional costs of producing the component in-house. The only additional costs involved appear to be the variable costs.

	Variable Cost per unit	
	£	
Material	3.45	
Mfg. Labour	3.00	
Mfg. Overhead		
Depreciation	-	
Supervision	0.06	(25% x 8% x £3.00)
Non-productive labour	1.20	(50% x 80% x £3.00)
Utilities	0.96	(80% x 40% x £3.00)
Rates	-	
Other	0.06	(10% x 20% x £3.00)
Total Manufacturing Cost	8.73	

Purchase price = £12.95 per unit, therefore the company should manufacture in-house at an incremental cost of £8.73 per unit.

5.5 USE-OF-CAPACITY DECISIONS

In the short term a business often cannot much alter its operating capacity, so management has to decide how to use the available facilities to best advantage.

Example 6: Maggie Stewart, the proprietress of Flair Hair, a ladies' hairdressing salon, is considering whether to start selling a limited range of inexpensive popular romance books which her customers might buy to read during and after their appointment.

Maggie reckons she can sell about 200 books per month. The books can be obtained for £1 each and sold at £1.50 each. A suitable book display and storage rack can be purchased for £50. It can fit into a corner with only a minimum of furniture rearrangement. The rent and rates on the property works out to be £30 per square foot per year. The rack will take up about 4 square feet, and should last a number of years. About two percent of staff time is reckoned to be required for book selling. Since staff currently have about 25 per cent unutilised time, no additional working hours are envisaged. Staff costs are £3,500 per month. Maggie believes that selling books will not affect the level of Flair Hair's hairdressing business.

What should Maggie do?

First we must identify the relevant costs and revenues. These are:

Increased Revenue £300 per month (200 books at £1.50 each)

Increased Costs

Books £200 per month (200 books at £1.00 each)
Book Display and Storage Rack £50 (once-off cost).

The net result is an extra £50 profit in the first month (£300 book sales - £200 book costs - £50 book rack) and £100 per month profit thereafter (£300 book sales - £200 book costs).

The cost of floor space is irrelevant since no extra floor space is required, merely a minor rearrangement. Staff cost information is not relevant unless staff are to be paid extra for selling books.

Unless Maggie has a better use for the spare floor space, she should sell the books and reap the extra profits.

Now examine the following case study:

Integrated Systems Ltd

Integrated Systems Ltd manufactures electronic control systems for steel making plants, water distribution systems and other major plant control purposes. The Production Superintendent has recently suggested that the dual reflex actuator (DRA) unit ought to be discontinued due to low and declining demand levels. The current sales volume is 200 units per month.

The DRA unit is sold separately and whilst little, if any, adverse customer reaction is likely, the Sales Director points out that it still makes a contribution to overall company profit, as follows:

	per unit	per month
Sales price	£42.50	
Manufacturing Cost		
Labour	£7.50	
Material	£18.75	
Mfg. O/hd. - Variable	£11.25	
Contribution	£ 5.00	£1,000

The Plant Facilities Manager reckons that if the DRA unit is discontinued, the machinery and equipment, which has a nil book value, could be disposed of probably for scrap value only, about £1,500. The cost of dismantling would be about £1,000. The vacated space (about 10,000 square feet) could be used for storing spare parts currently stored in a nearby warehouse which is rented at a cost of £1,500 per month. If the spare parts storage operation were moved to the main site the rearrangement and moving costs would amount to about £500.

The Accounts Office advise that floor space on the main site costs £12 per square foot per year.

What action would you recommend?

Work out your answer on a separate sheet of paper. When you have finished, compare your solution with the one provided on the next page.

Solution

Relevant information is:

(a) Loss of contribution	£1,000 per month
(b) Scrap value of machinery and equipment	£1,500
(c) Dismantling cost of machinery & equipment	£1,000
(d) Saving on warehouse cost	£1,500 per month
(e) Rearrangement and moving costs	£500

	Positive effects		Adverse effects	
Once-off	(b)	£1,500	(c)	£1,000
			(e)	£500
Monthly	(d)	£1,500 per month	(a)	£1,000 per month.

The result is a net positive cash flow of £500 per month. Integrated Systems Ltd should therefore cease producing the DRA unit and relocate the spare parts storage operation into the available space at the main site. Before effecting the decision, management will need to consider the personnel implications of this reduction in business activities.

5.6 CAPITAL INVESTMENT DECISIONS

5.6.1 Relevant cash flows

In the decisions we have made so far we have looked at the relevant costs both at a point in time, and over a period of time. When the estimates reveal an alternative that provides a better financial outcome both now *and* later we find it easy to reach a (financial) decision. But what if we have to pay out money now in order to become better off in future? How do we analyse instances with mixed financial outcomes which occur over a number of years?

Example 7: Rapid Transport Company Limited is considering expanding its fleet of vehicles by one 20 ton truck costing £18,000. It would operate for four years and then be scrapped, so the straight line depreciation charge will be £4,500 per year. The company expects net cash flows from the extra business to be £4,000, £5,500, £7,000 and £8,000 in years 1 to 4. Should Rapid Transport acquire the truck?

Cash Flows £	*Timing*
-18,000	*Now*
+ 4,000	*1st year*
+ 5,500	*2nd year*
+ 7,000	*3rd year*
+ 8,000	*4th year*
+ 6,500	*Total for four years*

The table above does not show depreciation which is not a cash flow. Instead, the table includes the initial cash payment of - £18,000 now rather than the annual depreciation charge of £4,500 (for four years). This explicitly recognises the importance of timing *in decision making.*

The cumulative cash flow over the four years is + £6,500, i.e. the company will receive an extra £6,500 by acquiring the extra truck.

But so far we have ignored financing costs. In choosing to invest money in capital projects we give up the chance of investing that money elsewhere, e.g. in a bank, building society, or in the stock market. Or, if we borrowed the money, we will have to make interest payments as well as eventually repaying the principal sum borrowed.

For business organisations, finance for long-term investments may be provided by shareholders (in the form of share capital and reserves) or by lenders (via long term loans or debentures). It is possible for an organisation to estimate its cost of finance (or 'cost of capital'), and this is normally done by the Finance Department. Determining the cost of finance can be rather complicated and is beyond the scope of this book. For illustrative purposes we shall assume the cost of finance to be 20% per year. But first we must appreciate the time value of money.

5.6.2 The time value of money

Capital investment involves spending money now in the expectation of getting returns later. To tell whether the returns are large enough, we need a way to compare returns in the future with investment now.

A given amount of money now is worth more than the same amount of money in future. Why? Because it can be invested today to yield a return in the meantime.

Interest rates do not merely represent inflation, they also allow for time preference and risk. Some types of investment (e.g. in the stockmarket) are more risky than others (e.g. bank deposits) and therefore command a higher return.

Let us suppose that money can be invested today to yield 20 per cent a year; then £1,000 invested today will accumulate (compounding annually) to the amounts shown below:

In 1 year's time, to £1,000 x 1.20	= £1,000 x 1.200	= £1,200
In 2 years' time, to £1,000 x $(1.20)^2$	= £1,000 x 1.440	= £1,440
In 3 years' time, to £1,000 x $(1.20)^3$	= £1,000 x 1.728	= £1,728.

Thus, using an interest rate of 20 per cent a year, the future value of '£1,000 now' is '£1,728 at the end of three years'. Or looking at it the other way round: the *present value* of '£1,728 to be received at the end of three years' is '£1,000 (now').

	Now = End of Year 0 (£)	End of Year 1 (£)	End of Year 2 (£)	End of Year 3 (£)
Future values	1,000 →	1,200 →	1,440 →	1,728
Present values	{ 1,000 ←	1,200		
	{ 1,000 ←		1,440	
	{ 1,000 ←			1,728

Figure 5.6 Future values of '£1,000 now' at 20 per cent a year.

What, then, is the present value of £1,000 to be received at the end of three years ? Clearly it must be £578.70, as shown below:

$$\frac{£1,000}{(1.20)^3} = \frac{£1,000}{1.728} = £578.70$$

We can prove this, by showing what would happen if we invested £578.70 at 20 per cent a year. Each year the effect of compound interest is to add 20 per cent of the start-of-year cumulative amount invested:

After 1 year the amount becomes	:	£578.70 + £115.74 = £694.44
After 2 years " " "	:	£694.44 + £138.89 = £833.33
After 3 years " " "	:	£833.33 + £166.67 = £1,000

Thus we can show the present value of £1,000 to be received at any future date.

		Now = End of Year 0 (£)	End of Year 1 (£)	End of Year 2 (£)	End of Year 3 (£)
Future values		578.70 →	694.44 →	833.33 →	1,000
Present values	{	833.33 ←	1,000		
	{	694.44 ←		1,000	
	{	578.70 ←			1,000

Figure 5.7 Present value of '£1,000 in future' at 20 per cent a year.

Assuming an interest rate of 20 per cent a year, the present value of any amount (call it *a*) to be received at the end of three years is 0.579*a*. Thus, 0.579 is the discount factor for three years at 20 per cent a year. It is equivalent to $1/(1.20)^3$. (We shall use discount factors correct to three decimal places. Whilst this results in some rounding errors, it is accurate enough for most applications).

In effect this gives us an 'exchange rate over time'. Just as compound factors tell us the future values of present money amounts, so discount factors tell us the present values of future money amounts. (See Appendix B for table of discount factors).

In Figure 5.8 the vertical (log-scale) axis shows the accumulating amounts connected by straight lines. Since the rate of increase is a constant 20 per cent a year, all the lines are parallel. (With an ordinary vertical scale, the chart would show upward-curving lines for the cumulative amounts, representing compound interest).

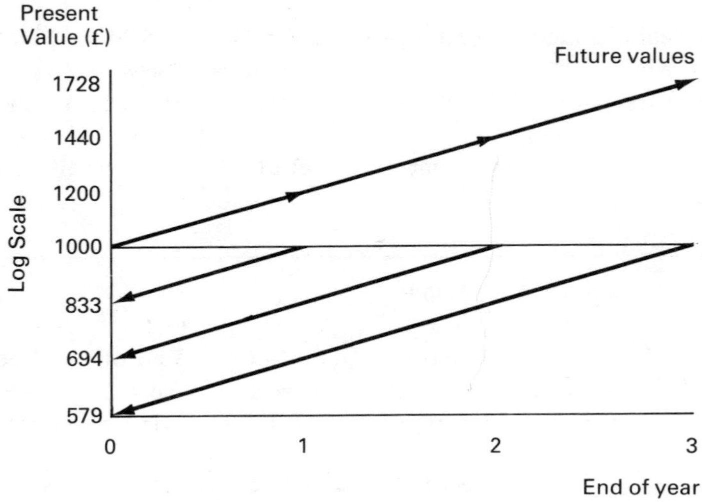

Figure 5.8 Present value chart at 20 per cent a year

You should be able to determine from Figure 5.8:

(a) what £500 invested today would accumulate to in two years' time,
(b) the 'present value' of £2,000 receivable at the end of year 3,
(c) how long it would take for £694 to accumulate to £1,440.

(Answers are shown below).

We have been assuming that we can always invest any sum of money now to yield an annual return of 20 per cent. In practice it is not always easy to estimate this rate of interest (the 'opportunity cost' of capital).

If the relevant opportunity cost is 20 per cent a year, then that is the required rate of return on a capital investment project. If money costs 20 per cent a year, why invest in a capital project expected to yield less than 20 per cent a year? We need to get a higher return from capital projects for the investment to be worthwhile.

Using an annual interest rate enables us to compare money amounts receivable, or payable, at different points in time.

Example 8: If we now consider the proposed truck purchase by Rapid Transport Company, the present value of the proposal can be determined as shown in Figure 5.9.

Answers: a = £720 b = £1,158 c = four years

	(1)	(2)	(1) x (2)
End of Year	*Cash Flow*	*Discount Factor (at 20% per year)*	*Present Value*
	£		£
0 (= now)	*-18,000*	*1.0*	*-18,000*
1	*+ 4,000*	*0.833*	*+ 3,332*
2	*+ 5,500*	*0.694*	*+ 3,817*
3	*+ 7,000*	*0.579*	*+ 4,053*
4	*+ 8,000*	*0.482*	*+ 3,856*
Net Present Value			*- 2,942*

Figure 5.9 Net present value for new truck proposal

Thus, with financing costs at 20% per year, the proposed purchase is not financially justified. Financing costs would need to be lowered for this proposal to be acceptable. The maximum *interest rate would be when the NPV = 0. This discount rate is known as the project's* internal rate of return.

We could have reached the same conclusion by compounding the cash flows forward to the end of year 4 as shown in Figure 5.10.

Why does the compounding approach show a different net amount from that determined by discounting? The net present value of -£2,942 is expressed in today's value, whereas the net terminal value of -£6,093 relates to four years time. To reconcile the two answers, we can either compound (forward) the - £2,942 for four years (-£2,942 x 1.2^4 *= -£6,093) or discount (backwards) the -£6,093 for four years (-£6,093 x 0.482 = -£2,942).*

Cash Flow		*Compound Factor*	*Amount at end of year 4*
£			*£*
- 18,000	*x*	$(1.2)^4$	*- 37,325*
+ 4,000	*x*	$(1.2)^3$	*6,912*
+ 5,500	*x*	$(1.2)^2$	*7,920*
+ 7,000	*x*	*(1.2)*	*8,400*
+ 8,000	*x*	*1.0*	*8,000*
		Net Terminal Value	*-6,093*

Figure 5.10 Net terminal value for new truck proposal

In determining the net present value and net terminal value we have assumed that cash flows only arise at year ends. If the cash flows occur evenly throughout the year we could adjust the discount rates as follows:

End of Year	*Discount Factor*	*End of Year*	*Discount Factor (approx.)*
0	*1.000*		
1	*0.833*	*½*	$\frac{1 + 0.833}{2} = 0.917$
2	*0.694*	*1½*	*0.917 x 0.833 = 0.764*
3	*0.579*	*2½*	*0.917 x 0.694 = 0.636*
4	*0.482*	*3½*	*0.917 x 0.579 = 0.531*

If the above revised discount factors are used the conclusion is the same (but the net present value becomes - £1,430).

In addition to the net present value calculations, other factors such as strategic considerations and competitors' actions may need to be considered. The final decision for marginal capital investment proposals often depends on the ability of the proposer to 'sell' his idea. A good track record for previous capital investment will also carry weight at the final decision stage.

Now consider the following case study.

Saturn Software Ltd

Problem:

Saturn Software, a small but growing software company, is considering installing a hot drinks machine to provide free hot drinks for staff during the working day. Management felt that if free, high quality hot drinks were immediately available then time spent by individuals brewing tea and coffee (using their own equipment) could be significantly reduced. This saving would result in less overtime being worked and postpone the need to recruit additional staff.

The hot drinks machine would cost £1,500 to buy and would incur further costs for provisioning and maintenance (by the machine manufacturer) of £2,000 per year. Savings, resulting from more efficient use of staff are estimated to be about £2,600 per year over the five years estimated life of the drinks machine.

What is the present value of the proposed Saturn Software investment in the hot drinks machine if a 20% discount rate is applicable? What decision should be made? (Ignore corporation tax and inflation).

Write your answer below.

Saturn Software Ltd

End of Year*	Cash Flow £	Discount Factor (at 20%)	Present Value £
0 (now)	....	....	....
1	....	....	....
2	....	....	....
3	....	....	....
4	....	....	....
5	....	....	....
Net Present Value:			______

* Assume that the provisioning and maintenance costs, and the staff savings occur at the ends of years 1 to 5.

Decision: ....

Now turn overpage and check your answer.

Solution

End of Year	Cash Flow £	Discount Factor (at 20%)	Present Value £
0 (now)	- 1500	1.0	- 1500
1	+ 600	0.833	+ 500
2	+ 600	0.694	+ 416
3	+ 600	0.579	+ 347
4	+ 600	0.482	+ 289
5	+ 600	0.402	+ 241
Net Present Value:			+ 293

Decision: Install Hot Drinks Machine

5.7 COST-BENEFIT ANALYSIS

Not all business decisions have measurable financial outcomes. For instance, it may be difficult to accurately determine the costs and/or benefits of:

(a) introducing flexible working hours;
(b) research and development expenditure; or
(c) providing an after-sales service.

Business decisions can result from:

(a) conceding to the demands of others;
(b) financial analysis indicating the best financial alternative (possibly modified by additional subjective factors);
(c) cost/benefit analysis; or
(d) pure 'gut feel'.

Cost-benefit analysis involves the financial quantification of all the costs and benefits relating to a specific business decision. This requires subjective estimates to be made for costs and benefits that are not the subject of market transactions. These estimates, or proxy values, are often based on 'shadow prices' - what the recipients of external benefits would be prepared to pay for them or what those who bear external costs would regard as fair compensation.

A business might use cost-benefit analysis to consider, for instance, the provision of free sports facilities for employees. The costs can be determined fairly accurately but the benefits (better employee relations, fewer strikes, less absenteeism, etc.) are difficult to assess. The 'fringe benefit' of free sports facilities might also assist in attracting and retaining higher quality staff. Either the financial cost (maybe on a per employee basis) could be compared with the estimated (subjective) benefits or an estimated 'valuation' of the benefits could be compared with the cost. The valuation of benefits might involve interviews with beneficiaries (e.g. asking employees how much they would expect to pay if the benefits were not provided free) or maybe analysing statistical information in an attempt to quantify the benefits.

Cost-benefit analysis is of particular interest to those in the public sector because of the absence of market conditions that exist in the private sector (where suppliers' costs and prices affect the supply and demand for goods and services).

5.8 CHAPTER SUMMARY

People making business decisions must identify the relevant costs and revenues, that is the incremental future cash flows for the whole enterprise. Three important decision areas where this applies are:

(a) make-or-buy;
(b) use-of-capacity;
(c) capital investment.

In looking at capital investment decisions we must take into account the time value of money. Capital investment means spending money now in the hope of benefits in future. To see whether capital investment is worthwhile, therefore, we need a way to compare the future returns with the initial cash outlay.

Receiving money now is better than receiving the same money amount in future. We can overcome cash flow timing differences either by compounding today's money forward into the future, or by discounting future cash flows back to 'present value'. Discounting is more usual, as it expresses net present value in terms of today's money, which is easier to understand.

Cost/benefit analysis is a more subjective approach to decision-making, where the benefits (and maybe the costs) are hard to measure. This technique, requiring an estimate of the value of benefits, often applies to the public sector where there is no market as such.

5.9 REVIEW QUESTIONS AND ANSWERS

5.9.1 Questions

1. Identify three business decisions that require relevant cost information.
2. What are the four basic principles that identify which costs and revenues are relevant?
3. How should on-going costs and revenues be dealt with in financial decision making?
4. Division A of a company is considering dropping one of its product lines. If Central Office overheads are apportioned to divisions on the basis of divisional revenue, how should Division A include savings of Central Office overheads in their decision analysis?
5. Are past expenditures relevant in decision making?
6. Since many businesses aim to make a profit, surely depreciation and profit implications are relevant in decision making! Do you agree?
7. What is discounted cash flow concerned with?
8. What is present value?
9. What is the difference between a discount rate and a discount factor?
10. What does cost-benefit analysis involve?

Write our your answers and then check with the answers over page

5.9.2 Answers

1. (a) Make-or-Buy Decisions.
   (b) Use-of-Capacity Decisions.
   (c) Capital Investment Decisions.

2. (a) Only *future* costs and revenues are relevant.
   (b) Only *incremental* costs and revenues must be considered.
   (c) *Cash flows* should be used rather than accounting profits, depreciation charges, or accounting book values.
   (d) The *whole enterprise* should be considered, not just the section making the decision.

3. Cost and revenues which continue unchanged regardless of the decision can be ignored for the purpose of decision making.

4. If the Central Office overheads in total are unaffected by Division A's decision, then overhead savings should be ignored since they would merely be re-distributed amongst other divisions. Savings of Central Office overheads should be included to the extent that they are incremental to the decision.

5. No. The past cannot be changed, but the future can.

6. Using the cash flow approach is preferable to just estimating the effect on profits, because:
   (a) using cash flows allows us to take into account the time value of money;
   (b) most non-accountants find it easier to prepare; and
   (c) it avoids over-emphasis on short-term book losses. However, it is advisable to be aware of the P&L account implications, especially if they are large.

7. Discounted cash flow is a means of coping with the time value of money, whereby future cash flows are discounted to their equivalent 'present value' by means of a suitable discount rate.

8. Present value is today's equivalent of a future sum of money (receipt or payment).

9. A discount rate is the interest rate used in present value calculations, whereas the discount factor is the factor which reduces future cash flows to their present value. The discount factor is determined by the discount rate and the time period into the future when the cash flow occurs.

10. Cost/benefit analysis involves the financial quantification of all the costs and benefits (financial and especially non-financial) relating to a specific business decision.

5.10 PROBLEMS

5.10.1 Questions

1. Nippey's Garage sells new and used cars and provides after-sales service. Business activity has grown rapidly in recent years. The servicing, repair and MOT test facilities, and the five garage staff, are fully utilised from 8.00 a.m. to 6.00 p.m. Monday to Friday, and from 8.00 a.m. to 1.00 p.m. on Saturdays (50 working hours). In fact some potential customers are going elsewhere rather than wait two weeks or more for an 'appointment'.

   Nippey's General Manager is considering recruiting five garage service and repair staff to work from 6.00pm to midnight on Monday to Friday (30 working hours). He believes this shift would rapidly become fully utilised.

   Existing financial information for the servicing and repair activities reveals the following:

	£ per hour
Charge-out rate to customer	15.00
Labour costs (including NIH pensions, etc.)	7.50
Equipment depreciation	2.00
Floor space costs (including rates)	2.50
Other overheads	1.50
Total costs	13.50
Profit margin	1.50
	15.00

   Higher labour rates of £9.50 would be incurred for the new late shift. With the additional proposed use of existing equipment, its estimated life is only two-thirds of its current estimated life. About one-third of the 'other overheads' are variable. Which is the better alternative:

   (a) commence a late shift operation; or
   (b) continue to limit customers due to capacity restrictions?

   What other alternatives would you consider before making a final recommendation?

2. A leading football club was considering introducing an away-supporters' ban, thus limiting attendance to home club supporters only. Attendance at matches would be adversely affected by the absence of away supporters but it was reckoned that this would be partly offset by attracting more home supporters. For the first season as a whole the following estimates were made:

	With away supporters' ban	Without
	£m	£m
Gate receipts	2.4	2.5
Programme sales	0.1	0.15
Policing costs	0.06	0.2
Cost of new system: equipment*	0.2	-
Cost of new system: running costs	0.1	-
Staffing costs on match days	0.04	0.1
Players costs	1.8	1.8
Other running costs	0.5	0.5

* the equipment was expected to last at least three years.

What is the financial effect on the football club? Are there any other factors that need to be considered?

3. Roy Essex was considering utilising six currently unused robots for a cost savings project. The robots had been replaced by more modern equipment after only two years of use and were now stored in a nearby warehouse. The robots cost a total of £2.4 million and were being depreciated on a straight-line basis over ten years. With eight years to go the net book value stood at £1.92 million. Roy gathered from the equipment supplier that the second hand value for the six robots was about £0.8 million.

Generally when equipment was transferred within the company it was transferred at its net book value. Roy knew his project could not afford the net book value cost, but he felt it was a shame that the robots should remain unutilised.

(a) What costs are relevant?
(b) How should the company deal with this situation ?

5.4 Jack Ladd is currently using his credit cards fully and is paying interest at the rate of 2 per cent per month. With recent overtime working his wages this week provide him with a rare surplus cash balance of £100. However his motor car licence fee is due for renewal at a cost of £100 for 12 months or £55 for six months. Should Jack buy a 12 month licence or buy only a six months' licence and use the remaining £45 to reduce his credit card balance?

5.10.2 Solutions

1. Additional profits of introducing late shift

	£ per hour	£ per week (150 man-hours)
Extra sales revenue	15.00	2250
Extra labour costs	9.50	1425
Extra depreciation of equipment*	1.67	250
Floor space costs	-	-
Other overheads ($^{1}/_{3}$ variable)	0.50	75
Total costs	11.67	1750
Profit margin	3.33	500
	15.00	2250

* Since equipment will last only two-thirds of its current estimated life, depreciation charge will increase by 50% (per week).

Depreciation now = £2.00 per hour x 50 hours x 5 staff
= £500 per week

Extra depreciation is therefore £250 per week

$$= \frac{£250}{30\text{x}5} \text{ per hour}$$

= £1.67 per hour

By commencing a late shift operation, Nippeys can expect an additional profit of £500 per week when this shift becomes fully utilised. The profit margin per hour is actually higher for the late shift than for the daytime shift. This appears to be a much more profitable alternative to the present arrangement of 'turning away' customers.

Other alternatives that might be considered before making a final decision:

(a) Extend the building and facilities to provide the necessary service on dayshift only.

(b) Increase prices to reduce unsatisfied demand, whilst increasing profits.

(c) Seek other alternatives which will allow more business to be handled with existing facilities.

2.

	Effect on profit of away-supporters' ban
	£m
Gate receipts	-0.1
Programme sales	-0.05
Policing costs	0.14
New system: equipment depreciation*	-0.07
New system: runnings cost	-0.1
Staffing costs on match days	0.06
Total effect on profit	-0.12

* £0.2m depreciated over three years

In the first season profit (before tax) is expected to be £0.12m lower as a result of the away-supporters ban. In subsequent seasons the adverse effect on profit might not be as large, particularly if more home-supporters attend and programme sales increase.

In addition to the financial effects on the football club, the local community may be effected on match days as follows:

less violence and property damage
less traffic
lower (perhaps higher?) retail sales of food, drink, etc.

If these effects are net benefits to the local community, the football club might consider the cost acceptable.

CHAPTER SIX

BUDGETS

6.1 BUDGETARY CONTROL

6.1.1 What are budgets?

Budgets are formal business plans comprising:

(a) quantitative statements;
(b) usually expressed in financial terms;
(c) covering a specific period of time;
(d) for all or part of a firm's operations;
(e) agreed in advance.

Budgets are not neutral forecasts of future events: managers accept a personal commitment to *help* make them happen. Nor are they merely ideal targets: budgets must be capable of achievement.

Budgetary control involves:

(a) setting objectives;
(b) motivating managers;
(c) co-ordinating activities;
(d) communicating information;
(e) assessing performance;
(f) facilitating effective action.

The following sections discuss each of these separately.

6.1.2 Achieving objectives through budgets

An organisation's aims (as discussed in Chapter 1) will clearly influence top management's approach to budgets for the various parts of a business. Objectives will be expressed in terms of sales revenue, production costs, fixed and working capital investment levels, etc. Many businesses prepare budgets for *balance sheet items* (e.g. debtors, stocks, cash) as well as for profit and loss items (e.g. sales, expenses).

Many budget techniques are also relevant in organisations which are not even aiming for profit, such as schools, churches, armed services, etc. In such cases specific budget objectives will serve as proxies for ultimate objectives other than wealth maximisation. Organisations which do not sell goods or services on the market may find it useful to budget their output in physical rather than money terms, paying attention both to quantity and quality. (Inputs can usually be expressed in terms of money, but physical quantities may be useful also).

It is important for top management to keep their long-term objectives in mind. Otherwise they may persist with short-term goals - originally chosen as steps on the way to the ultimate objectives - even after conditions have changed, now requiring different short-term goals in aiming for the same long-term objectives.

As a summary of the kinds of things that a financial budget aims to cover, Figure 6.1 sets out the main headings that a business ought to consider when trying to improve perhaps the single most important financial measure of operating performance - Return on Net Assets.

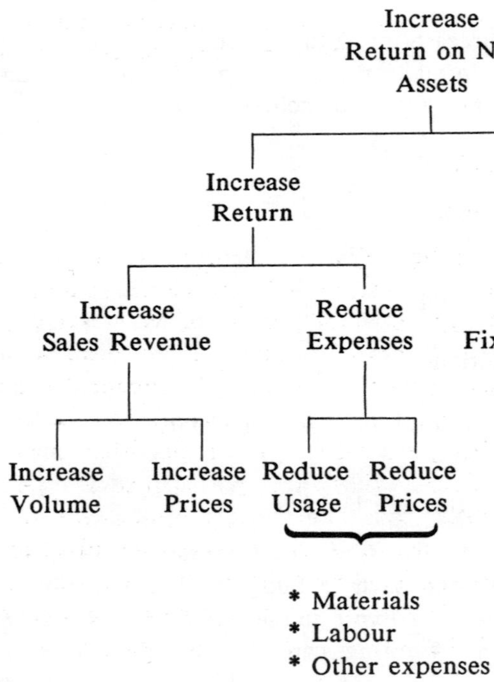

Figure 6.1 Financial Split of Operating Objectives

6.1.3 Motivating managers

Most students work with more purpose if they know they are going to be tested. Likewise, business managers tend to work more effectively if they know that their performance (or than of their business unit) is to be compared with a previously agreed budget. Managers may feel more personal commitment to achieving budgeted performance where they have themselves participated in preparing the budget. Their detailed knowledge may anyway make that a good idea.

Ultimately, however, it is for top managers to judge whether a proposed budget represents adequate performance. A budget that is either 'too easy' or 'too hard' to achieve will usually provide less effective motivation than a budget which is 'difficult but achievable'.

There can be danger in judging a business's performance entirely on the basis of current profits, if some decisions have longer-term effects. For example, a manager might be able to improve this years profits by spending less on research; but it could be disastrous in the long run. In practice, managers are normally judged on their 'track record' over a period of years. Business success has several aspects; and using more than one yardstick is wiser than judging managers or business units by any single accounting number, however cleverly devised.

6.2 PREPARING BUDGETS

6.2.1 Construction of budgets

Establishing a bottom-up budget for a business usually starts by estimating the sales revenue for the period. Individual salesmen can estimate the quantity and type of products or services likely to be purchased by both existing and new customers. If the business has a separate marketing department, then a further independent forecast of sales may be made. After any necessary reconciliation, sales and marketing can present their agreed sales forecast, detailing quantities, types of products or services, prices and perhaps some specified customers. For the forthcoming year, the budget is normally divided into monthly budgets. If the business is not seasonal, dividing the annual budget into twelve equal monthly budgets may be satisfactory. However if the business is seasonal or is growing (or declining) rapidly, greater care will be needed in setting realistic monthly budgets.

Some organisations, e.g. charities, churches, etc. don't have any sales. But they do have income. The budgeting of income becomes easier and more accurate if they have a commitment from givers. Charities invite people to sign a banker's order and a deed of covenant to ensure regular income. Many churches operate an 'envelope scheme' in which the churchgoer agrees to weekly offerings, even for the weeks they don't attend church.

Once a budget for sales revenue (and quantities) has been set it is then possible to establish a manufacturing budget. (In a service organisation this would be a budget for those directly involved in providing the services). People, materials and equipment need to be provided in the right amounts and types to achieve the level of output required.

Figure 6.2 outlines the early stages in building up a budget for a manufacturing organisation. Further budgets would be needed for any additional activities, e.g. R & D, Engineering and After-Sales Service functions. But by establishing the sales revenue budget first, all other business functions can be budgeted to achieve the sales objective. Any other objectives, e.g. developing new products can then also be planned and budgeted for.

The resultant budgeted Profit and Loss account, Balance Sheet and Cash Flows for the organisation constitutes the first draft of the master budget, i.e. the plan which the organisation as a whole will work towards achieving.

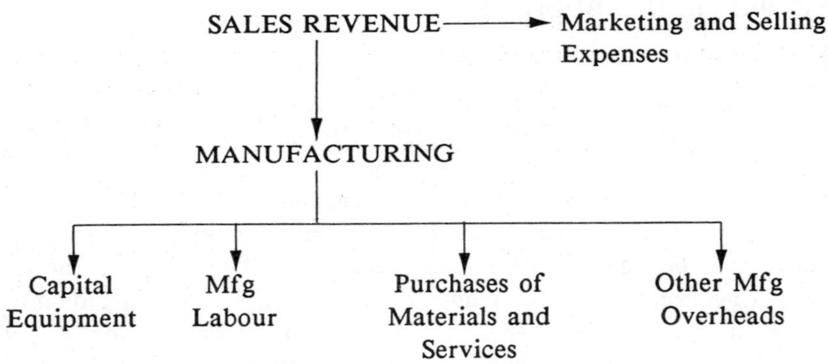

Figure 6.2 Construction of a Manufacturing Organisation Budget

6.2.2 The budget cycle

Developing the *master* budget involves the following steps:

(a) Stating basic assumptions and company objectives.

(b) Forecasting general economic and industry conditions.

(c) Developing detailed sales budgets, analysed suitably, e.g. between customers, products, areas, market sectors, etc.

(d) Preparing *production* budgets, including budgets for materials and labour, analysed between different products, locations, etc.

(e) Preparing *capital expenditure* budgets.

(f) Preparing *cash* budgets.

(g) Combining all the above into the master budget: the overall budgeted profit and loss account, balance sheet, and cash flow statement.

Many companies make some central assumptions about the business environment for a budget period such as the rate of population growth, the rate of inflation, etc., which they require all subordinate units to use in their own detailed budgets. It is a matter of judgement which assumptions are best made centrally and used consistently throughout an organisation, and which can be left to each unit or department to make for itself.

Most businesses prepare budgets annually; but the one-year budget is normally split into much shorter periods: quarters, months (or four-week periods), weeks, and perhaps even days. Most activities are not carried out precisely evenly throughout the year, so one would not usually expect an amount in a monthly budget to be exactly one-twelfth of the equivalent item in the annual budget.

Some businesses also prepare longer-term plans with the 'annual' budget representing only the first year of the longer period. There will often be extra refinement of detail in the one-year budget, as compared with longer-term three-year or five-year plans. Another difference will be in managers' stronger commitment to the one-year budget.

It is also possible to prepare 'rolling' budgets, which add a month at the end while dropping off the month just finished. This means that detailed budgets always stretch twelve months into the future; whereas with 'fixed' annual budgets there can come a time when they cover only a month or two ahead. The question is whether the benefit from rolling budgets outweighs the extra costs of preparing them.

6.2.3 Co-ordination

Budgets help to co-ordinate business operations, e.g. between production and sales, by revealing end-of-period inventories in budgeted balance sheets. They also *force managers to plan ahead*; and may often reveal needs for action which might otherwise have remained unnoticed, e.g. storage requirements, financing needs, etc.

Since lead times can often be extensive, it is clearly useful to plan far enough ahead to give adequate warning of such needs in good time.

The budget procedure nearly always contains elements of feedback, and, if the original budgets reveal unexpected problems in particular areas, suitable changes may be required. It may also be possible to adjust the *timing* of certain planned events to avoid bunching, especially in relation to so-called 'critical' resources (which may be money, manpower, raw materials, or physical facilities).

Capital budgets should be co-ordinated with operating budgets. Thus, if a new capital investment is justified on the basis of the operating savings it will produce, subsequent operating budgets should incorporate such savings.

The first draft of the master budget frequently fails to satisfy all the parties concerned. There may be doubts about achieving budgeted sales or production levels or perhaps surplus capacity is revealed. And clearly, the first draft may need changing if the budgeted level of profit does not satisfy top management. Alterations may be made to sales revenue or expenses, and part or all of the budgeting process may be repeated. Further iterations may be required to achieve an achieveable master budget that all parties can accept.

6.2.4 Negotiating budgets

At the two extremes, budgets could be dictated from on high ('top-down') or simply emerge from below ('bottom-up'). In practice, however, budgets are normally agreed by a process of negotiation between different levels of management. The final agreed budget will often lie somewhere between what top management would like and what junior managers reckon they can achieve. But ambitious lower managers might even budget for better results than top management demands.

A more satisfactory outcome is likely where there exists a high degree of 'trust' between different levels of management, the desire to set 'difficult but achievable' budgets, and experience in both setting and achieving them.

6.3 USING BUDGETS

6.3.1 Time lags

The pay-off from spending time and effort on budgeting comes not only from requiring managers to plan in adequate detail, but also from measuring actual performance against the plan. For effective use of budgets it is essential to report actual results as soon as possible after the budget period has ended. Delay in reporting actual results (versus budget) can delay the taking of necessary corrective (or opportunistic) action. Also long delays can reduce management motivation and lead to speculation that perhaps things have improved since the end of the latest reported budget period and therefore no action is required.

It is pointless producing and sending weekly reports if action is taken only once a month. For example, a business school improved its financial reporting system by using suitably summarised figures once a quarter instead of excessively detailed reports every month. On the other hand, timing *may* be important: small businesses, for example, may gain by being able to react *quickly* to changing events.

In many organisations 'flash figures' are reported to management within a few days of the budget period just ended. Flash figures are approximate financial figures, promptly reported, relating to the most essential aspects of a business performance, e.g. sales revenue, sales volumes, production (or service) output, profit. The detail of *which* flash figures are desirable will to some extent be determined by the nature of the business.

Even if flash figures are promptly provided, the main report of actuals against budget should follow quickly, perhaps in no more than a week or two. Businessmen most often prefer approximate figures soon to precise figures later.

6.3.2 Communication

Budgets, which aim to communicate, should be simple and easy to read. Filling reports with trivial items, or with needlessly accurate detail, obscures what really matters.

Figure 6.3 shows an example of a monthly profit and loss report (monthly balance sheets may also be useful). If required, attached schedules can give more details. In addition a brief report may highlight key aspects of the results. Also charts of past and projected future trends (possibly adjusted for inflation) may be valuable.

Signalling only important *exceptions* from an agreed standard can restrict needless detail, but requires judgement. If conditions have changed, deviation from budget may not be 'bad' (nor exactly attaining it 'good'). There may be perfectly sound reasons for a variance from budget.

	Latest month September				Cumulative to date 9 months			
	Budget £'000	%	Actual £'000	%	Budget £'000	%	Actual £'000	%
Sales Revenue								
Variable cost of sales:								
materials								
direct labour								
mfg. overheads								
Other variable expenses								
Contribution								
Fixed mfg. overheads								
Other fixed expenses								
Operating profit								

Figure 6.3 Monthly profit and loss report

If conditions change, the budget figures may not represent a good estimate of the current year's results. Monthly reports may then include a 'latest estimate for the current year', updated each month. This can help show whether a variance in one month is merely a *timing* difference, which will reverse itself next month, or the start of a trend resulting in large cumulative variances by the year-end. Clearly these could have different implications for management action.

6.3.3 Appraising Performance

When appraising performance one needs a *standard* against which to judge actual results. If the budget is properly set, there should be no need to include last year's actual figures. The budget should take them into account, together with expected changes, in setting the current year's standard. Their inclusion will clutter up the report and distract attention from what really matters: the budget and the current year's actual figures.

Flexible budgeting can often be very useful in allowing for changes in business conditions. Major changes may make it desirable to revise budgets, despite the time and effort involved. Otherwise managers may either become demoralised if actual results are compared with budgets which are now unattainable, or complacent if budgets are too easily achieved.

6.3.4 Management Action

Budgets should help managers manage: they are *not* rigid targets which must be exactly achieved at all costs, whatever has changed since they were agreed. There can be good reasons for actual results to differ from budget. Managers may not be able to control every item in their budgets, at least in the short run; but they are expected to react to changed conditions.

Budgetary control with monthly reporting may help managers to answer the following kinds of questions:

(a) What has performance been like recently? How does it differ from budget? Why?

(b) How if at all will these events cause latest estimates of current year results to differ from budget *if no action is taken*?

(c) What if anything can be done to counter unfavourable variances from budgets, or to increase favourable ones? (Successful managers cash in on good luck!)

(d) How soon will such action be effective? How much difference will it make?

(e) After all proposed actions, what is now the latest estimate of current year results?

6.4 THE BUDGET PROCESS

To illustrate how a business can develop its Master Budget, let's consider Green's Garden Sheds Ltd., whose accounting year runs from 1st October to 30th September.

6.4.1 Sales budget

The company makes three types of garden shed, Goliath, General and Gnome. Based upon previous sales volumes and prices, and taking account of their growing reputation for quality and sturdiness, the sales manager for Green's Garden Sheds estimates that sales for the year ending 30 September 1988, will be as follows:

Shed Type	Estimated Sales Volume units	Expected Price per unit £	Estimated Sales Revenue £
Goliath	190	240	45,600
General	320	150	48,000
Gnome	600	95	57,000
			150,600

6.4.2 Manufacturing budget

(a) Materials - Material costs have been estimated as follows:

	Cost per Shed		
	Goliath £	General £	Gnome £
Wood - Frame	40	25	16
- Door	15	11	9
Glass	5	4	3
Roofing	20	15	13
Handles, Hinges, etc.	6	5	5
Total	86	60	46

(b) Production Labour - estimated as follows:

2 employees full time at £160 per week plus 35% fringe costs (i.e. national insurance, pension costs, etc.) = 2 x £160 x 52 x 1.35 = £22,464.

4 temporary employees at £140 per week plus 20% fringe costs, for 15 weeks = 4 x £140 x 15 x 1.20 = £10,080.

(c) Production Overheads - estimated as follows:

Equipment Depreciation Charge	=	£8,200
Rent and Rates	=	£6,500
Utilities	=	£2,300

6.4.3 Purchases budget

In addition to purchasing materials to meet sales requirements, it has been considered appropriate to increase the year-end materials stock by four units of each shed type. Finished sheds and work-in-progress amounts are to remain the same as the previous year.

Therefore purchases will cost:

		£
Goliath	(190 + 4) x £86 =	16,684
General	(320 + 4) x £60 =	19,440
Gnome	(600 + 4) x £46 =	27,784
Total:		63,908

6.4.4 Capital equipment budget

Machinery, equipment and tools costing £8,950 are to be bought.

6.4.5 Administration budget

Estimated as follows:

		£
Sales Manager £14,000 + 45% fringe costs	=	20,300
Lease cost of company car	=	2,200
Advertising costs	=	1,500
Book-keeper £6,000 + 35% fringe costs	=	8,100
Auditing charges	=	800
		32,900

6.4.6 Profit budget

The budgeted profit for the year can now be determined by bringing together the budgets for Sales, Manufacturing and Administration. See Figure 6.4:

GREEN'S GARDEN SHEDS LTD
BUDGETED PROFIT AND LOSS ACCOUNT
FOR THE YEAR ENDING 30TH SEPTEMBER 1988

		£	£
Sales Revenue			
			150,600
Cost of Sales			
Materials	£86 x 190 =	16,340	
	£60 x 320 =	19,200	
	£46 x 600 =	27,600	
		63,140	
Production Labour		22,464	
		10,080	
		32,544	
Production Overheads		8,200	
		6,500	
		2,300	
		17,000	112,684
Gross Profit			37,916
Less Administration and Finance Costs			32,900
Budgeted Profit before Tax			5,016

Figure 6.4 Green's budgeted profit and loss account

So the budgeted profit before tax represents about 3% of the budgeted sales revenue. If management (Mr Green) is unhappy with this budget, then ways of increasing revenue (by increased volumes and/or increased prices) and/or reducing expenses (materials, production labour, production overheads, administration) must be found.

Before management can be satisfied that the budget, as outlined, is acceptable, it is also necessary to produce a budgeted balance sheet and a cash flow budget.

All three financial aspects of the master budget (profit and loss account, balance sheet and cash flow) should then be divided up into a number of budget periods, e.g. twelve one-month periods, for control purposes.

6.4.7 Balance Sheet Budget

At 30 September 1987 Green's Balance Sheet was as shown in Figure 6.5:

		£
Fixed Assets		
(Machinery, equipment, tools, etc.) net		45,200
Current Assets		
Stock	26,150	
Debtors	21,420	
Cash	3,790	51,360
Total Assets		96,560
Less Current Liabilities: Creditors		16,160
Total Assets less Current Liabilities		80,400
Less Other Liabilities		
Long Term Loan	22,500	
Warranty Provisions	15,000	
		37,500
Total Assets less Total Liabilities		42,900
Share Capital and Reserves		
Paid Up Ordinary Shares	30,000	
Accumulated Profits	12,900	42,900

Figure 6.5 Green's balance sheet

During the year to 30th September, 1988, the following were budgeted:

a) Materials stock level to be increased by four units of each type (total stock level budget = £26,150 + 4 x £86 + 4 x £60 + 4 x £46 = £26,918).

b) Debtors' level: 2 months (based on sales).

c) Cash balance at 30 September 1988 (see later) £925.

d) Creditors level: 3 months (based on purchases cost of £63,908).

e) £2,500 of the Long Term Loan would be repaid.

f) Warranty Provision would remain at £15,000.

g) No further cash was to be raised by the issue of shares.

h) No Corporation Tax was expected to be paid in the next few years.

Green's budgeted balance sheet at 30th September, 1988, is shown in Figure 6.6:

		£
Fixed Assets (£45,200 + £8,950 - £8,200)		45,950
Current Assets	£	
Stock	26,918	
Debtors (2/12 x £150,600)	25,100	
Cash (see later)	925	52,943
Total Assets		98,893
Less Current Liabilities - Creditors (3/12 x £63,908)		15,977
Total Assets less Current Liabilities		82,916
Less Other Liabilities	£	
Long Term Loan (£22,500 -£2,500)	20,000	
Warranty Provisions	15,000	
		35,000
Total Assets less Total Liabilities		47,916
Share Capital and Reserves		
Paid Up Ordinary Shares	30,000	
Accumulated Profits (12,900+5,016)	17,916	
		47,916

Figure 6.6 Green's budgeted balance sheet

Of particular importance within the Balance Sheet Budget is the Cash Budget. Let's see how Green's year-end cash balance is arrived at.

Cash Receipts

		£
Sales:	Amount owed by debtors at 30.9.87	21,420
	+ Sales for 1987/88 year	150,600
		172,020
Less debtors at 30.9.88		25,100
		146,920

Cash Payments

(i)	Materials: Amount owed to creditors at 30th September 1987	16,160
	+ Purchases for 1987/88 year (see section 6.4.3)	63,908
		80,068
	Less creditors at 30th September 1988*	15,977
		64,091

* $\frac{3}{12}$ purchases budget of £63,908

(ii)	Production Labour: from 1987/88 P&L Account	32,544
(iii)	Production Overheads	
	From 1987/88 P&L Account	17,000
	Less Depreciation charge (not a cash flow)	8,200
		8,800
(iv)	Administration and Finance Costs: from 1987/88 P&L Account	32,900
(v)	Capital Equipment Purchased during 1987/88	8,950
(vi)	Long Term Loan: Part Repayment during 1987/88	2,500

Therefore Total Cash Payments:	Materials	64,091
	Production Labour	32,544
	Production Overheads	8,800
	Administration & Finance	32,900
	Capital Equipment	8,950
	Loan Repayment	2,500
		149,785

Cash Balance at 30th September 1988

=	Cash Balance at 30th September 1987	3,790
+	Cash Receipts for 1987/88	146,920
	Less Cash Payments for 1987/88	(149,785)
		925

Cash budgets need to be produced for monthly (or even shorter) periods to ensure that the business does not run out of cash *during* the year. If the cash balance is expected to go negative (or fall to an unacceptably low positive balance) then the business will need to find other sources of cash (e.g. issue more shares, increase borrowing, etc.) or else modify the budget.

6.5 CHAPTER SUMMARY

Budgeting is now common in all but the smallest companies. Budgets focus management's attention on preparing and gaining commitment to detailed co-ordinated plans, as a means of achieving the firm's objectives.

Many businesses establish a budget for the profit and loss account, for the end-of-year balance sheet, and for cash flows over a future twelve-month period. This may apply for a specific annual period, or else be on a *rolling* twelve-month basis by updating the budget every month.

If there are major unexpected changes in business conditions, it may make sense to revise the budget completely during the year. This is likely to provide greater incentive for managers to meet a target which is 'difficult but achievable'. Otherwise the target may be either too easy or else too hard.

Preparing a budget has value in itself, but further advantage can result from prompt reporting of actual performance compared with budget, and by management taking suitable action quickly. This might be corrective action to mitigate adverse performance, or opportunistic action to 'cash in' on good luck.

The foundation of the budget process is normally the sales budget. This provides the basis for operating expenses such as materials purchases and direct labour costs, as well as for purchases of capital equipment. The level of sales will also affect working capital items such as stocks and debtors.

6.6 REVIEW QUESTIONS AND ANSWERS

6.6.1 Questions

1. What are budgets?

2. What benefits derive from budgetary control?

3. What is a master budget?

4. What are the steps involved in developing a master budget?

5. What is a rolling budget?

6. How does a budget differ from a neutral forecast?

7. Why may it be necessary to produce a number of draft budgets before establishing the master budget?

8. Which is most important to business managers; eventual provision of precise actual results reported against budget, or prompt provision of approximate figures reported against budget?

9. What are 'flash figures'?

10. What is flexible budgeting?

Write out your answers and then check with the answers provided.

6.6.2 Answers

1. Budgets are formal business plans comprising
   (a) quantitative statements;
   (b) usually expressed in financial terms;
   (c) prepared and approved in advance;
   (d) covering a specific period;
   (e) for (the whole or part of) a firm's operations.

2. Budgetary control
   (a) set objectives;
   (b) co-ordinates activities;
   (c) motivates managers;
   (d) communicates information;
   (e) helps assess performance; and
   (f) facilitates effective action.

3. The master budget is the plan which the organisation as a whole will work towards achieving. It comprises a budgeted profit and loss account, balance sheet and cash flow for the organisation.

4. The master budget involves:
   (a) stating basic assumptions and company objectives;
   (b) forecasting general economic and industry conditions;
   (c) preparing detailed sales budgets;
   (d) preparing detailed production budgets;
   (e) preparing capital expenditure budgets;
   (f) preparing cash budgets;
   (g) co-ordinating the various subsidiary budgets into the master budget.

5. A rolling budget is one in which figures for an extra budget period (e.g. one month) are added each time a budget period finishes. In this way the budget always covers the next twelve months.

6. Managers accept a personal commitment to achieve their approved budgets.

7. The first draft of the master budget frequently fails to completely satisfy all the interested parties. Therefore it is often necessary to perform one or more iterations to achieve an acceptable master budget.

8. Businessmen nearly always prefer approximate figures soon to precise figures later. In this way motivation is enhanced and necessary appropriate action may be taken sooner.

9. Flash figures are approximate financial figures, promptly reported, relating to the most essential aspects of a business performance.

10. Flexible budgeting is the revision of a budget necessitated by major changes in business conditions, which cause the existing budget to be either too difficult or too easy to attain.

6.7 PROBLEMS

Questions:

1. The Wardown Car Wash provides an automatic washing service for cars and small vans. In addition to the basic wash at £1.50 per vehicle, a 'wash 'n wax' option is available for £2.50. The washing equipment, which cost £60,000 installed, has been in use now for one year. It is estimated to have a useful life of five years or more.

   Rent and rates for the forthcoming year amount to £2,250 and will be paid half in April and half in October. In addition, annual operating costs (all paid in cash) are estimated at:

washing solution	20p per vehicle
wax (used only on wash'n'wax)	45p per vehicle
maintenance and repair	£50 per month.

   During the forthcoming year, customer usage is expected to be as follows:

	Basic Wash only		Wash'n'Wax	
April	1,000	vehicles per mth	150	vehicles per mth
May-Sept	1,300	"	230	"
Oct	1,200	"	220	"
Nov	1,050	"	210	"
Dec	900	"	205	"
Jan	850	"	200	"
Feb	500	"	80	"
March	700	"	130	"

   (a) Construct a profit and loss budget for the forthcoming year.
   (b) How much is the budgeted profit for February? How much is it for May?
   (c) Construct a monthly cash budget. In which month is the cash flow greatest? Which month is the worst for cash flow?

2. The Gerkin Delight Company buys and then bottles (pickled) gerkins. A standard costing system is used. Labour cost being the basis for absorbing production overheads.

The following data is to be used in establishing the 1988 budget.

Production Data

Production Volume	1,200,000 bottles
Estimated Variable Production Overhead	£540,000
Estimated Fixed Production Overhead (excluding depreciation)	£720,000
Standard Material Cost	£0.27 per bottle
Standard Labour Cost	£0.50 per bottle.

Selling and Administrative Data

Sales Volume	1,200,000 bottles
Fixed Administrative and Selling Expenses	£150,000
Variable Administrative and Selling Expenses	£0.32 per bottle

Investment Data

Estimated Plant and Equipment Depreciation Expense for 1988	£440,000
Tools, etc. Depreciation Expense for 1988	£70,000

Instructions

(a) Compute the selling price if the desired gross profit is $33^1/_3$ % of sales.

(b) Construct the budgeted profit and loss account (before tax) for 1988.

3. The Balance Sheet for The Gerkin Delight Company as at 31.12.1987 is as follows:

		£000	£000
Fixed Assets			
Plant and Equipment: at cost		2,600	
Less accum. dep.		340	
net book value			2,260
Tools, etc: at cost		175	
Less accum. dep.		80	
net book value			95
			2,355
Current Assets	£000		
Stocks	595		
Debtors	395		
Cash	40		1,030
Less Current Liabilities			
Creditors	76		
Corporation Tax	220		
Dividend	84		(380)
Total Assets Less Current Liabilities			3,005
Shareholders' Funds			
Share Capital: Ord. £1 shares			1,200
Share Premium Account			550
Profit and Loss Account			1,255
			3,005

Additional investment for 1988 is estimated at £450,000 (£370,000 for plant and equipment and £80,000 for tooling, etc.)

The stock level at the end of 1988 is planned to be £665,000.

By the end of 1988 it is planned to pay trade creditors (material suppliers) about two months in arrears. Other creditors are estimated to then be about £8,000. Customers are to be given one month's credit.

The Accounts department advise that a tax charge of £185,000 is likely for the year of 1988. Tax is paid nine months after the accounting year end.

The Managing Director wishes to pay a final dividend of £100,000 in respect of 1988. No interim dividends are paid.

It is planned to raise £200,000 net (of share issue costs) by a one-for-ten rights issue.

Using any necessary information from question 6.2, construct a budgeted balance sheet as at 31.12.1988.

4. Hackney Roof Racks Ltd. produces roof racks for cars and small vans. Two types are produced, designated as Economy and Super. Three materials are used, designated as A, B and C. There are two producing departments - Stamping and Assembly. The following budget estimates have been made for the year 1988.

(a) Sales Forecast (units)

	Cars	Vans
Economy	20,000	4,000
Super	30,000	10,000

(b) Unit sales prices to retailers

Economy	£15.00
Super	£20.00

(c) Stocks

	December 31, 1987		December 31, 1988	
	Units	Unit Cost	Units	Unit Cost
Direct Material				
A	3,000	£1.25	4,000	£1.25
B	10,000	£0.50	10,000	£0.50
C	4,500	£0.40	4,000	£0.40
Work-in-Progress	Nil		Nil	
Finished Goods				
Economy	2,000	£9.00	2,000	£8.90
Super	4,000	£12.50	3,000	£11.99

(d) Direct material requirements per unit:

Economy:	Two units of Material B and two units of Material C.
Super:	One unit of Material A and two units of Material B.

(e) 1988 estimated purchase prices per unit of material

Material A	£1.25
Material B	£0.50
Material C	£0.40

(f) Estimated direct labour cost per unit:

	Stamping Department	Assembly Department
Economy	£0.75	£2.50
Super	£1.00	£3.50

(g) Factory overhead budgets developed for 1988 indicate the following per unit overhead cost.

	Stamping Department	Assembly Department
Economy	£2.25	£1.60
Super	£3.00	£2.24

(h) other estimated costs:

Distribution expense	£150,000
Administrative expense	£70,000

Corporation Tax: 35% of profit before tax.

Instructions

Utilising the above information, prepare the following budget schedules for 1988:

(a) A summary of budgeted sales.
(b) A production (volume) budget.
(c) An estimate of direct material requirements.
(d) A purchases budget.
(e) A summary of estimated direct labour costs.
(f) A summary of factory overhead costs.
(g) A statement of estimated cost of goods sold.
(h) An estimated profit and loss account.

6.7.2 Solutions

1. (a) **The Wardown Car Wash Budgeted Profit & Loss Account**

	£	£
Sales (12,700 x £1.50 + 2,345 x £2.50)		24,912
Expenses		
Washing solution (15,045 x 20p)	3,009	
Wax (2,345 x 45p)	1,055	
Washing equipment: depreciation (£60,000/5 years)*	12,000	
Maintenance and repair (£50 x 12)	600	
Rent and rates	2,250	
		18,914
Budgeted profit		5,998

* Using most conservative estimate of useful life and straight-line depreciation method.

(b) **Budgeted Profit for February**

	£	£
Sales (500 x £1.50 + 80 x £2.50)		950
Expenses		
Washing solution (580 x 20p)	116	
Wax (80 x 45p)	36	
Washing equipment: depreciation	1,000	
Maintenance and repair	50	
Rent and rates	187	
		1,389
Budgeted profit/(loss)		(439)

i.e. a loss of £439 is budgeted for February.

Budgeted Profit for May

	£	£
Sales		2,525
(1,300 x £1.50 + 230 x £2.50)		
Expenses		
Washing solution (1,530 x 20p)	306	
Wax (230 x 45p)	103	
Washing equipment: depreciation	1,000	
Maintenance and repair	50	
Rent and rates	187	
		1,646
Budgeted profit		879

(c) **Monthly Cash Budget (£)**

Cash receipts	Apr	May Sept	Oct	Nov	Dec	Jan	Feb	Mar
Basic wash	1500	1950	1800	1575	1350	1275	750	1050
Wash 'n wax	375	575	550	525	512	500	200	325
Total receipts	1875	2525	2350	2100	1862	1775	950	1375
Cash payments								
Washing solution	230	306	284	252	221	210	116	166
Wax	67	103	99	94	92	90	36	58
Maintenance and repair	50	50	50	50	50	50	50	50
Rent & rates	1125	-	1125	-	-	-	-	-
Total payments	1472	459	1558	396	363	350	202	274
Net cash flow	403	2066	792	1704	1499	1425	748	1101

Cash flow is greatest in the period May - September.
Cash flow is worst (= lowest net cash inflow) in April.

2. (a) **Standard Cost per Bottle**

	£	
Material	0.27	
Labour	0.50	
Overhead:		
Variable production overhead	0.45	(£540,000/1,200,000 bottles)
Fixed production overhead	0.60	(£720,000/1,200,000 bottles)
Plant&equipment: deprec.	0.37	(£440,000/1,200,000 bottles)
Tools, etc: depreciation	0.06	(£70,000/1,200,000 bottles)
	2.25	

To give gross profit margin of $33^1/_3$%, selling price needs to be 1.5 x £2.25 = £3.37.

(b) **The Gerkin Delight Company Budgeted Profit & Loss Account for 1988**

	£'000	£'000
Sales revenue (1,200,000 x £3.37)		4,044
Cost of goods sold		
material (1.2m x £0.27)	324	
labour (1.2m x £0.50)	600	
variable production overhead	540	
fixed production overhead	720	
plant & equipment: depreciation	440	
tools, etc: depreciation	70	
		2,694
Gross profit		1,350
Fixed administrative & selling		150
Variable admin. & selling(1.2m x £0.32)		384
		534
Budgeted profit before tax		816

CHAPTER SEVEN

VARIANCE ANALYSIS

7.1 WHY BOTHER WITH VARIANCE ANALYSIS?

Variance analysis not only involves the comparison of actual results with the budget, but also aims to determine the reasons why differences (variances) have arisen. It often gives additional insight into which factors have affected performance and to what extent.

For example, suppose a company's actual profit turns out to be lower than budgeted, despite sales revenue being higher. It appears that the company has problems in controlling costs. But it could be that the higher sales revenue has been achieved by selling greater volume at lower prices. In which case it might be that the higher sales volume has given rise to increased output and hence higher production costs.

Without the benefit of variance analysis, management may jump to the wrong conclusion. By analysing variances and seeking explanations for them, management is more likely to determine the underlying cause. In this instance the underlying cause might be one or more of the following:

(a) desire to increase volume, thereby cutting prices;
(b) forced to follow competitors' price reductions;
(c) changing market needs;
(d) different product sales mix;
(e) poor quality, necessitating price discounts;
(f) lack of cost control.

The calculation of variances is the first stage in the analysis process. Significant variances direct management's attention to important *questions* that require explanation, rather than providing the *answers* themselves.

Variance analysis is one of the most important practical financial control procedures. Of course by itself variance analysis will not guarantee good business performance. A motivated, trained and experienced workforce is normally necessary if superior performance is to be achieved. Often too, managers are aware that things are going wrong even before they see their management accountant's report, giving the details. In these instances managers may have already taken appropriate action by the time variances are reported.

7.2 SALES VARIANCES

Sales variances occur when either:

(a) sales *volumes*;
(b) selling *prices*; or
(c) the *mix* of products or services (in a multi-product or multi-service business);

is different from that budgeted.

7.2.1 Volume variances

Sales volume variances arise when the actual volume of sales differs from that budgeted. The amount is calculated as follows.

Sales volume variance = (actual volume - budgeted volume) x budgeted price per unit

Example 1: Suppose Arsenal football club expect to sell 20,000 programmes for their match with Liverpool. Programmes are priced at 50 pence each. What is the sales volume variance if only 17,200 programmes are sold?

Sales volume variance = *(actual volume - budgeted volume) x budgeted price per unit*
= *(17,200 - 20,000) x 50p*
= *-£1,400 (i.e. an unfavourable variance of £1,400)*

When the answer is positive, the variance increases revenue compared with the budget and is said to be favourable. When the answer is negative, the variance reduces revenue and is therefore unfavourable.

7.2.2 Price variances

Sales price variances result from actual selling prices being different from those budgeted. It is calculated as follows:

Sales price variance = (actual price per unit - budgeted price per unit) x actual units sold.

Example 2: The UK Oil Company budgeted to sell 10 million barrels of oil during April 1986 at $30 per barrel. However oil prices unexpectedly collapsed and although 10 million barrels were sold, the average price for the month was $12 per barrel. What was the sales price variance?

Sales price variance = (actual price per barrel - budgeted price per barrel) x actual barrels sold = ($12 - $30) x 10 million, = -$180 million *(i.e. an unfavourable variance of £180m).*

In this example only the selling price varied, the volume sold remaining unchanged. The previous example (see section 7.2.1.) dealt with a volume change only, the price remaining unchanged. For situations like these it is relatively easy to calculate the variance. But what happens when both the volume and price turn out to be different from budget?

Example 3: The UK Oil Company budgeted to sell six million barrels of oil at $30 per barrel during May 1986. They sold only five million barrels at $15.00 per barrel. Determine the price and volume variances.

Figure 7.1 illustrates the budgeted and actual volumes and prices.

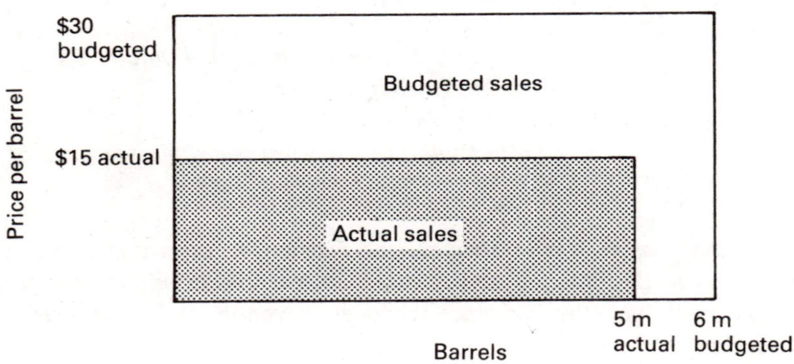

Figure 7.1 Actual versus budgeted sales

The variances are calculated as follows:

Budgeted sales = 6 million barrels at $30/barrel = $180 million.
Actual sales = 5 million barrels at $15/barrel = $75 million. Therefore sales volume variance + sales price variance = $ (75-180) million = -$105 million.

Sales volume variance = (actual volume - budgeted volume) x budgeted price per unit.
= (5m barrels - 6m barrels) x $30 per barrel = -$30m.

Sales price variance = (actual price per unit - budgeted price per unit) x actual units sold.
= ($15 per barrel - $30 per barrel) x 5m barrels = *-$75m.*

Figure 7.2 shows how these two variances combined equate to the difference between actual sales and budgeted sales.

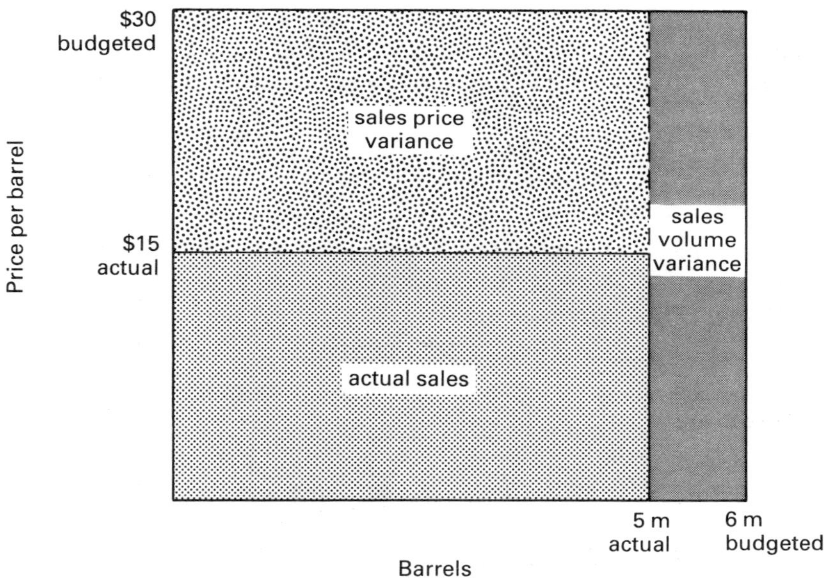

Figure 7.2 Sales - price and volume variances

Note that we have used the *budgeted price* when calculating the volume variance and the actual units sold for the price variance. This is the normal convention when separating variances into their volume and price components. It recognises (unlike other possible ways of splitting the sales variance) that managers are often more able to control volume than price.

7.2.3 **Mix variances**

In multi-product (or multi-service) business's actual sales revenue can also vary from budget even if the total volume and selling prices of the individual products remain unchanged. This can happen when the actual mix of products or services is different from that budgeted.

Example 4: The actual and budgeted sales of the Modern Milk Company for June 1987 are shown in Figure 7.3.

		Budgeted	*Actual*
Volume	- *Banana Flavour*	*600,000*	*400,000*
(gallons)	- *Chocolate Flavour*	*800,000*	*900,000*
	- *Strawberry Flavour*	*800,000*	*900,000*
	- *Total*	*2,200,000*	*2,200,000*
Price	- *Banana Flavour*	*£3.60*	*£3.60*
(per gallon)	- *Chocolate Flavour*	*£4.00*	*£4.00*
	- *Strawberry Flavour*	*£4.40*	*£4.40*
Sales Revenue	- *Banana Flavour*	*£2.16m*	*£1.44m*
	- *Chocolate Flavour*	*£3.20m*	*£3.60m*
	- *Strawberry Flavour*	*£3.52m*	*£3.96m*
Total Sales Revenue		*£8.88m*	*£9.00*

Figure 7.3 Modern Milk Company's budgeted and actual Sales for June 1987

From Figure 7.3 we can see that actual sales revenue exceeded budget by £120,000 (£9.00m - £8.88m) even though the actual prices of each of the different flavours and the actual total volume (2.2m gallons) were as budgeted. The favourable £120,000 mix variance arose by shifting 200,000 gallons of sales towards chocolate and strawberry flavours and away from banana flavour. The price differences (40p and 80p respectively) multiplied by the volume shift, gives the favourable sales mix variance of £120,000, as follows:

shift from banana to chocolate = *100,000 gallons x 40p per gallon (higher price)*	=	*£40,000*
shift from banana to strawberry = *100,000 gallons x 80p per gallon (higher price)*	=	*£80,000*
Total Sales Mix Variance	=	*£120,000*

It is relatively easy to calculate mix variances when the individual prices and total sales volume remain unchanged. But the calculations are more complicated when volumes, prices and product mix all vary from budget. The basis for splitting the total variance into volume variance, price variance and mix variance is to calculate the first two variances as if the actual product mix was the same as that budgeted. Having calculated the volume variance and price variance, the mix variance is the difference between the total sales variance and the (combined) volume and price variances.

In cases like this, where there are only a few products, it is probably simpler to calculate the price and volume variances for each product and add them together to give a total price variance and a total volume variance. This eliminates the need to calculate a mix variance.

7.2.4 Sales revenue variances versus contribution variances

So far we have calculated the extent to which actual sales revenue has varied from budget and the degree to which volume and price changes are responsible. This information is particularly useful in assessing sales performance. When seeking to explain differences between actual and budgeted *profit* it is often more useful to calculate the change in *contribution* resulting from changes in sales volume. This is referred to as the sales (contribution) volume variance and is dealt with in Section 7.3.1. Because changes in selling price affect the sales revenue, contribution and profit equally; the sales price variance is the same, whether calculating the effect on revenue or on profit.

7.3 OPERATING EXPENSE VARIANCES

Operating expenses include wages and salaries, cost of bought-out materials and services, and overhead costs not directly traceable to specific business outputs (i.e. products or services). Manufacturing companies generally (and some service organisations) budget for direct labour, direct materials, manufacturing overhead and non-manufacturing costs. Variances can be calculated for each item in the budget, and, where significant, investigated further.

7.3.1 Flexible budgets

Comparison of actual costs against budget must take into account the actual level of output achieved. Suppose a brewery was subject to a lengthy strike which resulted in output being only 80% of that budgeted, should we congratulate the brewery superintendent for meeting his operating costs budget (for materials, labour and overheads)? Clearly not. If output volume is reduced to 80% of budget we would expect ingredients used to be about 80% of that budgeted (although the stoppage might result in some additional wastage).

Where costs are expected to be proportional to output (e.g. direct labour, direct materials, and variable overheads), we need to 'flex' the budget in relation to the actual output. If actual output is only 80% of that budgeted then these variable costs should be only 80% of those in the original budget. Flexible budgets therefore provide a logical basis from which to evaluate operating expense variances.

Example 5: Radio Aerials Ltd. have budgeted their monthly sales revenue at £50,000 (25,000 units at £2.00 each); variable expenses were budgeted at £1.20 per unit (= £30,000 in total); and fixed expenses were budgeted at £12,000 for the month. Actual sales revenue was £42,000 (20,000 units at £2.10); actual variable expenses were £28,000; and actual fixed expenses were £11,200. Figure 7.4 shows how to analyse the difference between budgeted profit of £8,000 and actual profit of £2,800 in two stages by using a flexible budget.

	Original budget (25,000 units)	*Flexible budget (20,000 units)*	*Actual (20,000 units)*
	(£)	*(£)*	*(£)*
Sales revenue	50,000	40,000	42,000
Variable expenses	30,000	24,000	28,000
Contribution	20,000	16,000	14,000
Fixed expenses	12,000	12,000	11,200
Profit	8,000	4,000	2,800

Figure 7.4 Flexing a budget for variance analysis

The total profit variance of -£5,200 between the original budget profit (£8,000) and the actual profit (£2,800) is now split into two parts (-£4,000 and -£1,200) which can be analysed separately:

(a) The variance of -£4,000 in contribution, between the original budget (£20,000) and the flexible budget (£16,000), is due to the decline in sales:

sales volume is down by 5,000 units. This leads to a decline in:

sales revenue	*-5,000*	*x*	*£2.00*	=	*£10,000*
variable expenses	*-5,000*	*x*	*£1.20*	=	*£6,000*
sales (contribution) volume variance	*-5,000*	*x*	*£0.80*	=	*-£4,000*

Alternatively, sales (contribution) volume variance = (actual volume - budgeted volume) x budgeted contribution per unit = (20,000 - 25,000) x £0.80 = -£4,000

(b) The total variance of -£1,200, between the flexible budget and actual:

	Flexible budget	*Actual*	*Variance*
sales price	*£40,000*	*£42,000*	*+£2,000*
variable expenses	*£24,000*	*£28,000*	*-£4,000*
fixed expenses	*£12,000*	*£11,200*	*+ £800*
			-£1,200

The use of flexible budgets is a convenient way to break down the analysis of variances step by step, in particular distinguishing between variances due to a change in sales volume, and those due to expenses being different from expected at the actual sales volume. In practice this is helpful because different managers are likely to be responsible. Clearly it is essential to split the apparent £2,000 favourable variance on variable expenses (between the original budget's £30,000 and the actual £28,000) into the £6,000 favourable variance due to the decline in sales volume and the £4,000 unfavourable variance due to spending more than 'should' have been spent at the actual sales volume.

7.3.2 Input-cost variances

Even with flexible budgets, actual operating expenses might deviate from budget. This might be due to:

(a) the *cost* of materials and labour; or
(b) the *usage* of materials and labour, being different from budget.

In this section we look at variances relating to material and labour costs and in the next section we consider usage variances.

Input-cost variances are calculated as follows: (budgeted cost per unit of input - actual cost per unit of input) x actual units of input.

For material this cost variance is called the material price variance. For direct labour it is called the direct labour rate variance.

Example 6: Anne Teek Furniture Company produce high quality household furniture. They have budgeted to produce 120 teak tables a month using 10 kg. of wood costing £13.80 per kg. Because of increased demand, they produce 140 tables in September 1987, using 11 kgs. of wood per table. The cost of teak wood has risen to £14.50 per kg. What is the material price variance?

Material price variance = *(budgeted cost per kg. - actual cost per kg.) x kgs. of wood used*
= *(£13.8 - £14.5) x (140 x 11)*
= *<u>-£1078</u> (i.e. an unfavourable variance of £1078 - see Figure 7.5).*

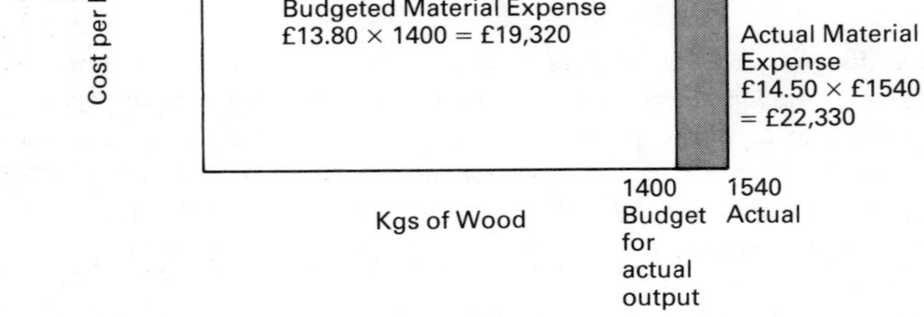

Figure 7.5 Material - price and usage variances

Note that we use the cost of wood per kg. not per table. The latter is affected not only by the cost of wood per kg, but also by the amount of wood used to produce each table.

A similar approach can be used to calculate the direct labour rate variance.

Example 7: Using the following information for Anne Teek Furniture Company, determine the direct labour rate variance for September 1987.

	Budget	*Actual*
No. of tables produced	*120*	*140*
Direct labour hours per table	*6.0*	*5.6*
Direct labour rate per hour	*£4.20*	*£4.60*

Direct labour rate variance = *(budgeted direct labour rate per hour - actual direct labour rate per hour) x actual direct labour hours used*

= *(£4.20 - £4.60) x (140 x 5.6)*

= *-(£0.40 x 784)*

= *-£313.60 (see Figure 7.6)*

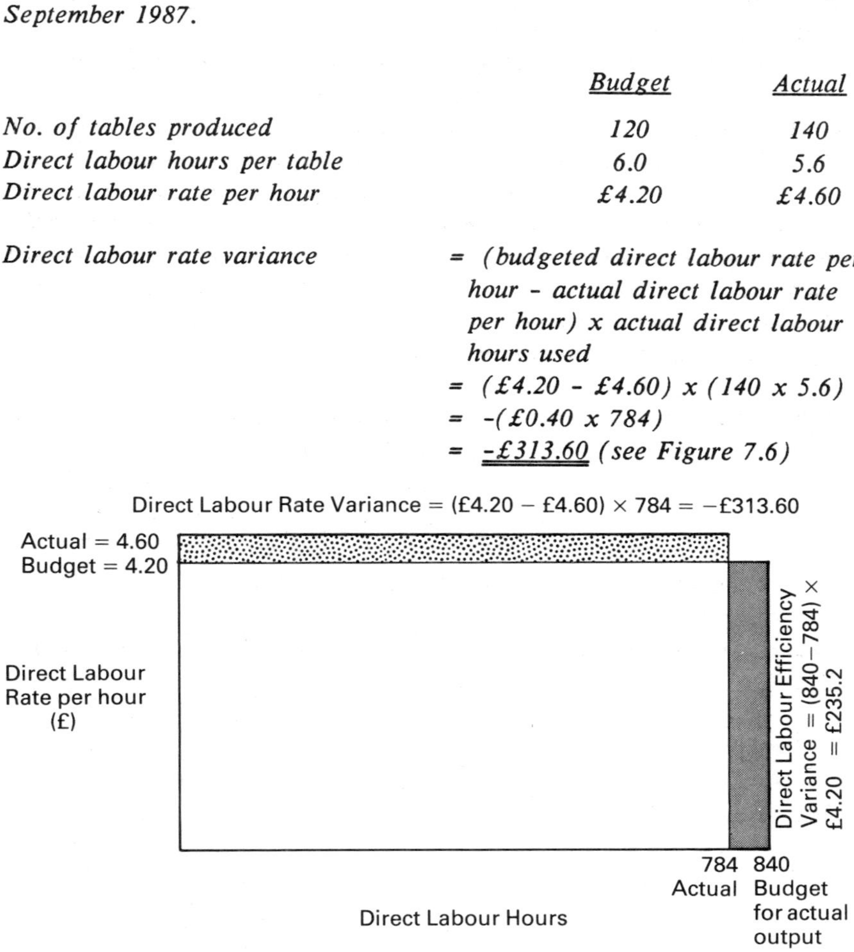

Figure 7.6 Direct labour - rate and efficiency variances

7.3.3 Usage variances

Actual operating expenses can exceed budget not only because input costs have risen but also because the actual amount of resources input (e.g. materials and labour) exceeds the budget.

Usage variances are calculated as follows:

(Budgeted usage for actual output - Actual usage) x Budgeted cost per unit of input.

Example 8: Given the following budgeted and actual September 1987 figures for the Anne Teek Furniture Company, determine the material usage variance and the direct labour efficiency variance.

	Budget	*Actual*
No. of tables produced	*120*	*140*
Kgs. of wood per table	*10*	*11*
Cost of wood per kg.	*£13.80*	*£14.50*
Direct labour hours per table	*6.0*	*5.6*
Direct labour rate per hour	*£4.20*	*£4.60*

Material usage variance = (Budgeted kgs. of wood for actual output - Actual kgs. of wood) x Budgeted cost per kg.

= [(10 x 140) - (11 x 140)] kgs. x £13.80 per kg.
= - (140 kgs. x £13.80 per kg.)
= - £1,932 (an unfavourable variance due to more material being used than should have been for the actual level of output - see Figure 7.5).

Direct labour efficiency variance = (Budgeted hours of direct labour for actual output - Actual hours of direct labour) x budgeted direct labour rate per hour

= [(6.0 x 140) - (5.6 x 140)] hours x £4.20 per hour
= 56 hours x £4.20 per hour
= £235.20 (a favourable variance due to more efficient use of direct labour than budgeted - see Figure 7.6)

We can now reconcile the material variances as follows:

	£
Budgeted material expense (£13.80 x 1,400)	*£19,320*
Plus*: unfavourable variances:*	
material price variance	*1,078*
material usage variance	*1,932*
Actual material expense (£14.50 x 1,540)	*22,330*

Likewise, the direct labour variances can be reconciled as follows:

	£
Budgeted direct labour expense for actual output (£4.20 x 840)	*3,528.00*
Plus *unfavourable direct labour rate variance*	*313.60*
Less *favourable direct labour efficiency variance*	*(235.20)*
Actual direct labour expense (£4.60 x 784)	*3,606.40*

Now attempt the following case:

Anne Teek Furniture Company have produced the following budget for October 1987.

No. of tables produced	130
Kgs. of wood per table	10
Cost of wood per kg.	£14.50
Direct labour hours per table	6.0
Direct labour rate per hour	£4.20

During October 1987 148 tables were produced, requiring 1,600 kgs. of wood and 810 hours of direct labour. The cost of wood was £15.00 per kg. and the direct labour rate was £4.60 per hour.

Determine:

(a) Material price variance
(b) Material usage variance
(c) Direct labour rate variance
(d) Direct labour efficiency variance.

When you have calculated the variances, turn over the page and check your answers.

SOLUTION

Anne Teek Furniture Company

(a) Material price variance = (Budgeted cost of wood per kg. - Actual cost of wood per kg.) x Actual quantity of wood used.

= (£14.50 per kg. - £15.00 per kg.) x 1,600 kgs.
= - (£0.50 per kg. x 1,600 kgs.)
= - £800

(b) Material usage variance = (Budgeted kgs. of wood for actual output - Actual kgs. of wood used) x Budgeted price per kg.

= [(10 x 148) - 1600] kgs. x £14.50 per kg.
= (1480 - 1600) kgs. x £14.50 per kg.
= -(120 kgs. x £14.50 per kg.)
= -£1,740

These two material variances combined (-£2,540) identify why the £24,000 actual cost of wood (1600 kgs. at £15.00 per kg.) exceeds the £21,460 budgeted cost (10 kgs. per table x 148 tables x £14.50 per kg.)

(c) Direct labour rate variance = (Budgeted direct labour rate - Actual direct labour rate) x Actual direct labour hours used

= (£4.20 - £4.60) per hour x 810 hours
= -(£0.40 per hour x 810 hours)
= -£324

(d) Direct labour efficiency variance = (Budgeted direct labour hours for actual output - Actual direct labour hours used) x Budgeted direct labour rate per hour.

= [(6.0 hours per table x 148 tables) - 810 hours) x £4.20 per hour
= (888-810) hours x £4.20 per hour
= £327.60 (i.e. a favourable variance)

These two labour variances combined (£327.60 - £324 = £3.60) identify why the £3,726 actual labour costs (810 hours at £4.60 per hour) were less than the £3,729.60 budgeted cost (888 hours at £4.20 per hour).

7.3.4 Overhead variances

When analysing overhead variances we need to split them into

(a) fixed overhead; and
(b) variable overhead.

(a) Fixed Overhead

Providing we do not dramatically change the actual level of output from that budgeted (i.e. we stay within the 'relevant range') then the *amount* of overhead required should be unchanged. The only reason for actual fixed overhead to vary from budget, therefore, is if the actual *cost* of fixed overhead is different from that budgeted. This variance is usually referred to as the *Fixed Overhead Expenditure Variance*. It is negative (unfavourable) when the actual fixed overhead costs exceed the budget, and positive when the actual cost is less than budget. The convention of positive variances relating to increased profit is therefore maintained.

(b) Variable Overhead

By definition, variable overhead is expected to change in line with output. If output is up by 20%, we would expect variable overhead to be up by 20%. Any difference between the expected variable overhead at actual output, and the actual variable overhead is called the Variable Overhead Expenditure Variance. It is calculated as follows:

Variable overhead expenditure variance = (Budgeted variable overhead per unit of output x Actual units of output) - Actual variable overhead.

Example 9: The Spot-On Watches budget for September 1987 included variable overhead costs as follows:

Variable Overhead	*£40,000*
Output of Watches	*20,000*

Budgeted variable overhead per watch produced is

$$\frac{£40{,}000}{20{,}000 \text{ watches}} = £2 \text{ per watch}$$

Actual variable overhead was £47,000 for an output of 22,000 watches.

Variable overhead expenditure variance = (Budgeted variable overhead per unit of output x actual units of output) - Actual variable overhead

= (£2 per watch x 22,000 watches) - £47,000
= £44,000 - £47,000
= -£3,000

7.3.5 Profit Variance Chart

We can now see how the sales and operating expense variances can be combined to 'explain' the profit (before tax) variance, see *figure 7.7*. Profit variance formulae are listed in *figure 7.8*.

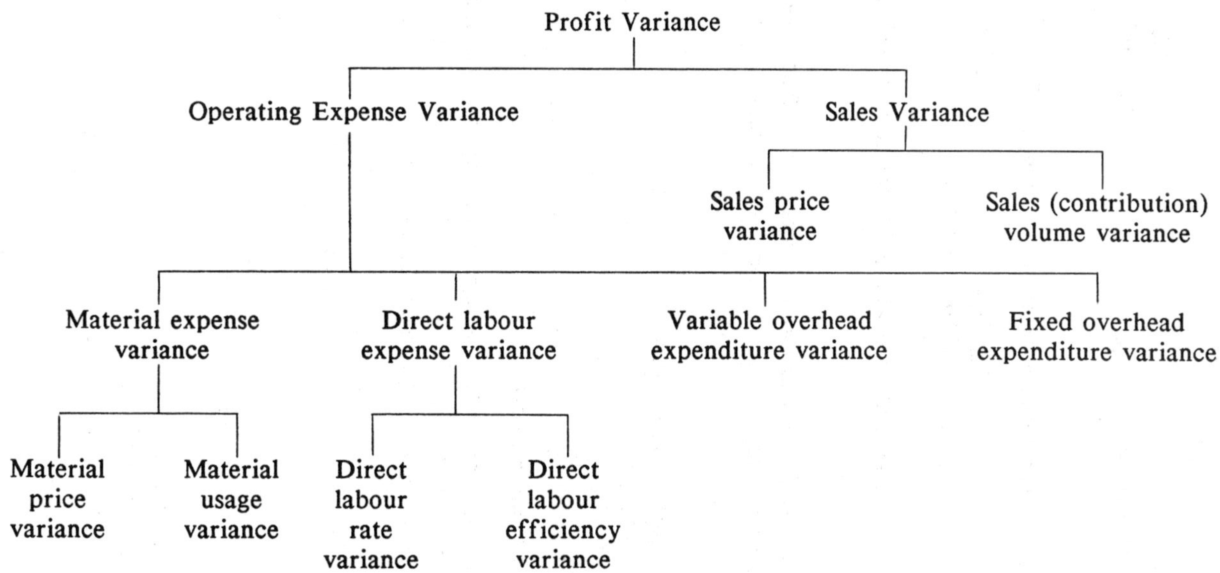

Figure 7.7 Profit variance chart for marginal costing system

1. Sales price variance = (actual price per unit - budgeted price per unit) x actual units sold.

2. Sales (contribution) volume variance = (actual volume - budgeted volume) x budgeted contribution per unit.

3. Material price variance = (budgeted material price per unit - actual material price per unit) x actual units of material used.

4. Material usage variance = (budgeted material units for actual output - actual material units used) x budgeted material cost per unit.

5. Direct labour rate variance = (budgeted direct labour rate - actual direct labour rate) x actual direct labour hours used.

6. Direct labour efficiency variance = (budgeted direct labour hours for actual output - actual direct labour hours used) x budgeted direct labour rate per hour.

7. Variable overhead expenditure variance = (budgeted variable overhead per unit of output x actual units of output) - actual variable overhead.

8. Fixed overhead expenditure variance = budgeted fixed overhead - actual fixed overhead.

Figure 7.8 Profit variance formulae for marginal costing system

7.4 ANALYSING PROFIT VARIANCES FOR STANDARD COSTING SYSTEMS

Standard costs include:

(a) material cost
(b) labour cost
(c) overhead charge (for both variable and fixed overheads).
(See section 3.5.2)

Because fixed overheads are included in the standard cost, it is necessary to make two changes to the Profit Variance formulae (for marginal costing system) listed in Figure 7.8. Firstly, the sales (contribution) volume variance (formula no. 2) is replaced by the sales (standard profit) volume variance. Secondly, a new variance is added. It is the fixed overhead volume variance. The formulae are as follows:

sales (standard profit) volume variance = (actual volume - budgeted volume) x standard profit per unit.

fixed overhead volume variance = (actual volume x standard fixed overhead rate) - budgeted fixed overhead.

Example 10: The original monthly budget and actual results for Radio Aerials Ltd are shown in Figure 7.4 (page 202). The original budget would be modified to show standard profit as in Figure 7.9.

	Per unit (£)	*Total for 25,000 units (£)*
Sales revenue	*2.00*	*50,000*
Variable expenses	*1.20**	*30,000*
Fixed expenses	*0.48**	*12,000*
Standard profit	*0.32*	*8,000*

* *standard cost per unit = £1.20 + £0.48 = £1.68*

Figure 7.9 Standard profit for Radio Aerials Ltd

The two new variances can now be calculated as follows:

Sales (standard profit) volume variance = (20,000 units - 25,000 units) x £0.32 per unit.

= -(5,000 x £0.32)
= -£1,600

This shows the reduction in total standard profit due to the lower sales volume.

Fixed overhead volume variance = (20,000 units x £0.48 per unit) - £12,000

= £9,600 - £12,000
= -£2,400

Because the budgeted fixed overhead was shared out over 25,000 units, a fall in actual volume to 20,000 units means that not all the fixed overhead is 'recovered'. Profit falls accordingly. Since we have assumed that production and sales are equal, these two variances combined (-£4,000) equal the sales (contribution) volume variance calculated in the marginal costing system.

Now consider the following case:

Munchy Crunch Limited

The latest quarter's results for Munchy Crunch Ltd, a small confectionery company, are shown below, together with the budgeted figures.

Actual results for latest quarter		**£'000**
Sales 460 tons @ £2,100/ton (average)		966.00
Cost of sales		
Direct labour: £4.25/hour x 22080 hours		93.84
Direct materials: £550/ton x 630 tons		346.50
Manufacturing overheads:	variable	117.00
	fixed	152.00
Other overheads:	variable	43.00
	fixed	203.00
Total costs		955.34
Profit before tax		10.66

Budget for latest quarter			**£'000**
Sales 500 tons @ £2,000/ton (average)			1,000
Cost of sales			
Direct labour:	£4/hour x 50 hours/ton x 500 tons		100
Direct materials:	£500/ton x 600 tons		300
Manufacturing overheads:		variable	110
		fixed	150
Other overheads:		variable	40
		fixed	200
Total costs			900
Profit before tax			100

Calculate and list the variances that explain the shortfall in Munchy Crunch's profit for the quarter, assuming they operate a marginal costing system.

Write out your answer, then turn over the page and check with the solution provided.

Solution

Munchy Crunch Limited

The profit variances for a marginal costing system are:

(a) Sales price variance = (actual price per unit - budgeted price per unit) x actual units sold
= (£2,100 - £2,000) per ton x 460 tons
= £46,000

(b) Sales (contribution) volume variance = (actual volume-budgeted volume) x budgeted contribution per unit
= (460 - 500) tons x £900 per ton*
= -£36,000

* budgeted contribution for 500 tons = £1,000,000 (sales) - £100,000 (direct labour) - £300,000 (direct materials) - £150,000 (total variable overheads)
= £450,000
= £900 per ton

(c) Material price variance = (budgeted material price per unit - actual material price per unit) x actual units of material used
= (£500 - £550) per ton x 630 tons
= -£31,500

(d) Material usage variance = (budgeted material units for actual output - actual material units used) x budgeted material cost per unit
= ((460 x $^{600}/_{500}$) - 630) tons x £500 per ton
= -£39,000

(e) Direct labour rate variance = (budgeted direct labour rate - actual direct labour rate) x actual direct labour hours used
= (£4-£4.25) per hour x 22,080 hours
= -£5,520

(f) Direct labour efficiency variance = (budgeted direct labour hours for actual output - actual direct labour hours used) x budgeted direct labour rate per hour

= ((50 hours/ton x 460 tons) - 22080 hours) x £4/hour

= £3,680

(g) Variable overhead expenditure variance = (budgeted variable overhead per unit of output x actual units of output) - actual variable overhead

$$= \frac{(£110{,}000 + £40{,}000) \times 460 \text{ tons}}{500 \text{ tons}}$$

- (£117,000 + £43,000)

= £138,000 - £160,000

= -£22,000

(h) Fixed overhead expenditure variance = budgeted fixed overhead - actual fixed overhead

= (£150,000 + £200,000) - (£152,000 + £203,000)

= -£5,000

Summarising,

	£'000
Budgeted profit before tax	100
Variances	
Sales price	46
Sales (contribution) volume	(36)
Material price	(31.5)
Material usage	(39)
Direct labour rate	(5.52)
Direct labour efficiency	3.68
Variable overhead expenditure	(22)

Fixed overhead expenditure	(5)
Actual profit before tax	10.66

Note that, for a standard costing system, the sales (contribution) volume variance is deleted in favour of the following two variances:

(a) Sales (standard profit) volume variance = (actual volume - budgeted volume) x standard profit per unit

$$= (460 \text{ tons} - 500 \text{ tons}) \times \frac{£100{,}000}{500 \text{ tons}}$$

$$= -40 \text{ tons} \times £200 \text{ per ton}$$

$$= \underline{-£8{,}000}$$

(b) Fixed overhead volume variance = (actual volume x standard fixed overhead rate) - budgeted fixed overhead

$$= \left(460 \text{ tons} \times \frac{£150{,}000 + £200{,}000}{500 \text{ tons}}\right) - £350{,}000$$

$$= (460 \text{ tons} \times £700/\text{ton}) - £350{,}000$$

$$= \underline{-£28{,}000}$$

Note that these two variances total *minus* £36,000, the same amount as for the sales (contribution) volume variance. This is always true when the levels of production and sales are equal.

7.5 BALANCE SHEET VARIANCES

Although the main emphasis of variance analysis is usually concerned with P & L account items, it is important not to ignore balance sheet variances. Three items in particular need to be monitored closely; stocks, debtors and cash. These three working capital items can change very quickly. Stocks and debtors may rise rapidly because of falling sales and slow customer payments. The cash balance is the net result of many cash inflows and cash payments. The volatility of these working capital balances can be much greater than for fixed assets, which usually require senior management approval for both acquisition and disposal. Stocks, debtors and cash balances however, depend very much more on short term *external* influences.

7.5.1 Stocks

Some managers are tempted not to worry about excessively high stocks. In manufacturing organisations, high levels of raw materials, bought-out items and work in progress reduce the likelihood of any losses in production output due to stock shortages. Production managers are often happy with this situation as it means one less problem to worry about.

In manufacturing and retail organisations high levels of goods ready for sale please the sales force since all customer needs can be instantly met. No sale is lost because of lack of (finished) stocks for sale.

However, the cost of holding stock is not insignificant. Insurance premiums, stock losses, spoilage, storage and financing costs combined together might amount to as much as 25% per year of the value of stock held.

Stock levels need to be set at a level that allows a *satisfactory* supply for production purposes and to provide an *adequate* customer service level to meet sales requirements. *Excessively* high stock levels need to be avoided. The Japanese 'Just-In-Time' stock policy is becoming the target for many firms. Fortunately many British managers have now recognised the high cost of their 'Just-in-Case' stock policy.

Significant variances between actual and budgeted stock levels indicate the need for management action. Perhaps customer needs are changing. Or maybe, manufacturing problems are causing excessively high levels of raw materials, bought-out items or work in progress. Alternatively, manufacturing problems may be causing shortages in finished goods.

It is probably worthwhile, therefore, to calculate and review stock variances on a monthly basis, or in some cases more frequently.

7.5.2 Debtors

Some salesmen have been led to believe that 'a sale is not a sale until the cash has been received'. We know from financial accounting that (with the exception of long-term contracts) a sale is made when goods are passed to the customer or when a service is rendered. Often this precedes the payment of cash. Between the time when the customer is invoiced and payment made, the unpaid invoice is shown (with others) as a debtor in the seller's balance sheet.

Failure to collect cash from debtors in accordance with the agreed payment terms can be very costly. Not only could the unpaid cash be put to better use by the business (e.g. investing in profit producing assets, earning bank interest, or reducing bank overdraft interest charges) but there is also the possibility that the customer might not pay at all. This latter risk is particularly high where the financial soundness of the customer is suspect. If the customer goes into liquidation, payment might not be made, or perhaps less than the full amount is paid. In any event a substantial time delay is likely.

Variances between actual debtors and budgeted debtors may require management action. Of course if recent sales are substantially different from budget, debtors are likely to be affected accordingly. Variance analysis of debtors will at least give rise to important questions (such as 'is our debtor collection performance deteriorating ?') that might otherwise be overlooked.

In addition to reviewing debtors in aggregate (perhaps on a monthly basis) many firms also produce an 'aged debtor analysis' which identifies debtors into groups relating to how long it is since the (unpaid) invoice was issued. Investigations can then be focused on overdue invoices. Some firms even discuss invoice payments before they are due just to make sure there are no problems (e.g. disputes) preventing payment.

7.5.3 Cash

Cash balances are the result of all the various inflows and outflows of cash. Although responsibility therefore relates to a number of different managers, it is necessary for variances to be reviewed and appropriate action taken. In addition to actions taken in other departments, the Finance department will need to decide how to acquire additional cash (or utilise spare cash). This latter activity is often dealt with on a day-to-day basis. For a business operating on an overdraft, this is a vital activity. Running out of money may well mean the end of the business, even if the business is profitable.

7.5.4 Creditors

It can be useful to look at total net working capital (i.e. current assets less current liabilities), as well as at the individual components. One reason why net working capital may not be out of line with expectations, (even if individual current asset components are higher than budgeted) is that creditors may also be higher than budgeted. This may be a matter for concern, since if 'too much' trade credit is taken from suppliers, they may cut off supplies, and possibly cause a good deal of inconvenience to operations.

7.6 PRESENTATION

7.6.1 Management by exception

Many Accounts departments produce comprehensive monthly management accounts. This is fine for reconciling the financial accounts with the budget but is often inappropriate for busy managers trying to run a business. What most busy managers prefer is a summary report highlighting the significant variances (determined as a minimum amount or percentage) together with an explanation of the cause of the variance. Their limited time can then be focused on determining what action needs to be taken, rather than wading through pages of accounting data.

Clearly where managers are not receiving the sort of information they need it is up to them to *demand* that information from their Accounts department. After all, the purpose of management accounts is to help managers manage the business better.

7.6.2 Avoiding spurious detail

Another important feature of a good presentation of variance analysis is the avoidance of spurious detail. As well as focusing on exceptions, variances should not be quoted to the nearest penny. Reporting to the nearest hundred or thousand pounds is probably quite adequate for most businesses. For larger firms variances may be rounded to the nearest ten thousand pounds (or larger still).

The summary accompanying the variance figures should focus on the main causes and avoid insignificant factors. This again will aid managers to direct their attention to where it is most needed.

The variances calculated in this chapter are not the full range of variances. It is useful in some cases to calculate additional variances. In other situations variance formulae may be modified to give more useful information. A balance must be struck between calculating every conceivable variance, resulting in a more complex analysis, and the need to provide information that business managers can understand and use.

7.7. MANAGEMENT ACTION

7.7.1 Minimising unfavourable variances

Calculating variances and presenting them to management is of no value unless management take appropriate action. Where variances are unfavourable the root cause needs to be determined. This might require discussions with a number of different managers. For instance, when sales are down the cause might be:

(a) reduced customer demand;
(b) prices too high;
(c) insufficient output from manufacturing or supply department;
(d) quality problems;
(e) customer's plant is stopped by strike action, etc.

As mentioned earlier, calculated variances provide the questions. Often the answers are known or easily determined. Sometimes the answers require detailed investigation before management is able to decide on appropriate action. Prompt remedial action (sometimes perhaps before the variances have been calculated and presented) should then be directed towards eliminating or, at least, minimising unfavourable variances. Positive action is desirable even if the unfavourable variance is caused solely by external factors.

7.7.2 Maximising favourable variances

Sometimes variances turn out to be favourable. The temptation is to feel grateful and then pass on to concentrate on the problem areas (unfavourable variances). However, an opportunity may be missed if favourable variances are glossed over too quickly.

Something has gone better than expected. Why? Perhaps circumstances have changed in the marketplace or perhaps procedures have been altered in the operating areas. Further improvements might now be possible.

Suppose a strike has been called at a competitor's plant. Some of their customers may be willing to buy elsewhere, at least whilst the strike continues. An opportunity may therefore exist to boost sales and profit above budget. This is a frequent occurrence in the newspaper industry, for example.

Budgets are an agreed plan for management to aim at but they need not be a straightjacket preventing management from cashing in on improved circumstances. In fact taking action to maximise the favourable variances may be more profitable than concentrating on minimising unfavourable variances, some of which may be outside management's control.

7.8 CHAPTER SUMMARY

Variance analysis can often help managers understand better why actual business results turned out to be different from budget. It will not always provide the answers directly; but it does help to identify relevant questions.

The main focus of variance analysis concerns items in the profit and loss budget, i.e. sales and operating expenses. It is often useful also to look at balance sheet items such as stocks, debtors and cash.

In presenting the results of variance analysis, it is important to avoid needless detail. Instead one should direct management's attention to the main issues, in order to make the best use of their time.

Comparing actual results with budget may often lead to management action. This may be to put an end to unfavourable variances, or to maximise variances arising from unexpected favourable conditions. In any event, management may wish to review the appropriateness of existing plans.

The essence of working capital mgt is a trade-off between costs & risks.

Working capital mgt. is to control the many actions affecting working capital which are taken at operating levels of the firm.

They will be recouped as working capital is liquidated with reductions in operating levels or at the end of the investment's life.

* Most working capital decisions are essentially short-run

7.9 REVIEW QUESTIONS AND ANSWERS

7.9.1 Questions

1. What is a variance?
2. What is the benefit of variance analysis?
3. Does the calculation of variances directly identify the cause of the variance?
4. What are the two variances that comprise the sales variance? (Ignore the mix variance).
5. What is a flexible budget? What is its purpose?
6. Why are volume variances calculated by using budgeted prices (rather than actual prices)?
7. What are the two variances that comprise:
   (a) material expense variances;
   (b) direct labour expense variance?
8. Why is there only one variance identified for:
   (a) fixed overhead (for marginal costing system);
   (b) variable overhead?
9. Why are there two fixed overhead variances for standard costing systems?
10. List the eight variances which together comprise the profit variance for a marginal costing system. How do these variances differ when analysing the profit variance for a standard costing system?
11. What variances, other than sales, operating expense and profit variances, might be worth calculating?
12. 'It is important to give management *all* the facts in order for them to be effective. We therefore provide them with all our variance analysis results'. Do you agree with this view?
13. Should management concentrate most of its efforts on minimising unfavourable variances?
14. Does a thorough analysis of variances, guarantee good business performance? If not, why not?

Write out your answers and then check with the answers over page.

7.9.2 Answers

1. Difference between the actual amount and the budgeted amount.

2. Variance analysis often provides additional insight into which factors have affected performance and to what extent.

3. Not necessarily, but it does direct management's attention to important questions that require explanations.

4. (a) Sales volume variance - when analysing the profit variance, this should be substituted by the sales (contribution) volume variance.

   (b) Sales price variance.

5. A flexible budget is one in which the budgeted variable costs are 'flexed' (increased or decreased) to represent the expected variable cost for the *actual* sales volume (as opposed to the budgeted sales volume). The purpose is to provide a more meaningful budget for costs which are expected to vary with output and sales.

6. Prices are usually less controllable, by managers, than volumes. Volume variances are therefore isolated from price movements (actual v budget) by using budgeted prices in order to focus management's attention on factors it can control.

7. (a) Material price variance and material usage variance.

   (b) Direct labour rate variance and direct labour efficiency variance.

8. (a) Providing the actual level of output stays within the 'relevant range' the *amount* of fixed overhead should be unchanged. This being so, a fixed overhead expenditure variance should arise only if the *cost* of fixed overhead varies from budget.

   (b) Variable overhead by definition changes in line with output. A variable overhead expenditure variance results from spending more (or less) on variable overhead than 'should' have been spent for the actual level of output.

9. Apart from the fixed overhead expenditure variance (which is the same as for marginal costing systems), the fixed overhead volume variance identifies the loss in profit due to fixed overheads being under-recovered (unfavourable variance) or over-recovered (favourable variance). It arises when the actual output volume is different from that budgeted.

10. The eight variances in a marginal costing system are:
    (a) Sales price.
    (b) Sales (contribution) volume.
    (c) Material price.
    (d) Material usage.
    (e) Direct labour rate.
    (f) Direct labour efficiency.
    (g) Variable overhead expenditure.
    (h) Fixed overhead expenditure.

    For a standard costing system:
    (a) delete sales (contribution) volume variance, and add
    (b) sales (standard profit) volume variance, and
    (c) fixed overhead volume variance.

11. Balance sheet variances, particularly for stocks, debtors and cash.

12. No. Management by exception is necessary in today's competitive climate. Therefore in the presentation of reports to managers, unnecessary detail should be avoided. It is easier for managers to ask for additional specific detail than to sort through masses of detail which may obscure more vital issues.

13. Not necessarily. There may be better opportunities for increasing profits by maximising favourable variances.

14. Business performance is often improved by a thorough analysis of variances. Other factors such as a motivated, trained and experienced workforce are also necessary if superior performance is to be achieved.

7.10 PROBLEMS

7.10.1 Questions

1. Smith and Son Ltd budget to sell 6,000 units during September, at a price of £4.80 per unit. Actual sales revenue in September, from selling 6,400 units is £28,160.

   (a) What is the total sales variance for September?
   (b) Analyse the total sales variance between volume variance and price variance.

2. Bob Strange Ltd budgeted total expenses in December at £144,000 on a sales volume of 2,800 units. This included budgeted fixed expenses of £60,000. Actual expenses in December were £156,000 (including £68,000 for fixed expenses). Actual sales volume was 3,000 units.

   (a) What is the variable expenses variance?
   (b) Why is it different from the total expenses variance? Reconcile the two figures.

3. Monty and Winston Ltd. budgeted sales revenue in 1986 at £1,800,000, variable expenses at £1,200,000 and operating profit at £175,000. Actual sales revenue was only £1,475,000 even though selling prices were 10 per cent higher than budgeted.

   (a) Prepare a flexible budget for 1986.
   (b) Analyse the variances, as far as possible.
   (c) As the General Manager, what use would you make of the calculated variances?

4. Design an outline monthly management report for the financial results of a business school. (Remember it will have to be used by people who are not financial experts!)

5. Mr Horwood has a small workshop at the back of his house, where he employs three people making bedside cabinets. They each work for 40 hours a week, at a wage of £4.00 per hour. It takes four working hours to produce a cabinet, which sells for £32.00 and contains £5.60 worth of timber. Heating, rent, rates, etc. normally average £100 per week.

One weekend, one of the workers catches the 'flu and is away for the whole of the next week. He receives no pay for that week. The other two workers work six hours overtime each, for which they are paid at 'time and a half'. They manage to produce 25 cabinets between them, but due to haste they use 10 per cent more material than usual. Also the timber price has risen by 20 per cent. The weather is extremely cold that week, so the bill for overheads rises to £120 because of additional heating for longer hours.

(a) Calculate the budgeted profit for the week.
(b) Calculate the actual profit or loss for the week.
(c) Prepare a statement explaining the difference between the actual financial result for the week and the 'budget'. Distinguish between (i) quantity differences, and (ii) price differences.

6. Karl Klem (Mainz) Gmbh produces two models of cuckoo clock. The company's budget for 1986 was as follows:

	Bigbird	Sparrow	TOTAL
Selling price each	DM60	DM25	
Sales quantities	2,000	8,000	
	DM'000	DM'000	DM'000
Sales revenue	120	200	320
Variable cost of sales	60	160	220
Contribution	60	40	100

The actual figures for 1986 were as follows:

	Bigbird	Sparrow	TOTAL
Sales quantities	1,800	9,000	
	DM'000	DM'000	DM'000
Sales revenue	90	240	330
Variable cost of sales	50	185	235
Contribution	40	55	95

Account for the drop in contribution between budget and actual.

7. Power Chain Ltd operates two small factories at Dudley and Wolverhampton in the West Midlands, each employing 100 people in production of bicycle chains. All employees work for 150 hours a month, at a wage rate of £4.00 per hour, each producing on average 10 chains per hour. Material costs amount to 30p per chain, and Power Chain normally sells 300,000 chains a month, for £1.20 each, mainly to bicycle manufacturers. Fixed costs are budgeted at £90,000 a month.

A dispute about working conditions closes the Dudley factory for the month of November, and all 100 Dudley production workers are laid off and receive no pay for that month. Fixed costs, however, fall by only £8,000. The 100 Wolverhampton workers are able to increase their productivity so that in November they actually produce 200,000 chains, all of which are sold at the usual price. They are rewarded by a productivity bonus amounting to 25 per cent of their normal wages. Thanks to a nearby metal manufacturer going bankrupt, Power Chain Ltd is able to buy materials for the month at a discount of 20 per cent off the normal cost.

(a) Calculate Power Chain's actual profit (or loss) for November.

(b) Prepare a table showing the difference between the actual result and the original budgeted contribution and profit for the month.

(c) Compare the actual result with a flexible budget, showing what the expenses 'should have been' at the actual volume of sales.

(d) Split the total labour cost variance for November between the difference due to efficiency (volume) and that due to rates of pay.

(e) Summarise all the variances to explain the difference between the originally budgeted profit and actual profit.

7.10.2 Solutions

1. Smith & Son Ltd

Budgeted sales revenue = 6,000 units x £4.80/unit =£28,800

Actual sales revenue = 6,400 units x £4.40/unit =£28,160

a) Total sales variance = £640 unfavourable

b) Volume variance = increase in volume x budget price
= + 400 units x £4.80/unit = +£1,920

Price variance = fall in price x actual volume
= -£0.40/unit x 6,400 units = -£2,560

Total sales variance = -£640

2. Bob Strange Ltd

	Budget	Flexible Budget	Actual
	£'000	£'000	£'000
Variable (£30 per unit budgeted)	84	90	88
Fixed	60	60	68
Total	144	150	156
Units	2,800	3000	3,000

	£		
Variable expenses variances:			
volume	-6,000)	=	-£4,000
expenditure	+2,000)		
Fixed expenses variance	-8,000		
Total expenses variance	-12,000		

CHAPTER EIGHT

DECENTRALISED MANAGEMENT

8.1 INTRODUCTION

Decentralised management means delegating some planning, control and decision making to lower levels of management within a firm. This may also involve a geographical split. Some functions (e.g. Research) may be decentralised away from top management's direct supervision. Of more interest from a management accounting point of view is the decentralisation of a self-contained business unit as a separate operating *division*.

A division of a company differs from a whole company with respect to:

(a) independence;
(b) reducing capital;
(c) financial policy; and
(d) internal transfer pricing.

(a) No division is entirely independent. The central top management of the company is likely to have some say in:

appointing senior divisional managers;
setting long-term objectives and overall product strategy;
approving annual budgets;
approving major capital expenditures;
arranging necessary finance;
agreeing to (perhaps initiating) possible disinvestments.

There may also be common corporate policies for personnel, accounting, etc.

(b) Until recently a company with limited liability was legally forbidden to reduce its nominal money capital (except under special circumstances). Recent changes in company law, allowing companies to buy back their issued shares, have not yet resulted in much change to the practice of re-investing within the company the funds arising from depreciation.

There is, however, no requirement to maintain a *division's* capital, so it is possible to run down a division's operations fairly rapidly simply by *not re-investing* in it. In this sense, *all* a division's annual funds inflows are 'external' to it, while a large proportion of a whole company's funds may be 'internal'. Any group or company which lets each subsidiary or division *automatically* retain and reinvest 'its' internally-generated cash is abdicating one of its most powerful strategic tools.

(c) Whereas a company has three major sources of long-term capital (i.e. retained profits, issuing more equity shares, or long-term borrowing), a division usually has only one (an allocation of funds from the corporate 'pool'). Divisional managers will therefore probably be much less concerned with long-term financial policy than with marketing, operations, and personnel management.

(d) Some goods and services may be transferred to or from other divisions of the same company. This leads to the subject of 'transfer pricing' (see section 8.6).

8.2 MEASURING DIVISIONAL PERFORMANCE

8.2.1 Measuring 'return'

Four problems arise when measuring profit or 'return'. These are as follows:

(a) Depreciation

Depreciation represents the charging (sharing out) of a fixed asset's net cost (i.e. original cost less ultimate proceeds) over its useful life. There are four main problems:

(i) *Determining cost* is relatively easy for fixed assets purchased from external suppliers, including legal costs and installation charges. When fixed assets are manufactured internally, however, overhead costs may not always be capitalised.

(ii) *Estimating ultimate proceeds* is often ignored in practice. This tends to result in charging 'too much' depreciation during the asset's life, and being left with a 'profit on sale' at the end.

(iii) *Estimating the economic life* of a fixed asset usually depends on economic (market) considerations rather than on technical (engineering) or legal ones. Hence it can be difficult, and in practice fixed assets are often grouped into classes in which all assets are assumed to have similar lives.

(iv) *Choosing a depreciation method*. The main methods are:

- Straight-line: charging an equal amount each year, i.e. a constant percentage of original cost. This is the simplest method, being easy to understand and apply.

- Declining balance: charging each year a constant percentage of the declining net book value.

- 'Machine-hour' (or 'usage'): relating the asset's 'life' not to time but to usage or output.

(b) Interest payable

Any external long-term borrowing will normally be incurred by the parent company or group, and not by separate divisions. So in calculations of Return on Investment, long-term 'capital employed' will usually be 100% 'equity', and no question of interest payable arises.

Where a division has its own bank overdraft, interest will be payable. Unless the divisional manager has authority to determine the size of his division's bank overdraft (which would be unusual), it is probably best to relate profit before interest to total capital employed (i.e. including bank overdraft). A possible alternative would be to relate profit after interest to 'equity' capital only.

There may be advantages in charging divisions interest on all net long-term capital employed, whether it is ultimately financed at corporate level by debt or by equity. This correctly emphasises that all capital has an economic 'opportunity cost'. The disadvantages are that it may tend to complicate the reporting system, and it may provoke arguments about the rate of (notional) interest being charged.

(c) Tax

A divisional manager may not 'control' his division's tax liability, since investment incentives and other tax rules may vary between different divisions (according to their location, capital intensiveness etc.). Some companies, therefore, do not allocate the total corporate tax charge between divisions, using profit before tax (and perhaps also before interest, i.e. EBIT) as the measure of divisional performance. If profit before tax is used, the current tax liability should probably not be deducted in calculating divisional capital employed. (Otherwise the higher the actual tax payable, the higher the 'before-tax' ROI!)

Tax charges of individual divisions may not add up to the company's total tax charge, for a number of reasons. Certain taxable income and expenses may not be allocated to divisions at all. It may not be thought desirable to employ deferred tax liability reserves in divisional accounting, even if that is done in external reporting for the whole company. And although a company can set off profits in one division against losses in another, there is a question whether one division's performance should be affected by the tax positions of other divisions.

(d) Inflation adjustments

The arguments for allowing for the effects of inflation in external financial reporting are just as strong in internal management accounting. These adjustments will help avoid misleading comparisons between divisions with fixed assets of varying average ages. They will also improve the usefulness of comparisons over time within a division.

It can be argued that current cost accounting is more appropriate (or less inappropriate) in divisional accounting than in external financial reporting. But constant purchasing power accounting would still be needed to make residual income (divisional profit less a nominal interest charge on divisional capital employed) comparisons over time (see section 8.2.5), though not for ROI comparisons over time. Many companies would presumably prefer to use the same method for both purposes.

8.2.2 Measuring 'Investment'

(a) Opening, average, or closing investment

In calculating 'return on investment' measures from external published accounts, convenience suggests using 'end-of-period' investment as the denominator. A 'beginning-of-period' figure may be available (as the 'end-of-period' figure from the previous year's balance sheet), but not a suitable 'average' figure. Internally, however, the choice seems to be between 'beginning-of-period' and 'average' investment. It will normally make little difference which figure is used consistently; but the longer the period concerned, and the bigger the changes within the period, the more reason there is to prefer an 'average' figure.

(b) Valuation of assets

Revaluing fixed assets upwards increases 'investment', and may also affect depreciation (and thus reduce 'return'). Unless explicit inflation adjustments are made, regular re-evaluations of fixed assets may be desirable, say at least every five years.

Methods of stock valuation can significantly affect short-term profits. Divisions in completely different kinds of business may want to use different methods of stock valuation, but these will need to be applied consistently over time.

(c) Accumulated depreciation on fixed assets

Unless there are regular replacements of fixed assets, using net book value of fixed assets may mean a division's 'capital employed' seeming to shrink as fixed assets grow older. One way to solve this (largely academic) problem is to have a budgeting system which allows for the apparent ROI (or Residual Income) increase over time (and the probable sharp fall when major new capital investment is undertaken).

(d) Leased assets

Both ROI and residual income can make it seem profitable to lease fixed assets rather than buy them, since the implicit interest rate in lease contracts is likely to be only slightly above the cost of borrowing. The required rate of ROI (or of RI capital charge), however, will normally be much higher than that: it will represent either the cost of *equity* capital alone, or at least a weighted average cost of capital.

Now that companies are required to capitalise financial leases (SSAP 21) it makes sense to capitalise them also in divisional reports.

(e) Cash and debtors

Using *actual* figures for both cash and debtors is simplest; but the critical question is whether a division really *controls* either amount. If cash is centralised (as is common), a division should be allocated some 'reasonable' amount - perhaps a fixed percentage of sales. Similarly with debtors, if trade credit policy and administration is centrally managed, then a division should be allocated an amount based on 'normal' ratios to credit sales volume. But where a division controls collection, actual trade debtors outstanding should be used.

(f) Current liabilities

Divisional 'investment' is sometimes taken as total assets, but there is a strong argument for deducting current liabilities, since they do reduce the amount of long-term company investment. Unless trade creditors are paid centrally, actual liabilities may be used; even though this may encourage divisions to delay payment unduly, with possible loss of goodwill to the whole company. Tax liabilities should probably not be deducted, unless 'return' is calculated after tax. Bank overdrafts should be deducted if, but only if, they are both (i) really short-term, and (ii) negotiated separately by each division.

(g) Long-term liabilities

Many divisions have no long-term liabilities. Even if they have, long-term financial policy (concerning capital structure) is nearly always decided by a company's top management. This suggests that any long-term liabilities should be included as part of (long-term) capital employed.

(h) Deferred tax liabilities

Deferred tax liabilities (tax equalisation accounts) should be included as part of capital employed, if indeed they are even set up for internal divisional accounting purposes.

8.2.3 Return on investment

Figure 8.1 shows a hypothetical summarised profit and loss account and balance sheet for Paradise Division:

Profit and loss account Year 1986	£'000	Balance sheet at 31 December 1986	£'000
Sales revenue	1,500	Fixed assets, net	400
Cost of goods sold	850		
Gross profit	650	Current assets	1,300
Admin. expenses	350	Current liabilities	(500)
EBIT	300		800
Interest payable	50	Net assets	1,200
Profit before tax	250		
Tax	100	Equity	900
		Long-term debt	300
Profit after tax	150	Capital employed	1,200

Figure 8.1 Paradise Division's accounts

Return on Investment (ROI) is calculated as follows:

profit before interest and tax (EBIT), divided by net assets* (= capital employed)

$$\text{ROI} = \frac{\text{EBIT}}{\text{Net assets}} = \frac{300}{1200} = 25\%$$

* In published financial accounts, net assets are often referred to as 'Total Assets less Current Liabilities'.

8.2.4 Characteristics of ROI

Return on Investment:

(a) relies upon adequate accounting measurement of profit (see section 8.2.1) and of capital employed (see section 8.2.2.);
(b) can be used to plan, control and evaluate divisional performance in decentralised companies;
(c) can (and probably should) use *budget* figures as a standard against which to compare actual results;
(d) can be used as the basis for compensation based on profit-sharing;

(e) assesses performance by a *percentage* measurement;
(f) implicitly involves the same percentage rate of return for all assets;
(g) profit (or loss) is related to the capital employed.

8.2.5 Residual income (RI)

Residual Income is calculated as follows:

profit, less interest on capital employed

EBIT	300
Less: Capital charge*	240
= Residual income (before tax)	60

* 20% (say) on net assets (1200).

In effect Residual Income adjusts accounting profit by charging a notional interest expense on Equity capital and other long-term capital. (Any interest charges on divisional bank overdraft would need to be deducted in calculating the EBIT only if the overdraft was actually negotiated directly by the division. In this case, the bank overdraft would be excluded from the 'Long-Term capital').

Residual Income can be calculated either before-tax or after-tax.

8.2.6 Characteristics of RI

Residual Income:

(a) relies upon adequate accounting measurement of profit and of capital employed;
(b) can be used to plan, control and evaluate divisional performance in decentralised companies;
(c) can use *budget* figures as a standard against which to compare actual results;
(d) can be used as the basis for compensation based on profit-sharing;
(e) assesses performance by a *money* amount;
(f) does not necessarily require the same minimum rate of return (notional interest) for all assets;
(g) profit (or loss) is the residual amount after charging (notional interest) for the capital employed.

The first four characteristics are the same as those for ROI. The last three are different for RI and ROI. *Figure 8.2* summarises these differences.

	Return on investment	Residual income
1. Emphasis	Percentage ratio	Money amount
2. Involves same rate of return for all assets?	Yes	No
3. Profit (or loss)	Relates to capital	is Residual

Figure 8.2 Differences between ROI and RI

8.2.7 A possible advantage of residual income

Using Residual Income, a division will want to *go on expanding* as long as it can find investment projects which promise a return higher than the 'required' rate of return. This makes economic sense, as the aim is to *maximise* residual income. Using ROI, however, a division may not want to accept such projects if they are expected to return less than the present rate of ROI.

Example 1: Division A of a company has been earning a 30% ROI, Division B 8%, and the company as a whole 17%. Two new capital investment projects of similar risk are being considered in each division, returning 10% and 20% respectively.

Using the Return on Investment approach, the company as a whole might want both divisions to reject the first project and take the second. But Division A might want to reject both projects (since they would both be expected to reduce the division's ROI); *whereas Division B might want to accept both.*

With the Residual Income approach, however, using an interest rate of 17% would presumably induce each *division to reject the 10% project and accept the 20% project - thus achieving* goal congruence *between each division and the company as a whole).*

8.3 MEASURING MANAGERIAL PERFORMANCE

8.3.1 Controllability

The basis of controlling a division's performance is usually the budget, which should be agreed as a result of informed discussion. No single measure can encompass all aspects of performance; and accounting problems can distort any financial measurement (such as ROI or RI). The 'single criterion' fallacy can lead division managers to concentrate on manipulating numbers; but it is one of top management's tasks to establish a sensible and realistic budget climate. For instance, there may be good reasons for failing to achieve an agreed budget.

The need to balance short-term and long-term aspects requires subjective judgement. The emphasis in the financial literature has changed from 'maximising profits' to 'maximising shareholders' wealth'; but the latter requires the use of an interest rate to discount expected future cash flows back to their present day value. Choosing a suitable interest rate is itself subjective and difficult, and liable to a large margin of error.

There is a difference between measuring a business unit's results and measuring its manager's performance. Unless top management understands this, a 'good' manager may be unwilling to accept responsibility for a 'bad' division (which may badly need his services).

Some expenses may not be fully controllable by a division manager, especially in the short-term (for example, depreciation and rent). Leaving them out may give a misleading picture of a business unit's financial performance, but including them may make it hard to hold the division manager fully responsible for results.

Including apportioned expenses *informs* division managers about expenses which contributions from the divisions must cover, and may also *induce* them to query seemingly high corporate overheads. On the other hand it can cause pointless argument about the basis of apportionment.

Even where one can distinguish between 'controllable' and 'non-controllable' expenses, the resulting report form may be in danger of being too complicated (see Figure 8.3).

	£'000	£'000
Sales to outside customers	XXX	
Transfers to other divisions at market value	XXX	XXX
Less: variable cost of goods sold and transferred	XXX	
variable divisional expenses	XXX	
		XXX
Contribution to fixed costs and profit		XXX
Less: Controllable divisional overhead	XXX	
Depreciation on controllable fixed assets	XXX	
		XXX
Controllable operating profit		XXX
Less: interest on controllable investment		XXX
Controllable profit before tax		XXX
Less: non-controllable divisional overhead	XXX	
central expenses chargeable to division	XXX	
interest on non-controllable investment	XXX	XXX
Net profit before tax		XXX
Less: Corporation Tax		XXX
Net profit after tax		XXX

Figure 8.3 Divisional profit statement

8.3.2 Motivation

One of the major benefits of decentralised management is the chance it offers to develop managers for more senior positions. Giving division managers responsibility and authority can lead them to behave in a much more entrepreneurial way, almost as if they were running their own firm. However, top management cannot abdicate completely, since they must answer to shareholders for earning adequate profits.

When a company comprises divisions which neither compete nor trade with each other, a high degree of divisional autonomy is often healthy. However, if divisions are competing with each other, or if there is much trading between them, then allowing managers to do what is best for their divisions might harm the best interests of the group as a whole.

The aim is 'goal congruence', which means inducing division managers in trying to improve their own divisions' results, also to act in the best interests of the group. This requires an effective system of performance appraisal, and suitable transfer pricing rules. It also means that division managers need to *know* what corporate objectives are. Where there are problems, Head Office may need to arbitrate; but if this happens too often, it can undermine divisional management's autonomy, and thus impair motivation.

The balance is often difficult between:

(a) developing top-level managers;
(b) giving division managers a high degree of autonomy; and
(c) achieving goal congruence between divisional and group objectives.

Getting the balance more or less 'right' will go a long way towards enabling managers to demonstrate superior performance.

A division manager may not view *risk* in the same way as a corporate manager. The latter will assess not only an activity's specific risk, but also its ('portfolio') effect on the rest of the group's business. The division manager may be reluctant to take risks that could result in 'failure' for the division. In contrast, the corporate manager may be willing to accept such risks if he thinks the chance of outstanding returns is high enough. Thus, a division manager may be more averse to high-risk projects than a corporate manager.

8.4 BEFORE AND AFTER

There may be important differences, as Figure 8.4 shows, between methods used for prospective capital investment project evaluation in advance, and those used for retrospective divisional performance appraisal after the event. Some writers have suggested that using cash flows, instead of accounting profits or losses, as the basis for the latter, could avoid many of the differences. The asterisks against each item in Figure 8.4 show which way cash flow accounting would probably tend.

In Advance Main methods: NPV, IRR		After the Event Main methods: RI, ROI	
1a.	Incremental amounts	1a.	Overall totals
1b.	Relating to discrete 'projects'	*1b.	Relating to whole business unit
1c.	Over all (or most) of project's life	*1c.	For a single period (often one year)
	(Usually ..)		
*2a.	Cash flows	2a.	Profits (or losses)
*2b.	Ignoring depreciation	2b.	After charging depreciation
*2c.	After tax	2c.	Often before tax
3a.	May be constant purchasing power units (= year 0 money)	*3a.	Usually monetary units (distorted by inflation)
3b.	Often discounted	*3b.	Not discounted
3c.	With implicit re-investment assumption	*3c.	With no re-investment assumption
4.	Uncertainty clearly relevant	4.	Uncertainty often ignored

Figure 8.4 Prospective investment evaluation in advance compared with retrospective performance appraisal after the event

Items 1a. and 4. would remain difficult points to overcome. After the event it may often be very hard to identify 'incremental' amounts resulting from projects which the on-going business has thoroughly absorbed. (This is a major difficulty in attempting 'post-project audits'). Nor will it be possible to make useful guesses after the event about the actual degree of risk involved. (This, of course, is not easy *before* the event either!)

Figure 8.5 illustrates point 1. in Figure 8.4, the contrast between looking at incremental amounts relating to discrete 'projects' over a project's whole life and looking at overall totals relating to the whole business unit for a single period. Modern thinking has tended to downgrade techniques which strongly emphasise discrete 'projects', and to re-instate older approaches which try to consider the impact of particular decisions on the business as a whole.

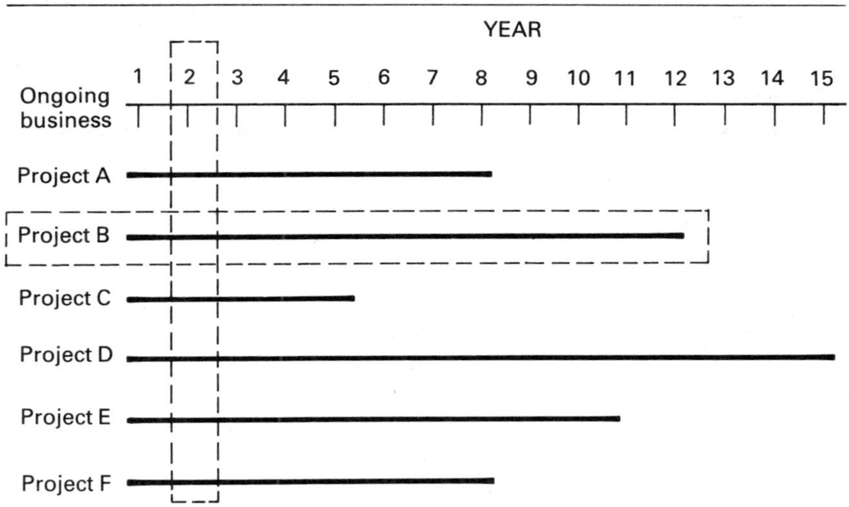

Figure 8.5 Project lives and accounting years

8.5 PROFIT CENTRES

8.5.1 Advantages

Profit centres may be suitable for a decentralised organisation where:

(a) divisions have access to markets both for suppliers and customers;
(b) inter-divisional business is not too important; and
(c) divisional managers are allowed considerable independence.

Where any of these conditions are not met, it becomes more difficult to judge whether on balance profit centres are beneficial. Some possible advantages of treating divisions of a company 'as if' they were (largely) independent of top management control are listed in Figure 8.6.

---

* Motivates managers to perform well in areas they control.
* Encourages initiatives.
* Uses divisional managers' specialised market knowledge.
* Gives local managers responsibility for making trade-offs.
* Emphasis on 'bottom line' spotlights poor performance anywhere.
* Permits management by exception.
* Frees top management time and energy for other tasks.
* Helps train future top managers.

Figure 8.6 Possible advantages of treating divisions as profit centres

8.5.2 Disadvantages

Where a divisional manager's freedom is limited as to:

(a) who he can buy from;
(b) who he can sell to;
(c) prices charged;
(d) what products (or services) are made,

profit centres may be inappropriate. Consider an extreme case where Division S produces only for Division C and the transfer price is decided by central management. If Division S is not allowed to sell to any other customers, but is required to make only to Division C's orders, and cannot amend the price, then their ability to influence profits is severely limited. Controlling and reducing costs (whilst achieving an acceptable quality level) is the only real controllable financial factor. In this case it is probably more appropriate to regard Division S as a cost centre and judge the divisional performance on that basis. (Cost centre performance is measured by comparing actual cost with the budgeted or standard cost for the actual level of output. ROI and RI are not used in assessing cost centre performance.)

Profit centres are therefore not always the most appropriate form of divisional organisation. Some possible disadvantages of treating divisions as profit centres are shown in Figure 8.7.

---

* Confuses division's results with manager's performance.
* Over-emphasises short-term results.
* Risks mistakes by divisional managers which top managers might avoid.
* Under-utilises corporate competence.
* Duplicates staff activities.
* Difficult to identify suitable profit centres.
* Hard to arrange for goal congruence.
* Complicated by transfer price problems.

Figure 8.7 Possible disadvantages of treating divisions as profit centres.

8.6 TRANSFER PRICING

Corporate management will usually make ultimate decisions about *sourcing* (or at least establish rules to enable divisions to decide), and lay down rules for negotiating *transfer prices* between divisions. Any system for establishing transfer prices should be reasonably simple, and needs to be accepted as fair by divisional managers. Some arbitration system may be required to settle disputes; but only exceptionally will top management want to get involved in setting a particular price for a specific transfer of goods or services between divisions.

8.6.1 Sourcing

There may be sound business reasons for transferring goods between two divisions, rather than letting one division buy from outside. Control of supply may be important, there may be commercial secrets involved, or the outside supplier may be seeking to expand operations at the company's expense. An inside division which can meet outside competition in price (and, of course, in quality) will normally be entitled to the business if it wants it. Even if another division can supply equivalent products at competitive prices, divisions may wish to buy outside, either to maintain more than a single source of supply, or to ensure that outside supplier price quotations continue to be realistic.

8.6.2 Pricing

Assuming there is no over-riding economic reason for two divisions to deal with each other, a common rule is to transfer goods and services between divisions at *long-run market price*, with either buying or selling division free to choose whether or not to deal with another division. This requires divisions to have access to outside markets, and to be free to negotiate with each other. For example, ICI's 1986 Annual Report says (page 38): 'The Group's policy is to transfer products internally at external market prices'.

In some cases there may be no outside market (e.g. for specialised intermediate products); or the market price may be difficult to discover; or the goods dealt in may not be exactly equivalent. Sometimes it may be possible to reach an acceptable proxy for a market price (e.g. by explicitly allowing for known differences in quality). Where no equivalent market price is available, there are three main possibilities:

(a) Transfer goods at 'cost plus mark-up';
(b) Use different prices for buyer and seller;

(c) Change from a profit centre organisation.

(a) Cost plus mark-up

Some kind of *standard cost* should be used, since using actual cost would enable the selling division to pass on the cost of manufacturing inefficiencies. To provide an incentive to *reduce* costs, it may be desirable to allow the selling division to continue charging the former price for a limited period.

If full costs are used, the selling division's *fixed costs* will appear to the buying division as *variable costs*. This might induce decisions which are inappropriate from the corporate viewpoint. Where volume is small, this may not matter much; but in principle it may be better to use *marginal costs*. Where volume is substantial, there may be a case for a two-part transfer price, consisting of:

(i) an explicit share of the selling division's fixed costs; plus
(ii) a variable cost per unit transferred.

In order to determine the transfer price, some mark-up needs to be added to whichever 'cost' figure is used. Otherwise a profit centre will nearly always prefer to sell outside, at a profit, rather than inside, at cost. The simplest method is to use a 'normal' profit margin on sales or a 'normal' rate of return on the assets employed. A fairly crude rule of thumb may be preferable to a complicated, spuriously accurate calculation.

(b) Different prices for buyer and seller

One way to avoid the seller's fixed overheads being seen as variable by the buying division is to credit the seller with standard full costs, and to charge the buyer only standard marginal costs. That procedure should avoid distorting buyer-division decisions away from corporate interests. Then the total of all the divisions' reported 'profits' would exceed the total company profit. The difference would become a corporate overhead: it would be charged to a special Head Office 'suspense account', and be eliminated on consolidation. One major disadvantage with this method is that neither the buyer nor the seller would really feel responsible for controlling the seller's fixed overheads. Without supervision from Head Office these fixed overheads could increase rapidly.

(c) Change the organisation of profit centres

If there is no suitable market price, and neither (a) nor (b) above seems acceptable, the profit centre organisation itself may be questioned. When the volume of internal business is large, two divisions may be so closely linked economically that it doesn't really make sense to treat them both as independent profit centres.

8.6.3 Capacity and competition

When the supplying division is operating at or near full capacity, then the transfer price ought to cover (at least) the full cost of production. To use its limited capacity for inter-group work at less favourable rates than can be achieved by dealing with external customers, might not be the free choice of the supplying division's management.

When the supplying division is operating well below full capacity there is some merit in transferring goods or services at (or a little above) marginal cost. In this way the buying division is more likely to buy from group divisions than external suppliers. In times of severe over-capacity in an industry, many suppliers might resort to 'distress pricing', i.e. variable cost plus a small percentage contribution. If the supplying division maintains its full-cost policy, they may rapidly find themselves without any (voluntary) customers.

8.7 CHAPTER SUMMARY

Most large companies are split into a number of more or less independent divisions, whose performance can be measured separately. The basis of measurement may be either *return on investment*, or else *residual income*. In measuring divisions' performances, there must be agreement about what constitutes 'return' and what constitutes 'investment'.

It may be misleading to relate a division's performance directly to that of its management. Managers can be responsible only for those aspects which they 'control' (or at least significantly influence).

Treating divisions as profit centres may have advantages. But profit centres may not be suitable for divisions where management freedom is limited, e.g. where group management decides about the division's suppliers or customers or selling prices.

Transfer pricing policy determines the prices that supplying divisions charge to other group companies. This might be as low as variable cost, or as high as full plus mark-up, or market price. Transfer pricing policy should aim at maximising group profits: it needs to consider management motivation, use of capacity, and the competitive position.

8.8 REVIEW QUESTIONS AND ANSWERS

8.8.1 Questions

1. What are the two main ways of measuring divisional performance?
2. What is the formula for return on investment?
3. What problems arise when measuring the 'return'?
4. What issues have to be decided to determine the amount of the 'investment'?
5. How is residual income measured?
6. How might residual income be superior to return on investment, in enhancing goal congruence?
7. What does 'goal congruence' mean?
8. Identify five differences between methods used for capital investment project evaluation and those used for divisional performance appraisal.
9. List four possible advantages of profit centres.
10. List four possible disadvantages of profit centres.
11. What options are available when selling a transfer price between two divisions, if there is no market price available?

Write out your answers and then check with the answers over page.

8.8.2 Answers

1. (a) Return on investment (ROI);

   (b) Residual income (RI).

2. $\text{ROI} = \dfrac{\text{EBIT}}{\text{Net assets}}$

3. How to deal with:

   (a) depreciation;
   (b) interest payable;
   (c) tax;
   (d) inflation.

4. (a) Whether to use opening, average or closing investment;

   (b) Whether to use historical cost or revalued figures for assets;

   (c) Whether to use gross fixed assets (at cost or re-evaluation) or just their net book value;

   (d) How to cope with leased assets (probably by capitalising financial leases);

   (e) Whether to include actual cash and debtors;

   (f) Whether to use total assets as the investment figure, or to deduct (some or all) current liabilities;

   (g) Whether to include long-term liabilities (e.g. loans) as part of the capital employed;

   (h) Whether deferred tax liabilities should be included in capital employed.

5. RI = EBIT less capital charge (a predetermined percentage of Net Assets).

6. All divisions would undertake projects expected to give a return better than the group's minimum return. With ROI this

would not be likely where the division's return is expected to be different (either higher or lower) from that of the group.

7. Goal congruence is the motivation of divisional managers towards improving their own division's results, also to act in the best interests of the company or group as a whole.

8. Any five from Figure 8.4.

9. Any four from Figure 8.6.

10. Any four from Figure 8.7.

11. (a) Transfer goods at 'cost plus mark-up'.
    (b) Use different prices for buyer and seller.
    (c) Change from a profit centre organisation.

CHAPTER NINE

MICROCOMPUTERS IN MANAGEMENT ACCOUNTING

9.1 WHY USE MICROCOMPUTERS ?

Microcomputers are increasingly being used for business applications, particularly for management accounts. And this is in spite of the feelings of fear and distrust that many managers have towards them.

The main reasons why microcomputers are of particular use in management accounting are that they can:

(a) Calculate rapidly and accurately;
(b) Store and quickly retrieve data;
(c) Manipulate data according to a series of commands.

However, there is a *set-up time* involved at the start of any new application. In order to gain the benefits of the fast *run time*, compared with 'manual' calculations, the frequency of use and the amount of savings in run time must more than compensate for the set-up time and cost.

Microcomputer applications require the use of both hardware and software. (See sections 9.2 and 9.3)

9.2 HARDWARE

The essential equipment (hardware) involved in microcomputing is:

(a) **visual display unit** (VDU) cabinet, incorporating the screen and data storage system;
(b) **keyboard,** essentially an expanded typewriter; and
(c) **floppy disks** - the system master disk, software package disks, etc.
(d) **fixed (hard) disks**

In addition to physical items of equipment (hardware) it is essential to have appropriate software and suitable applications for use.

9.3 SOFTWARE

Without a series of logical control instructions microcomputers cannot meet user needs. These instructions (software) may be given in a variety of ways which include:

(a) programming - the writing of logical control instructions for manipulating data.

(b) software packages.

(i) **applications packages** - a pre-programmed standard solution to a problem of general concern. These are specific packages used for example for payroll, sales ledger, purchase ledger, etc.

(ii) **flexible packages** - a 'friendly' framework in which the user applies both data and logic.

Programming requires the use of computer languages (e.g. BASIC), some of which are easy to learn. By addressing a particular problem, programming can provide the solution in the form required. Response time and computer resources are minimised. However, writing programs is often very expensive in time and money, typically about 3 times that of an applications package.

Applications packages may be bought from software houses. The user simply applies his data to the pre-programmed package for a speedy and economical solution to his problem. It is vital that the package is suitably relevant and flexible to meet the user's needs. Although packages can be modified, it is costly to do so and results in less efficient use of computer resources.

Flexible packages are a compromise between (specific) programming and (general) applications packages. Of particular importance are *spreadsheets* (see section 9.4). Flexible packages are more flexible than applications packages, although the user must develop his own logic. Implementation time is therefore longer than with a ready-made applications package. But the greater flexibility and lower costs of flexible packages often over-ride the benefits of 'instant' packages.

9.4 SPREADSHEETS

A spreadsheet is essentially a matrix comprising information. Many companies use *manual* spreadsheets for planning and reporting purposes (e.g. for presenting budgets and actual performance). Whereas a manual spreadsheet is produced (handwritten or typed) on paper, microcomputers are able to display a spreadsheet on screen. Of course it may be printed out as well, if needed. Making input data changes to manual spreadsheets is often tedious, untidy and prone to errors, due to the fact that there may be many interrelationships and dependancies. Conversely changing input data on a microcomputer spreadsheet is quick, neat and accurate, as the interrelationships can be specified and stored.

Spreadsheet packages, such as Lotus 1-2-3, enable people to model and process financial information. Spreadsheets can be used for many purposes, including:

(a) *costing* - maintaining up-to-date costs on products (or services) that comprise many cost inputs;

(b) *budgeting* - especially in budget preparation where the budget is likely to be modified a number of times before it is agreed;

(c) *capital investment decisions* - net present values and internal rates of return can be rapidly calculated.

Modelling, i.e. the generation of the calculating logic, allows the consideration of 'what if' questions. The input data is changed and the effect on the output result is observed. In this way managers' questions such as 'what if material costs rise by 5%?' can be answered before future plans are finalised.

Although spreadsheets are often used as a separate system, they may be combined with other spreadsheets to provide a larger system. In addition to the spreadsheet itself some packages also include graphics (x-y graphs, bar charts, pie charts, etc.) and a database facility (for storage and retrieval of selected data).

The construction of a spreadsheet is based upon a series of cells, identified by a row and column reference. See Figure 9.1. The number of cells is often very large. The Lotus 1-2-3 (version 2) spreadsheet package, for instance, has about 7,800 rows and 250 columns, giving about two million cells.

	A	B	C	D	E etc.
1	A1	B1	C1	D1	E1
2	A2	B2	C2	D2	E2
3	A3	B3	C3	D3	E3
4	A4	B4	C4	D4	E4
5	A5	B5	C5	D5	E5
6	A6	B6	C6	D6	E6
7	A7	B7	C7	D7	E7
etc.					

Figure 9.1 Construction of a spreadsheet

Each cell is uniquely referenced, e.g. C3 is the cell in Column C, row 3. Contained within each cell may be one of the following:

(a) text;
(b) input data;
(c) 'hidden' formulae (i.e. the calculating logic) with the result displayed.

Suppose that column A is direct labour hours and column B is direct labour rate of pay per hour. To determine the direct labour cost in column C we would multiply columns A and B together. The 'hidden' formula, in cell C3 for instance, would then be A3 x B3.

The 'hidden' formulae once entered can be viewed on the screen, but, unlike the calculated formulae results, would not appear on the completed spreadsheet.

9.5 APPLICATIONS IN MANAGEMENT ACCOUNTING

9.5.1 Costing

For products comprising a number of components the total product cost is likely to be changing constantly, perhaps daily. In times of increasing costs, calculating product costs infrequently may result in selling prices becoming too low. By using spreadsheets, changes to component costs can be input as they occur, and the total product cost instantly recalculated. In this way management is continually aware of the relationship between a product's cost and its selling price.

Example 1: Norman Bicycles Ltd. have constructed a spreadsheet to keep up-to-date standard costs for their new 'Swift Mover' range, incorporating a low friction rubber-compound chain. Part of the spreadsheet is shown in figure 9.2. Text (e.g. column and row headings), input data (columns 2, 3 and 4), and formulae results (column 5 and the last row) appear. The hidden formulae are:

(a) multiply column 3 by column 4 to give column 5; and
(b) add the column 5 amounts to give the total material cost.

Swift Mover - GT Model
Standard Cost

Part Name	Part No.	No. off	Unit Cost £	Material Cost £
Frame	4001	1	4.20	4.20
Wheel	4002	2	4.80	9.60
Tyre	4008	2	2.20	4.40
Innertube	4009	2	1.95	3.90
Valve	4020	2	0.60	1.20
Pedal	4040	2	2.80	5.60
Chain	4052	1	6.50	6.50
Pump	4090	1	2.10	2.10
etc.	etc.	etc.	etc.	etc.
Total material cost				45.80

Figure 9.2 Standard cost spreadsheet - material cost

The spreadsheet shown in Figure 9.2 may be extended to include fabrication labour costs by adding further columns as follows:

Column	Input	Formula Result
6	Labour time (minutes)	-
7	Labour rate (£ per minute)	-
8	-	Labour cost (Col.6 x Col.7)

Beyond column 8 could be added overhead costs and then a total components fabrication cost.

Below the total material cost line is the assembly cost detail, see Figure 9.3. The hidden formulae in Figure 9.3 calculate the labour cost (labour time, column 3 x labour rate, column 4), and the total cost for each assembly operation (labour cost, column five x 5, i.e. 1 + 400% overhead on labour cost). The total assembly cost is then the sum of the amounts in column 7.

If desired, the labour rates and overhead percentage rate could be omitted from the presentation as shown in Figure 9.3. This would simplify the presentation. The hidden formulae would still include the labour rates and the overhead percentage rate, but these now would also be 'hidden'. An alternative would be to show commonly used data (labour rates, overhead percentage rates, etc.) in a table elsewhere on the spreadsheet.

Assy.Op.	Op.No.	Lab.Time mins.	Lab.Rate £/min.	Lab.Cost £	0/hd %	Total £
Wheels - Frame (2)	025	1.90	0.14	0.2660	400	1.3300
Wheel - Tyre (2)	021	1.42	0.16	0.2272	400	1.1360
Tyre - Inner T (2)	020	0.80	0.14	0.1120	400	0.5600
Wheel - Valve (2)	023	0.68	0.14	0.0952	400	0.4760
Frame - Crank	035	2.10	0.14	0.2940	400	1.4700
Crank - Pedal (2)	040	1.76	0.14	0.2464	400	1.2320
etc.	etc.	etc.	etc.	etc.	etc.	etc.
Total Assembly Cost						9.3200

Figure 9.3 Standard cost spreadsheet - assembly cost

The material cost, fabrication cost and assembly cost can now be added together to give a total production cost. This summary information will in most cases be sufficient for managers.

9.5.2 Budgeting

Spreadsheets are particularly useful in the preparation of budgets for profit and loss accounts, balance sheets and cash flows. The benefit is greatest where the budget is intricate and is likely to undergo a series of amendments before the budget is finally agreed.

Example 2: Bland, Bland and Bland Chartered Accountants were preparing their budget for the forthcoming year. Starting with the income budget, they have estimated client fees (= income) by client group and by service type (i.e. auditing, preparing accounts, consultancy and personal services). See *figure 9.4*.

Income Budget - Fees (£'000)

Client	Audit	Accounts	Consult.	Personal	Total
Major Co's	524	-	116	-	640
Other PLC Co's	205	-	30	-	235
Private Co's	62	115	12	-	189
Partnerships	-	56	4	-	60
Sole Traders	-	29	-	-	29
Individuals	-	18	-	18	36
Total	791	218	162	18	1189

Figure 9.4 Income budget

Staff numbers and associated cost for the year are identified by staff grade. See Figure 9.5.

Staff Budget

Staff	Number	Salary (£)	Total (£)	Total inc. Benefits (£)
Senior	2	22,500	45,000	67,500
Junior	6	16,200	97,200	136,080
Assistant	20	12,000	240,000	312,000
Consultant	2	32,000	64,000	96,000
Typists	3	8,400	25,200	32,760
Clerks	2	6,600	13,200	16,500
			484,600	660,840

Figure 9.5 Budgeted staff numbers and costs

Similarly other costs may be budgeted in detail and then brought together with the income budget to provide a budgeted profit and loss account. See Figure 9.6.

	Profit Budget £
Income	1,189,000
Staff Costs	660,840
Rent and Rates	105,200
Heat and Light	2,900
Telephone	4,150
Travel Expenses	87,800
Equipment	9,250
Stationery	3,700
Misc.	1,800
Total Costs	875,640
Profit Before Tax	313,360

Figure 9.6 Profit Budget

If the partners are dissatisfied with the level of budgeted profit they may wish to amend income and costs in some way. The effect of these amendments would then be immediately apparent in the revised profit budget.

9.5.3 Capital investment decisions

Larger enterprises are regularly involved in making capital investment decisions. Spreadsheets are beneficial here not only in rapidly calculating a project's net present value (or internal rate of return) but also in taking account of perceived risks. The amount of sales revenue is often the most uncertain aspect in many projects. The microcomputer allows us to alter the sales revenue input (and adjust any other related input, e.g. sales commissions) to quickly see the affect on the project's viability.

Example 3: Mr Jones, the proprietor of Roger's Refuse Service, was considering expanding his business by acquiring 20 refuse mini skips and a specially equipped truck. With this equipment he would offer a refuse collection service for householders and businesses. With building extension and repair activity growing he believed that by recruiting a driver he could generate £60,000 of revenue per year (20 skips x £15 per collection x 200 collection days per year). Mr Jones would proceed with the venture providing the expected return was in excess of 30% (before tax).

Figure 9.7 shows the detailed cost and revenue (input) figures, and the (calculated) present value row and Net Present Value of the project. (The net present value and internal rate of return are functions built into the spreadsheet).

Mini-Skip Project

	Now	Year 1	Year 2	Year 3	Year 4	Year 5
Skips		20	20	20	20	20
Price per collection		15	16	17	18	20
Days		200	200	200	200	200
Revenue		60,000	64,000	68,000	72,000	80,000
Costs						
Truck:						
- *purchase*	22,000	-	-	-	-	-
- *maint/repair*		600	1,000	1,800	3,000	4,000
- *fuel*		1,500	1,800	2,100	2,200	2,300
- *other*		1,200	1,320	1,450	1,600	1,650
Driver:						
(inc. benefits)		16,000	17,000	19,000	21,000	24,000
Skips:						
- *cost*	24,000					
- *replacement*		1,200	1,400	1,500	3,200	5,000
Admin.		6,000	6,400	7,000	7,500	8,000
Total costs	46,000	26,500	28,920	32,850	38,500	44,950
Cash flow	-46,000	33,500	35,080	35,150	33,500	35,050
Discount factor	1.0	0.769	0.592	0.455	0.350	0.269
Present value	-46,000	25,761	20,767	15,993	11,725	9,428
Net present value		£37,674				

Figure 9.7 Mini-skip project evaluation

Mr Jones can now use the calculating ability of the microcomputer to consider the following questions:

What will the net present value be if:

(a) Only 15 skips are bought instead of 20?
(b) Skips are utilised only 160 days per year?
(c) Driver costs are increased by 20%?
(d) Skip costs are 20% higher?

9.6 CHAPTER SUMMARY

Because of their ability to calculate rapidly, microcomputers are increasingly becoming part of the 'office furniture' for managers, management accountants and others.

In addition to the hardware, software must be chosen to suit the applications planned. The cost and set-up time involved needs to be less than the benefits from its fast and frequent use.

Of particular use in management accounting are spreadsheets, essentially a matrix of rows and columns. The microcomputer can facilitate calculations and recalculations when input data is changed. 'What if' questions can be answered rapidly, giving managers a prompt appreciation of the sensitivity of their proposals.

Management accounting applications of microcomputers include costing, budgeting and capital investment. Product costs can be quickly updated when component costs change. Budgets can be modified several times within a short space of time. Capital investment decisions benefit from the sensitivity analysis that microcomputers provide by varying assumptions.

9.7 REVIEW QUESTIONS AND ANSWERS

9.7.1 Questions

1. What are the main features of microcomputers that make them useful in management accounting?
2. When should microcomputers be used?
3. What does microcomputing equipment comprise?
4. What is software?
5. What are the two main types of software packages?
6. What is a spreadsheet?
7. Name three management accounting applications of spreadsheets.
8. What are the three types of content within spreadsheet cells?
9. In what circumstances are spreadsheets particularly useful for product costing applications?
10. Why is budgeting a good application for microcomputers?
11. How can the microcomputer help deal with risk in capital investment decisions?
12. What is meant by 'what if' questions?

Write out your answers and then check with the answers over page.

9.7.2 Answers

1. Microcomputers can:
   (a) calculate rapidly and accurately;
   (b) store and quickly retrieve data;
   (c) manipulate data according to a series of commands.

2. When the benefits of the faster run time offset the set-up time and cost involved.

3. (a) VDU cabinet;
   (b) Keyboard;
   (c) Floppy disks;
   (d) Fixed (hard) disks.

4. A series of logical control instructions.

5. (a) Applications packages;
   (b) flexible packages.

6. A table of rows and columns comprising information.

7. (a) Costing;
   (b) Budgeting;
   (c) Capital investment decisions.

8. (a) Text;
   (b) input data;
   (c) 'hidden' formulae, with the result displayed.

9. For keeping up-to-date costs of multi-component products where cost changes happen on a frequent basis.

10. Budgeted P&L accounts, balance sheets and cash flows often undergo a series of amendments before a final version is agreed. The more detailed the budgets, the more time-consuming and prone to error are those prepared manually.

11. Sensitivity analysis is possible with the help of 'what if' questions.

12. 'What if' questions seek to determine the effect on outcome (e.g. profit) as a result of a change of input data (e.g. sales volume).

CHAPTER TEN

MANAGEMENT ACCOUNTING IN ACTION

10.1 RISK AND UNCERTAINTY

In preparing budgets and making business decisions, managers often use only the *most likely* figures. Some figures may be known for sure, e.g. some suppliers' prices for the next few months. But usually managers have to plan, control, and make decisions on the basis of *uncertain* estimates.

Some authors distinguish between 'risk' and 'uncertainty'. They use the term 'risk' where the chance of each outcome occurring is *known* (as in roulette). 'Uncertainty' exists when, as is usual in business, the odds can only be estimated subjectively (i.e. *guessed*).

Where adverse events could seriously damage their business, managers need to understand the range and likelihood of possible outcomes. Two ways to cope with uncertainty are:

(a) sensitivity analysis;
(b) subjective probabilities and 'expected values'.

10.1.1 Sensitivity analysis

In budgeting and decision-making the first step is usually to make a single 'best estimate' for each item. One might then also make 'optimistic' and 'pessimistic' estimates for each variable; though this does raise questions such as how to *define* 'optimistic' and 'pessimistic', and how to make use of the three estimates. The spreads may not be symmetrical: for instance, capacity constraints may prevent budgeted sales volume from being exceeded by more than a small margin, whereas there could be a drastic decline in a severe recession.

Another approach is to vary the 'most likely' estimate for each item in turn, to see how much difference it makes to the overall result. Large changes to particular items will often not be important, so we need to identify those critical variables where even a fairly small change can make quite a large difference to the overall result.

It is not much use to try changing each item by a fixed percentage, say 10%, for some items may be much more variable, while others may be unlikely to change by nearly as much as 10%. A better method is to define an 'optimistic' estimate of income as one which would have only (say) a one in ten chance of being exceeded, while there would be only a one in ten chance of falling short of the 'pessimistic' estimate of income. (It would be the other way round for estimates of *expenditure*).

Ideally, one should allow for any inter-dependence among variables, though this is much easier said than done! But merely to combine the 'pessimistic' estimates of the most sensitive variables would be far too gloomy. If 'pessimistic' meant a one in ten chance of a 'worst' outcome, for example, with four independent variables there would only be a one in 10,000 chance of such a combined outcome!

10.1.2 Subjective probabilities and 'expected values'

Suppose that for a new product, sales of 600, 400, 300 or 100 units are thought possible, with the chances of each outcome being reckoned respectively as 0.1, 0.3, 0.4, and 0.2. By weighting the possible outcomes by their estimated chances of happening, we can calculate an 'expected value' of sales volume of 320 units. We can do the same for the profit estimates linked with each possible level of sales, to arrive at an 'expected profit' of £42.

Sales Volume	Probability	'Expected Sales'	Profit	'Expected Profit'
600	0.1	60	£210	£21
400	0.3	120	£90	£27
300	0.4	120	£30	£12
100	0.2	20	(£90)	(£18)
	1.0	320		£42

Attaching subjective 'probabilities' to uncertain future events allows arithmetical manipulation of the numbers. It may even mislead people into thinking their decision-making is 'scientific'. But what confidence can we have in guesses about the chances of various outcomes? Can we even be sure we have considered every possible event? (Events which in advance were thought to be 'impossible' often seem afterwards to turn out to have been 'inevitable').

What does it really mean to apply subjective estimates of probabilities to important events which are not going to be repeated? In deciding whether or not to become a professional footballer, for instance, does it make sense for someone to say: 'I guess the odds against my becoming a top-class football star are 200 to 1, against my becoming a run-of-the-mill third division player five to one, etc.'; to multiply the estimated rewards in each case by the estimated chance of it happening; and then to *decide* by choosing the alternative with the highest 'expected value'? Not many people would really have much confidence in such a procedure.

If we know the true odds there is no 'uncertainty', only insurable 'risk'. But we are not safe in extrapolating frequencies for future events from statistics of past occurrences in 'similar' cases. For we are then merely *assuming* that the past will repeat itself. And what about unprecedented events? What are the odds against Prince Charles becoming king between 14 March 1989 and 27 September 1996?

When dealing with unique events, we can never know if our estimates of the odds were correct even *after* the event. Some approaches may help us to think about a problem, by breaking it up into a number of simpler sub-problems. But it is not easy to identify, let alone properly allow for, inter-relationships between the main variables.

10.1.3 Risk perception and preference

Whose risk preferences should guide business decisions? Consider a major capital investment project in a division of a company organised into semi-autonomous investment centres. The project, let us suppose, conforms with overall company strategy, and if the division wants to go ahead with it, corporate management will be unlikely to object. But the project involves quite a large risk, in terms of what could go wrong and what that might cost.

The problem is that what seems 'quite a large' risk to the division may seem small to the top management of a group with eight equally large divisions. Head office may think the expected return ample reward for the risk involved. But while division management's *perception* of the risk may be the same, its *willingness to* bear a particular risk may differ from head office's. In many firms, avoiding visible mistakes may seem more important than missing out on invisible (because never actually undertaken) profit opportunities.

Why should head office's risk preferences matter? Why shouldn't it be *shareholders'* risk preferences which determine what risks companies should be prepared to take? One possibility would be to let shareholders determine the amount of dividends payable, instead of boards of directors being entitled to retain profits inside companies entirely at their own discretion. This might prevent companies using funds unprofitably in order to reduce the risk in their own operations.

The point is that company managers may value 'survival' for themselves and their companies even though shareholders (and the economy as a whole) may benefit far more on balance if some companies do not survive! The question is: how can institutional arrangements encourage *goal congruence*?

Preventing individual firms from going bankrupt by nationalising them all into one huge 'lame duck' may lead to a far more serious crash if the whole industry runs into trouble (as in the steel industry). Pretending that nationalised industries cannot be 'allowed' to fail implies expensive open-ended support from tax payers, which itself is possible only so long as enough profits are being earned elsewhere in the economy. What seems a low-risk short-term emphasis on security at all costs may turn out in the longer term to be a highly risky approach. (British Leyland - now the shrinking Rover Group - is an expensive example).

The risk-taker inside a company bears a different kind of risk from the external risk-taker. The internal risk-taker risks losing his job, or his chances for promotion; whereas the external risk-taker risks losing his capital (or some of it). The employee who loses his job retains his skills, but loses his company-specific knowledge (which may be very valuable as long as he is employed by the company). The entrepreneur may lose some or all of his capital, but perhaps retains his alertness to profitable opportunities. Because the balance of risk is different in each case, the amount of possible reward is also likely to differ as between the internal and the external risk-taker.

10.1.4 Managing risk and uncertainty

Business risk refers to how a business *invests* its resources, financial risk to how it *finances* them. Financial risk means borrowing to finance net assets. It is 'risky' because the business is then legally committed to making the fixed interest payments regularly, and to repaying the amount borrowed on the due date. Such 'financial gearing' has the effect, for any fluctuation in profits before interest, of increasing the volatility of the profits available for ordinary shareholders. In contrast, equity capital is less risky for the business, since it implies no legal commitments in terms of dividends or capital repayments.

Business risk can be reduced in a number of ways. Figure 10.1, which is certainly not comprehensive, groups various kinds of uncertainty-reducing business activities into three categories:

(a) contractual;
(b) flexible;
(c) uncertainty-reducing.

Some actions may be regarded either as reducing risk or as increasing it, for example:

(a) diversifying into different (less well-understood) businesses;
(b) building spare capacity.

	Contractual	Flexible	Uncertainty-reducing
Sales	Produce goods only against firm orders, not for stock	Avoid over-dependence on a few customers	Extensive market research before developing new products
Purchases	Arrange long-term supply contracts	Arrange alternative sources of supply	Stockpile raw materials
Assets	Insure as much as possible	Use general-purpose rather than highly specialised equipment	Retain high liquidity
Employees	Pay salesmen by commission, rather than flat rate		Promote from within rather than hire from outside

Figure 10.1 Ways of reducing uncertainty

A general approach to reducing uncertainty may be to spend time, as well as money, in trying to gain more information. This too may be risky! It is hard to avoid the conclusion that in a sense nearly all human action which commits resources in one way rather than another is speculative.

10.2 STRATEGIC ISSUES

10.2.1 Life cycle costing

Often we can identify an asset's 'cost' as its purchase price or perhaps the cost of making it. Sometimes, however, the cost of *acquiring* an asset is substantially less than the total extra costs related to its use over a prolonged period. For management purposes we may then need to identify *all* the asset's costs over its whole life cycle.

Life cycle costing is likely to be relevant for physical assets which have a useful life of many years. In the engineering field, life cycle costing (or 'terotechnology') is the interaction of management, financial, engineering and other disciplines, applied to physical assets in pursuit of economic life cycle costs.

In the planning, design, manufacture or purchase of plant, equipment and buildings, managers should consider the total costs over the asset's whole life rather than just the initial acquisition costs.

The life cycle of a physical asset may comprise a number of stages as follows:

(a) specify;
(b) design;
(c) manufacture/Build,
(d) install;
(e) commission;
(f) operate;
(g) maintain/overhaul;
(h) dispose.

Many assets will have life cycle costs of several times the initial cost. Managers require knowledge of the causes, the amount and the timing of the major elements of these costs.

They should base an acquisition decision on the estimated (discounted) life cycle costs together with technical performance and user satisfaction.

Example 1: a hospital is about to replace its rapidly deteriorating boiler equipment. Three types of boiler system are being considered as a suitable replacement:

(a) coal-fired;
(b) gas-fired;
(c) oil-fired.

The associated costs are as follows:

Boiler system	A	B	C
	£'000	£'000	£'000
Cost of boiler (including installation and commissioning)	55	74	67
Annual fuel cost	27	23	25
Annual operating labour costs	8	-	-
Annual maintenance costs	4	3	3
Annual electricity costs	1	1	1
Total annual operating costs	40	27	29

The new boiler system is expected to last at least ten years. The hospital has an opportunity cost of finance of 15% per year. Which system should be chosen?

If the decision was taken on the basis of initial cost only, then the coal-fired boiler system would be selected. However, over its life-time (at least ten years) the annual operating costs are much higher than for the gas-fired and oil-fired systems. The life-cycle costs for ten years are as follows:

Boiler system	A	B	C
	£'000	£'000	£'000
Cost of boiler	55	74	67
Operating costs (annual costs x 10)	400	270	290
Total life cycle costs	455	344	357

However, we need to discount the annual costs at a 15% discount rate to arrive at the present value cost of each system. The discount factor for years 1-10 at 15% is 5.019. (Simply add up the discount factors for years 1-10 in Appendix B).

The present value of each system then is:

Boiler System	*A*	*B*	*C*
	£'000	*£'000*	*£'000*
Cost of boiler	*55*	*74*	*67*
Operating costs			
(annual costs x 5.019)	*201*	*136*	*146*
Present value of costs	*256*	*210*	*213*

On the basis of financial considerations only, the gas-fired system is the most economical. Unless there are other important considerations the gas-fired system should be chosen.

A more intricate analysis might attempt to forecast the likely changes in each of the annual operating costs (e.g. fuel costs, maintenance costs, etc.). But some might consider this less predictable than forecasting the winner of the Grand National! It might be useful, however, to see how much each of the three fuel costs would need to change to alter the decision.

In addition to looking at the importance of fuel costs to the decision, we can also check the sensitivity of the expected system life. For instance, if the expected life is reduced to five years, the oil-fired system (C) becomes the most economical, as follows:

Boiler system	*A*	*B*	*C*
	£'000	*£'000*	*£'000*
Cost of boiler	*55*	*74*	*67*
Operating costs			
(annual costs x 3.353)	*134*	*91*	*97*
Present value of costs	*189*	*165*	*164*

If the expected life is reckoned to be six years or more, the decision is in favour of the gas-fired system.

Life cycle costing may be especially useful in organisations which:

(a) operate in capital intensive industries;
(b) have a sizeable, on-going construction programme;
(c) are dependent on expensive or numerous items of plant with consequent substantial replacement programmes;
(d) are considering major expansion;

(e) are contemplating the purchase/design/development of expensive new technology;
(f) are sensitive to disruption due to down-time.

10.2.2 Zero-based budgeting

Chapter 6 dealt with preparing next year's budget. In many firms this is an extra task to be done without disrupting normal on-going business. As a result it is easy to overlook gradual changes taking place in the environment which may affect the cost structure of the business. In contrast, zero-base budgets challenge the existence and amount of all budgeted items. The intention may often be to reduce costs, but sometimes it can pay to *increase* them. Figure 10.2 lists the main differences between 'normal' and zero-base budgeting.

The essence of zero-base budgeting is dividing a business into specific *decision packages* which together comprise the whole business. Figure 10.3 shows a possible set of decision packages for a business school.

Further sub-divisions may be possible. For instance, each taught course could be divided between the various component subject areas. For each decision package, the following need to be identified:

(a) purpose of the activity;
(b) expected outcome;
(c) performance measures;
(d) personnel involved;
(e) cost;
(f) possible alternative courses of action;
(g) likely effects if activity is not performed.

Managers evaluate decision packages and rank them in order of importance; 'musts' first and then 'wants'. This makes it easier to decide whether to approve a particular decision package and how much to spend on it. Also, consideration is given to alternative ways of achieving the same end result.

This zero-base budgeting process often requires a team which is familiar with the enterprise as a whole. It may sometimes be a good idea to delegate some of the work to people with a better detailed knowledge.

Because zero-base budgeting absorbs so much time and effort, few organisations would have enough spare managers available to review the entire business annually. (Nor would the benefits be likely to support an annual process). A three- to five-year cycle is probably more appropriate, perhaps reviewing only part of the enterprise each year.

Zero-base budgeting may be most effective where setting budgets involves a high degree of discretion. But it is unlikely to be worthwhile in businesses where legal and operational constraints 'control' costs.

	'Normal' budgeting	Zero-based budgeting
Frequency	Annual	Every 3-5 years
Starting point	Last year's budget	Zero
Basis for setting budget	Last year ±%	Careful analysis of decision packages
Budgeted amount	Usually single amount	Depends upon analysis of benefits from incremental spend
Priority of activities	'Musts' and 'wants' not differentiated	Distinguishes 'musts' and 'wants', and ranks priorities.
Alternatives	Often ignored	Considered
People involved	Boss and subordinate	Cross-functional team
Awareness Necessary	Knowledge of own function	Comprehensive understanding of how the whole business works
Preparation cost (Time and effort)	Can be minimal	Substantial
Appropriateness	General	Most effective in support-type activities

Figure 10.2 'Normal' budgeting vs zero-based budgeting

Long Courses

1. Full-time MBA
2. Full-time PhD
3. Part-time MBA
4. Part-time PhD

Short Courses

5. General Management
6. Subject-specific
7. Company-specific

Research Activities

8. Contract research
9. Faculty research
10. Student research

Administrative Activities

11. General administration
12. Computer facilities and services
13. Library facilities and services
14. Building maintenance
15. Equipment provision and maintenance
16. Marketing and Public Relations

Figure 10.3 Decision packages for a business school

10.2.3 External analysis

Management accounting information is often directly concerned only with the organisation itself. But most businesses operate within a competitive market and some consideration should therefore be given to the market itself and the other competitors therein.

In determining the company's future business strategy, it is necessary to have an understanding of the market size and growth (or decline) and a knowledge of competitors' prices, costs and output levels.

In section 2.4.4, we discussed the learning curve and saw in Figure 2.9 how the marginal cost per unit often falls as the cumulative output increases. Those firms with large market shares are therefore likely to have lower costs than firms with smaller market shares. Of course this may not hold true if a competitor makes a major breakthrough in terms of new products, materials or processes. Also, costs can be reduced by lowering quality standards, product specification and advertising, but this is likely to result in falling sales.

Long-term product profitability is also dependent upon obtaining satisfactory product prices. When the market is growing, prices are likely to be high enough to allow (at least) satisfactory profits for the 'average' supplier. In shrinking markets, fewer suppliers, if any, will tend to make profits.

Analysis of the market size and growth will be of substantial help in the long-term business plan concerning which products to make and sell. Ideally, a knowledge of the trends in competitors' prices, costs and output levels will be useful too, probably best shown in 'real-terms', i.e. adjusted for inflation. Decisions about which products to expand, maintain or drop should then be more soundly based.

Any clues obtained concerning competitors' costs may provide a useful 'standard' for comparison. If competitors' costs are lower, questions may be raised about internal cost control practices. Also, value analysis exercises may be prompted by such information.

Looking outside the business to competitors and the marketplace, as well as internally, should help improve the organisation's strategic decision making.

10.3 EFFECTIVE IMPLEMENTATION

Most of this book is concerned with accounting information and how managers can use that information to improve business performance. However, even the best information on its own will not achieve the best results. Usually the co-operation of other people is necessary. Managers, therefore, need to have some understanding of people's behaviour within organisations.

Often the co-operation of people is sought through a system of control. This might involve:

(a) identifying appropriate performance measures;
(b) setting standards;
(c) reporting actual performance;
(d) taking appropriate action.

This is easier said than done, especially since the goals of employees, managers and owners are likely to be very different. But there must be a satisfactory degree of overlap in goals if the enterprise is to succeed. Managers can seek to improve their control over the business by:

(a) recruiting suitable people for available jobs;
(b) providing appropriate training and instructions;
(c) designing an appropriate organisation structure, (e.g. jobs, relationships, responsibilities and authority);
(d) co-ordinating the efforts of others and resolving conflict;
(e) establishing policies and rules, including reward and punishment systems;
(f) implementing budgetary control procedures.

Perhaps the 'people problems' that plague some organisations can be dealt with by replacing people with machines. But even so, some people are still needed to operate the machines.

In addition to their intellectual grasp of management accounting, managers will find it useful to have an appreciation of human needs (physiological, safety, belonging, esteem and self-actualisation) and their effect on motivation. Individuals may be motivated to behave in a certain way if that behaviour increases their chances of achieving a desired outcome (more money, promotion, etc.). Appropriate reward/punishment systems can help, but may not be completely able to overcome group pressure to behave *against* the organisation's interest (e.g. restrictive practices, restricted output).

Since managers are expected to take the lead on many occasions they need to possess and develop leadership qualities and vary their style of leadership to suit the occasion.

As well as an effective grasp of management accounting, managers need adequate people skills if they are to achieve planned results.

10.4 CHAPTER SUMMARY

Most business plans and decisions are subject to uncertainty in input data and outcome. To appreciate better the likely variations from the most likely outcome, sensitivity analysis, subjective probabilities and 'expected values' may be used.

Uncertainty is an inherent feature of business and because of it opportunities for big returns (and big losses) exist. Whilst managers may prefer less risky ventures in order to maintain their jobs, shareholders are more enthusiastic to bear risks. They can of course reduce their exposure to risk by holding a portfolio of shares.

For physical assets where the initial cost is not the major portion of its life cycle costs, the latter needs to be used in acquisition decisions.

Zero-based budgets require a rigorous examination of an organisation's cost structure. Unlike annual budgets, zero-based budgets are considered perhaps only every 3-5 years. By analysing the business into a set of decision packages, 'must' and 'want' activities are differentiated, priorities ranked and funds allocated accordingly.

Comparing actual performance against a pre-determined standard is aimed at getting the co-operation of people. Control systems are enhanced if good recruitment, training and organisation procedures exist. Managers are likely to be better leaders if they understand human needs and motivation.

10.5 REVIEW QUESTIONS AND ANSWERS

10.5.1 Questions

1. What is the difference between risk and uncertainty?
2. Name two ways of dealing with uncertainty.
3. What is sensitivity analysis?
4. Is it satisfactory to always adjust 'most likely' figures by 10% when analysing sensitivities?
5. In what circumstances are 'subjective probabilities' useful?
6. What are the drawbacks to using 'subjective probabilities'?
7. How are 'expected values' calculated?
8. Are division managers, corporate managers and shareholders likely to have similar perceptions and preferences regarding risk within a division? Why, or why not?
9. Identify two ways of reducing risk by:
   (a) contractual arrangements;
   (b) flexible operating;
   (c) uncertainty-reducing.
10. What is life cycle costing?
11. What are the life cycle stages for a physical asset?
12. Which organisations are likely to benefit from 'life cycle costing'?
13. How does 'zero-base budgeting' compare with 'normal' annual budgeting?
14. What is a decision package?
15. In what ways can managers utilise people better to improve business control?

Write out your answers and then check with the answers over page.

10.5.2 Answers

1. The term 'risk' is used for situations where the probability of each outcome is known. 'Uncertainty' exists in situations where the odds can only be estimated.

2. (a) sensitivity analysis;
   (b) subjective probabilities and expected values.

3. Sensitivity analysis is the technique whereby input variables (e.g. sales volume) are adjusted by a specific percentage and the effect on the dependent result (e.g. profit) determined.

4. No. Some 'most likely' figures (e.g. sales volume) are likely to vary by much more than 10%. Other 'most likely' figures may be relatively certain.

5. Subjective probabilities are more useful in estimating outcomes of occurrences that are likely to be repeated a number of times.

6. (a) People might believe that using subjective probabilities gives a scientifically correct decision.

   (b) Difficult to estimate the probabilities for each variable.

   (c) It may not be easy to identify the inter-relationships between variables.

   (d) Likely to be time-consuming.

   (e) Not useful in assessing unique events.

7. The expected value is the sum of the probability multiplied by the outcome, for each possible outcome.

8. No. A risky venture within a division is likely to be seen as less risky by corporate managers with responsibility for a 'portfolio' of divisions. Shareholders will be even less at risk with their diversified shareholding.

9. (a) i. Produce goods only against firm orders
   ii. Arrange long-term supply contracts

(b) i. Avoid over-dependence on a few customers
ii. Arrange alternative sources of supply

(c) i. Carry out extensive market research before developing new products.
ii. Stockpile raw materials.

(See also Figure 10.1)

10. Life cycle costing is the interaction of management, financial, engineering and other disciplines, applied to physical assets in pursuit of economic life cycle costs.

11. Specify, design, manufacture/build, install, commission, operate, maintain/overhaul, dispose.

12. Those which:
(a) operate in capital intensive industries;
(b) have a sizeable, on-going construction programme;
(c) have substantial replacement programmes;
(d) are considering major expansion;
(e) are considering introducing expensive new technology;
(f) are sensitive to down-time disruptions.

13. Zero-base budgeting challenges the existence of all costs in a very thorough way but on less frequent basis (every 3-5 years). See Figure 10.2 for more detail.

14. A decision package is a discrete set of business activities which can be analysed for cost-effectiveness. The whole business is made up of a number of decision packages.

15. (a) Recruit suitable people.
(b) Provide training and instructions.
(c) Design an appropriate organisation structure.
(d) Co-ordinate efforts and resolve conflicts.
(e) Establish policies and rules.
(f) Implement budgetary control.

ABBREVIATIONS

B/E	=	Breakeven
C/B	=	Cost/Benefit
COGS	=	Cost of Goods Sold
CV	=	Current Value
DCF	=	Discounted Cash Flow
EOQ	=	Economic Order Quantity
FC	=	Fixed Costs
FG	=	Finished Goods
FIFO	=	First in First Out
IRR	=	Internal Rate of Return
LIFO	=	Last in First Out
NBV	=	Net Book Value
NPV	=	Net Present Value
NRV	=	Net Realisable Value
P & L	=	Profit and Loss (account)
RI	=	Residual Income
RM	=	Raw Materials
ROI	=	Return on Investment
RPI	=	Retail Price Index
SSAP	=	Statement of Standard Accounting Practice
VC	=	Variable Cost
WIP	=	Work in Progress
W/O	=	Write off.

GLOSSARY

Abnormal spoilage
Spoilage of material exceeding amount allowed for in standard costs.

Absorbed overhead
Overhead costs which, by means of *overhead absorption*, are included in product costs.

Absorption costing
(See *full costing*)

Accounts
Profit and loss account for a period, balance sheet as at the end of that period, and notes to the accounts, together with the auditors' report. (For larger companies, also a funds flow statement).

Allocation
Allotment of direct cost to a cost centre.

Amortisation
Depreciation, usually of an intangible fixed asset such as patent rights, leases or goodwill, or a 'wasting asset' such as a mine.

Apportionment
Allotment to two or more cost centres of proportions of indirect costs (on the basis of estimated benefit received).

Asset
Valuable resource owned by a business, acquired at a measurable money cost.

Audit
External examination of financial accounts (and records and systems) by independent professional accountants, to report whether accounts give a true and fair view. (See also *internal auditor*.)

Auditor
Independent professional accountant appointed by shareholders to check the company's financial accounts.

Average cost
(a) Total cost of a product or process divided by the number of units produced.
(b) Method of stock valuation.

Avoidable cost
Cost which will not be incurred if a particular action is not taken.

Balance sheet
Classified statement of financial position of a business, showing assets, liabilities, and shareholders' funds at a particular date.

Batch costing
Method of costing a specific batch of products.

Breakeven (B/E) chart
Chart plotting fixed and variable costs and sales revenue against volume, showing profit or loss at different volumes, within a limited ('relevant') range.

Breakeven point
Volume of output (x) at which sales revenue (R) exactly equals total costs. Breakeven point (x units) is found where sales revenue Rx = variable costs (Vx) + fixed costs (F). In other words, the breakeven volume equals fixed costs (F) divided by contribution (R-V) per unit.

Budget
Financial or quantitative statement, prepared and agreed prior to the budget period by those responsible, reflecting the policies to be pursued during that period to attain agreed objectives.

Budgetary control
System requiring managers to accept responsibility for achieving budget commitments.

Budgeted variance
Variance allowed for in budget, e.g. due to expected monthly inflation in a system using constant prices.

Burden (US terminology)
(See *overhead cost)*

By-product
Low value output produced incidentally in process of making main product.

Capacity cost
Fixed cost of providing a given productive capacity for a period.

Capital allowance
Tax equivalent of depreciation of fixed assets, calculated according to Inland Revenue rules.

Capital expenditure
Expenditure treated as an asset on balance sheet because it is being matched with expected future benefit; in contrast to revenue expenditure, which is treated as an expense in the profit and loss account.

Capitalise
To record expenditure as an asset, in contrast to writing it off as an expense.

Carrying cost
Cost of carrying inventory, e.g. interest, storage, insurance, etc.

Cash flow
Cash receipts less cash payments, for a period.

Common costs
Costs incurred in production of more than one product, needing to be apportioned between them.

Consistency
Principle in accounting, and other statistics, of treating similar items in the same way, to produce meaningful results and to allow comparisons over time.

Consolidated accounts
Accounts for a group of companies, 'consolidated' by combining the separate assets and liabilities of all subsidiaries with those of the 'holding' ('parent') company.

Continuous budget
Budget kept constantly up-to-date by adding new period at end when dropping most recent past period. (See also *rolling budget*).

Contract costing
System of costing a specific contract.

Contribution
Sales revenue minus variable costs (perhaps on a per-unit basis) is the contribution to fixed costs and profit. (Sales revenue less direct costs is the contribution to indirect costs and profit).

Control
Process of managing the present and immediate future. Often consists of comparing actual performance with budget; investigating reasons for any variance; and taking action to improve matters.

Controllable
Cost reckoned to be under control of responsible manager, the extent perhaps depending on time period involved.

Corporation tax
Tax payable by companies on UK taxable profits.

Cost
Amount given up in exchange for goods or services received. May be treated in accounts either as an asset or as an expense. Usually what is given up is either cash or a promise to pay cash in future; but see also opportunity cost. Not normally employed without some further

explanatory qualifying adjective, e.g. variable cost, historical cost, marginal cost, etc.

Cost accounting
Method of identifying costs of operating parts of a business, particular products, etc.

Cost/benefit (C/B) analysis
Process of trying to assess 'profitability' of something where either costs or benefits or both are hard to measure in financial terms. Often applied to social costs or benefits.

Cost centre
Unit or operation in respect of which costs are determined.

Cost of goods sold (COGS)
Costs identifiable with stocks, e.g. raw materials and components, direct labour, production overheads; but excluding selling expenses and administrative expenses.

Critical resource
Sometimes called 'limiting factor'. Factor of production which, at a particular time, may limit activity, often due to temporary shortage of supply.

Current asset
Cash or any asset expected to be converted into cash, or consumed in the normal course of business, within 12 months from the date of the balance sheet, e.g. stocks, debtors.

Current liabilities
Amounts owing to others, expected to be paid within 12 months from date of balance sheet, e.g. creditors, bank overdraft, tax, dividends.

Current value (CV)
Usually means current replacement cost of asset, but may refer to net realisable value. Unlike historical cost, which is usually a definite known fact, current value is usually only a hypothetical estimate.

Depreciation
Process of writing off as expense the cost (or valuation) of fixed asset to spread total cost (or valuation) over its economic life.

Differential cost
Cost incurred if certain activity is undertaken, but not otherwise. (= incremental cost).

Direct cost
Cost that is directly identifiable with particular process or product.

Direct costing (US terminology)
(See also *marginal costing*).

Direct labour
Labour cost directly identifiable with production.

Direct labour hour rate (for overhead)
Estimated total overhead costs attributable to a cost centre divided by appropriate number of direct labour hours for a period (either 'expected' or 'standard'), forming the basis for absorbing overheads.

Discounted cash flow (DCF)
A means of coping with the time value of money, whereby future cash flows are discounted to their equivalent 'present value' by means of a suitable discount rate.

Discount factor
The factor which reduces future cash flows to their present value.

Discount rate
The interest rate used in making present value calculations.

Discretionary cost
Cost which does not vary directly with production, but which is not necessarily fixed either. A discretionary cost changes at management's discretion, e.g. training, advertising, research. (Sometimes called non-variable cost.)

Economic life
Of fixed assets. May differ from physical life.

Economic order quantity (EOQ)
Calculated optimal number of units to order, balancing (carrying) costs of holding stock against costs of running out.

Economies of scale
Reductions in average costs per unit arising from increase in scale of operation, e.g. due to greater technical efficiency of larger plant sizes, spreading of fixed costs over more units, etc.

Effectiveness
Accomplishment of a predetermined objective.

Efficiency
Technical relationship between inputs and outputs.

Efficiency variance
Standard price for a resource multiplied by difference between budgeted and actual quantity used. For materials the term used is usage variance.

Engineered cost
Any cost that has an explicit, specified physical relationship with a selected measure of activity.

Equivalent units
Notional number of completed units substituted for actual greater number of incomplete units. For example, 200 units, 75% completed, might be reckoned as equivalent to 150 completed units.

Exception reporting
System of reporting only exceptions to budget or standard.

Expected value
Result of weighting the value of various possible future outcomes by the estimated chances of each happening.

Expenditure
Amount spent. May be either revenue (expense), or capital (asset).

Expenditure Variance
Usually a price variance related to overhead. (Sometimes called spending variance.)

Expense
Amount written off against profit in an accounting period in respect of goods or services consumed.

Factory cost
Cost of production, usually comprising materials, direct labour, and production overheads.

Feedback
Link between planning and control; modification of an activity as a result of comparing actual result with budget.

Financial accounting
External accounting, leading to published accounts for shareholders and other outsiders.

Financial year
The 12-month period for which a firm chooses to prepare its financial accounts.

Finished goods (FG)
Stocks of completed manufactured products, held for sale.

First in first out (FIFO)
Method of valuing stock, assuming stock at the end of an accounting period consists of most recent purchases.

Fixed asset
Resource, either tangible or intangible, with relatively long life, intended to be held for use in producing goods or services, not for sale in the ordinary course of business.

Fixed cost (FC)
Cost which is fixed for a given period (within the relevant range of output). (= period cost)

Flexible budget
System of 'flexing' budget when actual sales volume differs from original budget, so that variable costs in flexed budget represents expected amount at actual sales volume.

Forecast
Neutral term, implying nothing about desirability of or commitment to the result. (= estimate)

Fringe benefits
Costs of employment other than direct wages or salaries. May exclude employer's social security contributions, but include (e.g.) cost of motor vehicles provided, low-rate loans, etc.

Full costing
Costing method which allocates direct costs and apportions indirect (overhead) costs to products or cost centres. Required for valuing stocks in financial accounts. Contrast marginal costing.
(= absorption costing)

Funds flow statement
Accounting statement required for larger companies, showing sources and uses ('applications') of funds for a period.

Goal congruence
Compatibility of goals of one individual (or part of organisation) with overall goals of the organisation.

Going concern
Assumption that a business entity will continue in operation for the foreseeable future (as opposed to being wound up).

Group accounts
(See *consolidated accounts*)

Hardware
Physical items of equipment. For a microcomputer this comprises (a) VDU cabinet; (b) keyboard; (c) floppy disks; (d) fixed disks.

Idle time
Unproductive time due to circumstances beyond worker's control

Imprest account
System of control, often used for petty cash, with agreed fixed amount of 'float' replenished at regular intervals. Enables manager to check amount consumed during the period. The whole float can be accounted for at any time either in vouchers for usage or in physical units.

Imputed cost
(See *notional cost*)

Incremental cost
Cost incurred if certain activity is undertaken, but not otherwise. (= differential cost)

Indirect cost
Cost not directly identifiable with product or cost centre; may be apportioned on some reasonable basis, in full costing, or not apportioned at all, in marginal costing. (= overhead cost)

Inflation
Rise in the 'general' (weighted average) level of money prices, usually measured by the (annual) rate of increase in the Retail Price Index.

Intangible asset
Valuable, relatively long-life non-tangible asset owned by a business, acquired at a measurable money cost, and not yet written off (either against reserves or against profit), e.g. leases, patents, goodwill.

Interest
Compensation for borrowing or lending money for a period of time, comprising (a) pure time-preference, (b) inflation premium, and (c) risk premium.

Interim accounts
Financial accounts prepared for publication to shareholders, covering a period shorter than 12 months, and not subject to audit. Required, in abbreviated form, for larger companies.

Internal auditor
Employee responsible for reviewing the internal accounting system, preferably independent of the firm's accountants. Not to be confused with the external auditor.

Internal rate of return (IRR)
That discount rate which, for a capital project, produces a net present value of zero.

Inventory
(See *stock*)

Investment centre
Operation where manager is responsible not only for costs ('cost centre'), nor only for costs and revenues ('profit centre'), but also for investment in assets.

Job costing
Method of costing specific jobs.

Joint costing
Cost incurred before split-off point in producing joint products.

Joint products
Two or more products, separated at some stage in the course of processing, each with sufficiently high saleable value to merit recognition as a main product (rather than one being a by-product).

Key factor
The limiting factor of production (if any) reckoned to limit the volume attainable.

Last in first out (LIFO)
Method of valuing stock, rarely used in UK, which assumes that most recent purchases have been used up in the current accounting period, leaving earlier purchases in stock at the end of the period.

Lead time
Period elapsing from decision to start of operation; or from placing an order to receiving delivery.

Learning curve
Phenomenon where production costs based on time may fall as producers learn.

Life cycle costing
The interaction of management, financial, engineering and other disciplines, applied to physical assets in pursuit of economic life cycle costs.

Limited company
Form of business organisation in which liability of owners (shareholders) for the company's liabilities is limited to the nominal amount (fully paid) of their shares. Abbreviated to 'Ltd'; in larger companies to 'plc' (=public limited company).

Long run
Period of time in which all fixed costs are reckoned to be variable.

Long-run costs
Costs expected to be incurred in the long-run (as opposed to short-run costs, which may be much less). In the long-run all fixed costs are reckoned to be variable, so long-run costs may be synonymous with total costs, where short-run costs are synonymous with variable costs.

Loss
Negative profit, where expenses exceed sales revenue. Though not the aim, often the result of business.

Machine hour rate(for overhead)
Method of apportioning overhead costs based on machine hours used. Overheads attributable to one or more machines are divided by the number of machine hours expected to be worked.

Management accountant
Member of the Chartered Institute of Management Accountants.

Management accounting
Accounting internally for management's own use, as opposed to external financial accounting for shareholders and other outsiders.

Manufacturing costs
Material, direct labour, and production overheads.

Marginal cost
The extra cost incurred as a result of producing one more (one less) unit. Definition of 'the marginal unit' depends on the decision to be made.

Marginal costing
Costing method which allocates only variable costs, not fixed costs, to products. (Also sometimes called 'direct costing', but this may mislead, since a 'direct' cost can be fixed, or an indirect cost variable.

Master budget
Overall aggregation of various budgets for parts of a business, perhaps for part of a year, into a single profit and loss account budget, balance sheet budget, and cash budget for the whole company.

Matching principle
The accounting principle according to which expenditures are carried forward as assets on the balance sheet only if there are expected to be sales revenues in future periods against which they can be matched. Expenditures which cannot be matched against sales revenues, or which can be matched against sales in the current period, are written off as expenses in the current period's profit and loss account.

Material cost
Cost of commodities other than fixed assets incorporated in manufactured products.

Mix variance
Variance due to change in <u>mix</u> of products produced or sold.

Net book value (NBV)
Cost (or valuation) or fixed assets, less accumulated depreciation.

Net current assets
Calculated as current assets less current liabilities. (= working capital)

Net present value (NPV)
The net result of discounting future cash flows at a pre-determined discount rate.

Net realisable value (NRV)
Net amount for which asset could currently be sold; if less than cost, used for valuing stock.

Non-controllable
Applied to a cost, means not easily controllable by a manager, especially in the short-run, e.g. local rates.

Normal capacity
Productive capacity under normal conditions.

Normal spoilage
Spoilage which is anticipated, and built into product costs.

Normal volume
Standard long-run estimate of sustainable volume.

Notes to the accounts
Detailed notes forming part of the financial statements, explaining many items in more detail than on the face of the accounts.

Notional cost
Cost which does not represent actual 'out-of-pocket' expenditure, e.g. interest on equity capital.

Opportunity cost
The hypothetical revenue or other benefit that might have been obtained by the 'next best' alternative course of action, which was foregone in favour of the course actually taken.

Out-of-pocket cost
Cash payments resulting from doing something (rather than doing nothing).

Over-absorption
Overhead absorbed exceeding overhead incurred (or budgeted to be incurred at actual volume). Happens when standard overhead recovery rate is applied to actual volume greater than budget.

Overhead absorption
Apportionment of overhead costs to cost units by means of overhead recovery rates (often based on direct labour hours) separately calculated for each cost centre. Requires estimating what overhead costs should amount to at expected (or 'normal') volume, to set absorption rate, which is then applied to actual volume.

Overhead cost
A cost not directly identifiable with a product or cost centre. (= indirect cost)

Overhead recovery rate
Rate (often per direct labour hour) at which overheads are 'recovered' (absorbed) by products.

Partnership
Form of enterprise with two or more partners (owners), each with unlimited personal liability to meet the firm's debts in full.

Period cost
Fixed cost, incurred in a period regardless of volume of output.

Planning
Establishing objectives and formulating policies to achieve them. Budgets are short-term plans, often for one year ahead, expressed in financial terms.

Present value
Today's equivalent of a future sum of money (receipt or payment). Net present value is the sum of the present values for both positive and negative cash flows.

Price variance
Variance due to difference between budget price and actual price, calculated using actual volume. See also volume variance.

Prime cost
Direct labour plus material cost.

Process costing
Method of costing specific process.

Product cost
Cost attributed to product, maybe equivalent to direct cost.

Production cost
Direct labour plus material cost plus production overheads.

Profit
Surplus of sales revenue over expenses for a period.

Profit and loss (P&L) account
Accounting statement showing result (profit or loss) of business operations for a period.

Profit centre
Business unit with manager responsible for sales revenue as well as for costs.

Prudence
Conservatism. An accounting concept sometimes clashing with the convention of consistency. Inclination of accountants to recognise sales revenue (and therefore profit) only when reasonable certainty exists, but to make provision for all known liabilities (losses and expenses) whether their amount is known with certainty or is a best estimate.

Public limited company (plc)
Name given to public limited company, in place of former 'limited company' (abbreviated to 'Ltd').

Published accounts
Accounts, usually for a year, of a public company.

Purchasing power
= Value of money. What money will buy in real terms, usually measured by the 'basket of goods and services' comprising the constituent items in the Retail Price Index.

Qualified (accountant)
Professional accountant, member of one of the six main accountancy bodies.

Qualified (audit report)
Audit report including a 'qualification', i.e. an explanation of, or expression of disagreement with, some aspect of the financial accounts (for which the company's directors are responsible).

Rate variance
Price variance applied to labour.

Raw materials (RM)
Input to manufacturing process, held for a time as stocks.

Realisation
The concept in accounting that sales revenue (and therefore profit) is recognised only when it is 'realised' in cash or in other assets, the ultimate cash realisation of which can be assessed with reasonable certainty.

'Real' terms
Amounts expressed after adjustments to allow for inflation.

Relevant cost
Any cost relevant to a particular decision (i.e. ignoring costs which would be unaffected by it).

Relevant range
Range of output within which fixed costs are expected not to change during a period.

Replacement cost
Amount for which it is estimated that an asset held could currently be replaced. Not the expected ultimate cost when the asset is actually replaced in the future.
Reserves
Shareholders' funds other than issued share capital, including: share premium, revaluation reserve, cumulative retained profits.

Residual income (RI)
Operating profit less a capital charge representing interest on total capital employed (whether debt or equity). May be calculated before or after tax. Represents accounting profit less (notional) interest on equity capital.

Retail Price Index (RPI)
Monthly government statistic measuring the weighted average of money prices of representative 'basket of goods'. Based on January 1987 = 100. The year-on-year rate of increase in the RPI is usually regarded as 'the' rate of (general) inflation.

Retention money
Proportion of price of goods supplied or work completed temporarily withheld by purchaser for agreed period as security against possible failure by supplier to fulfil contract.

Return on investment (ROI)
Profit divided by capital employed. In management accounts usually represents operating profit divided by operating assets employed. (In financial accounting may represent profit after tax divided by shareholders's equity).

Revenue
(a) sales revenue, (b) Inland Revenue, the tax authorities, (c) contrasted to capital, relating to the profit and loss account, rather than to the balance sheet.

Revenue centre
Business unit whose manager is responsible for sales revenue (but not, to any major extent, for expenses).

Revenue expenditure
Expense, charged in profit and loss account, as opposed to capital expenditure which relates to assets.

Risk
Chance of occurence in future where the odds are known (e.g. as in roulette or throwing dice). Contrasted with *uncertainty*.

Rolling budget
Budget which is continually updated by adding a new period at the end as the most recent past period is dropped. (= continuous budget)

Safety stock
Minimum stock level providing a cushion against reasonably expected fluctuations in maximum demand and in lead times.

Sales mix
Combination of quantities of various goods or services sold.

Sales revenue
Turnover. A firm's trading income for a period from selling its products.

Scrap
Useless material resulting from production processes.

Semi-variable cost
Cost which is partly fixed and partly variable.

Sensitivity analysis
Process of determining which variables matter most, and how much it affects outcome if each varies.

Set-up cost
Fixed cost necessary prior to production, often in respect of a single machine.

Shareholders
Usually refers to ordinary shareholders, who own company in proportion to number of shares held; but legally may also refer to preference shareholders.

Short-run
Period within which not all factors of production are variable.

Short-run cost
Often synonymous with variable cost. Cost which may be changed within 'short' time horizon.

Shut-down cost
Incremental cost incurred in ceasing production (e.g. redundancy payments).

Single criterion fallacy
Attempt to measure (some aspects of) business success by reference to only one criterion. Nearly always a 'fallacy' because of inter-relationships between units, time periods, etc., and because of tendency to concentrate on what is measurable at expense of important qualitative aspects.

Software
A series of logical control instructions which enable microcomputers to meet user needs.

Split-off point
Point beyond which cost of joint products become separately identifiable.

Spoilage cost
Expected (normal) cost of spoilage as unavoidable part of production process.

Spreadsheet
A matrix comprising information. May be manual (handwritten or typed) or displayed on a microcomputer VDU screen.

Standard cost
Pre-determined cost, maybe per unit, that 'should' be attained.

Standard performance
Expected attainable level of performance.

Standard volume
Expected (normal) volume. May differ from budgeted volume in the short-term.

Start-up cost
Cost of initiating production, probably referring to larger scale operation than set-up cost.

Statement of standard accounting practice (SSAP)
Mandatory requirements issued by accountancy bodies regarding accounting treatment of certain items, e.g. SSAP 9 on stock valuation, SSAP 12 on depreciation (see Appendix A).

Step-down method
Allocation and apportionment of service department costs to other service departments as well as to production departments.

Stock
Holdings of goods, either as raw materials and components, work-in-progress, or finished goods, with a view to sale (perhaps after further processing) in the ordinary course of business.

Stock turnover
Cost of goods sold in a period divided by value of stocks held.

Straight-line depreciation
Method of writing off cost of fixed asset in equal instalments over its estimated economic life. If life is n years, annual depreciation expense will be $1/n$ x (cost - expected residual value).

Sunk cost
Cost already incurred which cannot be reversed.

Target
Outcome aimed for; but not necessarily expected, forecast or committed.

Taxable profit
Differs from 'profit before tax' in financial accounts (a) by deducting tax capital allowances instead of (book) depreciation, and (b) by taking account of any accounting expenses 'disallowed' by tax authorities, and of any timing differences.

Taxation
In company accounts, means UK corporation tax on taxable profits, plus any foreign tax on profits earned abroad. Excludes other taxes, such as local rates, employers' national insurances, etc., which are included in operating expenses.

Terotechnology
Life cycle costing.

Total cost
Implies both fixed plus variable cost; both direct plus indirect cost.

Transfer price
Internal price at which goods or services are transferred from one part of a firm to another. Can be important in evaluating performance of profit centres.

True and fair view
Aim of financial accounting, implying that generally accepted accounting concepts and conventions have been followed.

Turnover
Sales revenue, the 'turnover' of the products being sold for a period.

Unallocated cost
Cost which cannot conveniently or usefully be allocated, e.g. because it would be unduly expensive or arbitrary.

Uncertainty
Chance of occurence in future where (as is common in business) the odds are not known - hence have to be estimated subjectively (i.e. guessed).

Under-absorption
Balance of overhead cost not 'absorbed' by products due to actual volume falling short of budget.

Unit cost
Cost of a unit produced.

Usage variance
Efficiency variance applied to materials.

Value added
Difference between sales revenue and cost of bought-out materials and services. Roughly = profit plus wages.

Variable budget
Flexible budget.

Variable cost (VC)
Cost which varies directly in proportion to output.

Variance
Difference between budget and actual amount. (Not to be confused with a statistical variance, which is a dispersion around the mean (average) value of a group of data).

Volume variance
Variance between budget and actual attributable to difference between budget and actual volume (both priced at budget price).

Wages cost
Cost of employees' remuneration; gross wages, possibly plus employers' social security contributions; possibly plus fringe benefits.

Waste
Normal loss of material in process of production.

Working capital
Net current assets. Excess of current assets over current liabilities.

Work-in-progress (WIP)
Partly-completed stocks in manufacturing process.

Write-off (W/O)
To charge an expenditure as an expense in the profit and loss account, as opposed to capitalising it, i.e. recording it as an asset at cost on the balance sheet.

Zero-base budgeting
Budgeting from the ground up, as though the budget were being utilised for the first time. Implication: nothing is justified except what can be explicitly defended. (In contrast most actual budgets start from existing levels).

APPENDIX A

STATEMENTS OF STANDARD ACCOUNTING PRACTICE*

SSAP	Subject
1.	Associated companies.
2.	Accounting policies.
3.	Earnings per share.
4.	Government grants.
5.	Value added tax.
6.	Extraordinary items and prior year adjustments.
8.	Taxation under the imputation system.
9.	Stocks and work in progress.
10.	Statements of source and application of funds.
12.	Depreciation.
13.	Research and development.
14.	Group accounts.
15.	Deferred taxation.
17.	Post balance sheet events.
18.	Contingencies.
19.	Investment properties.
20.	Foreign currency translation.
21.	Leases and hire purchase contracts.
22.	Goodwill.
23.	Acquisitions and mergers.

* As at 30th June 1987

APPENDIX B

PRESENT VALUE TABLE

Present value of £1

Years Hence	1%	2%	4%	6%	8%	10%	12%	14%	15%	16%	18%	20%	22%	24%	25%	26%	28%	30%	35%	40%	45%	50%
1	0.990	0.980	0.962	0.943	0.926	0.909	0.893	0.877	0.870	0.862	0.847	0.833	0.820	0.806	0.800	0.794	0.781	0.769	0.741	0.714	0.690	0.667
2	0.980	0.961	0.925	0.890	0.857	0.826	0.797	0.769	0.756	0.743	0.718	0.694	0.672	0.650	0.640	0.630	0.610	0.592	0.549	0.510	0.476	0.444
3	0.971	0.942	0.889	0.840	0.794	0.751	0.712	0.675	0.658	0.641	0.609	0.579	0.551	0.524	0.512	0.500	0.477	0.455	0.406	0.364	0.328	0.296
4	0.961	0.924	0.855	0.792	0.735	0.683	0.636	0.592	0.572	0.552	0.516	0.482	0.451	0.423	0.410	0.397	0.373	0.350	0.301	0.260	0.226	0.198
5	0.951	0.906	0.822	0.747	0.681	0.621	0.567	0.519	0.497	0.476	0.437	0.402	0.370	0.341	0.328	0.315	0.291	0.269	0.223	0.186	0.156	0.132
6	0.942	0.888	0.790	0.705	0.630	0.564	0.507	0.456	0.432	0.410	0.370	0.335	0.303	0.275	0.262	0.250	0.227	0.207	0.165	0.133	0.108	0.088
7	0.933	0.871	0.760	0.665	0.583	0.513	0.452	0.400	0.376	0.354	0.314	0.279	0.249	0.222	0.210	0.198	0.178	0.159	0.122	0.095	0.074	0.059
8	0.923	0.853	0.731	0.627	0.540	0.467	0.404	0.351	0.327	0.305	0.266	0.233	0.204	0.179	0.168	0.157	0.139	0.123	0.091	0.068	0.051	0.039
9	0.914	0.837	0.703	0.592	0.500	0.424	0.361	0.308	0.284	0.263	0.225	0.194	0.167	0.144	0.134	0.125	0.108	0.094	0.067	0.048	0.035	0.026
10	0.905	0.820	0.676	0.558	0.463	0.386	0.322	0.270	0.247	0.227	0.191	0.162	0.137	0.116	0.107	0.099	0.085	0.073	0.050	0.035	0.024	0.017
11	0.896	0.804	0.650	0.527	0.429	0.350	0.287	0.237	0.215	0.195	0.162	0.135	0.112	0.094	0.086	0.079	0.066	0.056	0.037	0.025	0.017	0.012
12	0.887	0.788	0.625	0.497	0.397	0.319	0.257	0.208	0.187	0.168	0.137	0.112	0.092	0.076	0.069	0.062	0.052	0.043	0.027	0.018	0.012	0.008
13	0.879	0.773	0.601	0.469	0.368	0.290	0.229	0.182	0.163	0.145	0.116	0.093	0.075	0.061	0.055	0.050	0.040	0.033	0.020	0.013	0.008	0.005
14	0.870	0.758	0.577	0.442	0.340	0.263	0.205	0.160	0.141	0.125	0.099	0.078	0.062	0.049	0.044	0.039	0.032	0.025	0.015	0.009	0.006	0.003
15	0.861	0.743	0.555	0.417	0.315	0.239	0.183	0.140	0.123	0.108	0.084	0.065	0.051	0.040	0.035	0.031	0.025	0.020	0.011	0.006	0.004	0.002
16	0.853	0.728	0.534	0.394	0.292	0.218	0.163	0.123	0.107	0.093	0.071	0.054	0.042	0.032	0.028	0.025	0.019	0.015	0.008	0.005	0.003	0.002
17	0.844	0.714	0.513	0.371	0.270	0.198	0.146	0.108	0.093	0.080	0.060	0.045	0.034	0.026	0.023	0.020	0.015	0.012	0.006	0.003	0.002	0.001
18	0.836	0.700	0.494	0.350	0.250	0.180	0.130	0.095	0.081	0.069	0.051	0.038	0.028	0.021	0.018	0.016	0.012	0.009	0.005	0.002	0.001	0.001
19	0.828	0.686	0.475	0.331	0.232	0.164	0.116	0.083	0.070	0.060	0.043	0.031	0.023	0.017	0.014	0.012	0.009	0.007	0.003	0.002	0.001	
20	0.820	0.673	0.456	0.312	0.215	0.149	0.104	0.073	0.061	0.051	0.037	0.026	0.019	0.014	0.012	0.010	0.007	0.005	0.002	0.001	0.001	
21	0.811	0.660	0.439	0.294	0.199	0.135	0.093	0.064	0.053	0.044	0.031	0.022	0.015	0.011	0.009	0.008	0.006	0.004	0.002	0.001		
22	0.803	0.647	0.422	0.278	0.184	0.123	0.083	0.056	0.046	0.038	0.026	0.018	0.013	0.009	0.007	0.006	0.004	0.003	0.001	0.001		
23	0.795	0.634	0.406	0.262	0.170	0.112	0.074	0.049	0.040	0.033	0.022	0.015	0.010	0.007	0.006	0.005	0.003	0.002	0.001			
24	0.788	0.622	0.390	0.247	0.158	0.102	0.066	0.043	0.035	0.028	0.019	0.013	0.008	0.006	0.005	0.004	0.003	0.002	0.001			
25	0.780	0.610	0.375	0.233	0.146	0.092	0.059	0.038	0.030	0.024	0.016	0.010	0.007	0.005	0.004	0.003	0.002	0.001	0.001			
26	0.772	0.598	0.361	0.220	0.135	0.084	0.053	0.033	0.026	0.021	0.014	0.009	0.006	0.004	0.003	0.002	0.002	0.001				
27	0.764	0.586	0.347	0.207	0.125	0.076	0.047	0.029	0.023	0.018	0.011	0.007	0.005	0.003	0.002	0.002	0.001	0.001				
28	0.757	0.574	0.333	0.196	0.116	0.069	0.042	0.026	0.020	0.016	0.010	0.006	0.004	0.002	0.002	0.002	0.001	0.001				
29	0.749	0.563	0.321	0.185	0.107	0.063	0.037	0.022	0.017	0.014	0.008	0.005	0.003	0.002	0.002	0.001	0.001	0.001				
30	0.742	0.552	0.308	0.174	0.099	0.057	0.033	0.020	0.015	0.012	0.007	0.004	0.003	0.002	0.001	0.001	0.001					
40	0.672	0.453	0.208	0.097	0.046	0.022	0.011	0.005	0.004	0.003	0.001	0.001										
50	0.608	0.372	0.141	0.054	0.021	0.009	0.003	0.001	0.001	0.001												

RECOMMENDED FURTHER READING

GENERAL

1. L R Amey and D A Egginton: 'Management Accounting: A Conceptual Approach', Longman, 1973.

2. Robert N Anthony and Regina Hozlingt: 'Management Control in Non-Profit Organisations', Irwin, 1975.

3. E H Caplan: 'Management Accounting and Behavioural Science', Addison-Wesley, 1971.

4. Charles B Handy: 'Understanding Organizations', Penguin, 1976.

5. A G Hopwood: 'Accounting and Human Behaviour', Prentice-Hall, 1974.

6. H Mintzberg: 'The Nature of Managerial Work', Harper & Row, 1973.

7. D S Pugh, ed.: 'Organisational Theory: Selected Readings', Penguin, 1971.

8. Robert W Scapens, David T Otley, Roger J Lister: 'Management Accounting, Organisational Theory and Capital Budgeting', MacMillan, 1984.

9. Michael Schiff and Arie Y Lewin, Eds.: 'Behavioural Aspects of Accounting', Prentice-Hall, 1974.

10. John Sizer, Ed.: 'Readings in Management Accounting', Penguin 1980.

11. V H Vroom and E L Deci, Eds.: 'Management and Motivation', Penguin, 1970.

OLDER CLASSICS

(More than 20 years old)

1. R M Cyert and J G March: 'A Behavioural Theory of the Firm', Prentice-Hall, 1963.

2. A H Maslow: 'Motivation and Personality', Harper and Row, 1954.

3. D C McClelland: 'The Achieving Society', Van Nostrand, 1961.

4. D McGregor: 'The Human Side of Enterprise', McGraw Hill, 1961.

5. A C Stedry: 'Budget Control and Cost Behaviour', Prentice-Hall, 1960.

Chapter One

PLANNING AND CONTROL

R N Anthony: 'Planning and Control Systems: A Framework for Analysis', Irwin, 1965.

R N Anthony and John Dearden: 'Management Control Systems', Irwin 4th Ed, 1980.

John Argenti: 'Corporate Collapse: The Causes and Symptoms', McGraw-Hill, 1976

Clive Emmanuel and David Otley: 'Accounting for Management Control', Van Nostrand, 1985.

E A Lowe and J L F Machin: 'New Perspectives in Management Control', Macmillan, 1983.

Chapter Two

THE NATURE OF COSTS

James Buchanan and G F Thirlby, Eds.: 'LSE Essays on Cost', Weidenfeld and Nicolson, 1973.

James M Buchanan: 'Cost and Choice', Chicago, 1969.

Chapter Three

PRODUCT COSTING

J Dearden: 'Cost Accounting and Financial Control Systems', Addison-Wesley, 1973.

D Solomons (Ed.): 'Studies in Cost Analysis', Sweet and Maxwell, 2nd Ed., 1968.

H R Anton and P A Firmin (Eds.): 'Contemporary Issues in Cost and Managerial Accounting', Houghton-Miflin, 3rd ed., 1978.

C T Horngren: 'Cost Accounting', Prentice-Hall, 5th ed, 1982

Chapter Four

COSTS AND REVENUES

D C Hague: 'Pricing in Business', Unwin, 1971.

Harry Townsend (Ed.): 'Price Theory', Penguin, 1971.

A Gabor: 'Pricing, Principles and Practices', Heinemann, 1977.

Chapter Five

RELEVANT COSTS FOR DECISIONS

J L Bower: 'Managing the Resource Allocation Process', Irwin, 1972.

J Arnold and T Hope: 'Accounting for Management Decisions', Prentice-Hall, 1983.

A M Pettigrew: "The Politics of Organizational Decision-Making", Tavistock, 1973.

Brian J Loasby: 'Choice, Complexity and Ignorance', Cambridge, 1976.

Chapter Six

BUDGETS

G H Hofstede: 'The Game of Budget Control', Tavistock, 1968.

W J Vatter: 'Operating Budgets', Wadsworth, 1969.

A Wildavsky: 'Budgeting: A Comparative Theory of the Budgeting Process', Little, Brown, 1975.

Chapter Seven

VARIANCE ANALYSIS

Earnest Laidler: 'Variance Accounting', CIMA, MacMillan, 1985.

Chapter Eight

DECENTRALISED MANAGEMENT

Harold S Geneen: 'Managing', Granada, 1985.

David Solomons: 'Divisional Performance: Measurement and Control', Irwin, 1965.

R Vancil: 'Decentralisation: Ambiguity By Design', Irwin, 1979.

C Tomkins: 'Financial Planning in Divisionalised Companies', Haymarket, 1973.

H C Verlage: 'Transfer Prices for Multinational Enterprises', Rotterdam University Press, 1975.

Chapter Nine

MICROCOMPUTERS IN MANAGEMENT ACCOUNTING

Chris Edwards and Nigel Bryant: 'Developing Business Systems Applications', Prentice-Hall International, 1987.

Jacquetta Megarry: 'Computers Mean Business', Kogan Page, 1984.

Chapter Ten

MANAGEMENT ACCOUNTING IN ACTION

E Berne: 'Games People Play', Andre Deutsch, 1964.

A Jay: 'Management and Machiavelli', Hodder and Stoughton, 1967.

David A Buchanan and Andrzej Huczynski: 'Organisational Behaviour: An Introductory Text', Prentice-Hall, 1985.

S Beer: 'Brain of the Firm', Penguin, 1971.

John L J Mackin: 'The Expectations Approach', McGraw-Hill, 1980.

John Sizer: 'Perspectives in Management Accounting', ICMA, 1981.

W B Taylor: 'The Management of Assets: Terotechnology in the Pursuit of Economic Life-Cycle Costs', ICMA, 1980.

INDEX